SQL
Interview Questions

A complete question bank to crack your ANN
SQL interview with real-time examples

by

Prasad Kulkarni

FIRST EDITION 2019

Copyright © BPB Publications, India

ISBN: 978-93-89328-462

Distributors:

BPB PUBLICATIONS
20, Ansari Road, Darya Ganj
New Delhi-110002
Ph: 23254990 / 23254991

DECCAN AGENCIES
4-3-329, Bank Street,
Hyderabad-500195
Ph: 24756967 / 24756400

MICRO MEDIA
Shop No. 5, Mahendra Chambers,
150 DN Rd. Next to Capital Cinema,
V.T. (C.S.T.) Station, MUMBAI-400 001
Ph: 22078296 / 22078297

BPB BOOK CENTRE
376 Old Lajpat Rai Market,
Delhi-110006
Ph: 23861747

Published by Manish Jain for BPB Publications, 20 Ansari Road, Darya Ganj, New Delhi-110002 and Printed by him at Repro India Ltd, Mumbai

Dedicated to

My loved ones
Baba, Aai, Jadi, Mau, Bundu

About the Author

Prasad Kulkarni is a Microsoft MVP reconnect, Technical leader, Author, Agile Scrum Master, and Blogger. He has 13 years of core experience in Microsoft technologies such as SQL, ASP.NET, MVC, ASP.NET Core, VB.NET, SQL server, Word Automation, Office development, etc. and other technologies such as HTML, CSS, jQuery, JavaScript, Bootstrap, XML, etc. He is very passionate about Microsoft .NET technology. He likes to write articles and blogs on different aspects of SQL and .NET. He also likes to help developers resolve their issues and boost them on Microsoft Technologies.

Prasad has impressive certifications such as Microsoft Certified Professional (MCP), Microsoft Certified Technology Specialist (MCTS), and Agile Scrum Master. Prasad was awarded the most valuable member at dotnetspider, most popular curator, most active curator, and featured curator at Microsoft Curah, and editor at dotnetspider. He has been awarded for his articles on CodeProject.

He started his journey with Microsoft technologies in 2007 with Visual Basic 6 and SQL 2000. Then, he gradually moved to C#, ASP, ASP.NET, MVC and now .NET Core with SQL 2019.

About the Reviewers

Manavya is a Technical leader by profession, enthusiast about cutting edge technologies. He has completed Master's in computer science from Pune university and then after working as software professional from last 13 years. He likes to work on Microsoft technologies like SQL, .NET, MVC, jQuery.

Development is his hobby and Coding is passion

Acknowledgement

I would like to thank my mother, Mrs Lata Kulkarni, and my wife Mrs Apoorva, for their support. They deserve to have their name on the cover of this book as much as I do for all their support that made this possible. I would also like to thank my father, Shrikant Kulkarni, and my children, Mau and Manasi, for their love and support to help achieve my goals.

Last but not least, I would like to thank everyone at BPB Publications for giving me this opportunity to publish my book.

— Prasad Kulkarni

Preface

The database is the most essential or a crucial part in any modern technology. It is developed for web-based, desktop/laptop-based or any smart device-based application. We need the database to maintain data security, data storage, data integrity, handling large/huge data, create and maintain relationship between data, fetching of data in a well-organized way, increase the efficiency of the end user, avoid duplication and redundancy of data, and data sorting. For all these activities, we must know about the database concepts. Are you not aware of all these concepts? Don't worry, this book will give you a complete idea about the SQL database. This book is divided into three parts: Beginner, intermediate, and advanced level.

This book starts with very basic concepts like what is data, database and DBMS. What are the advantages and disadvantages of SQL? Gradually, we move on to concepts of SQL datatypes and keywords.

In the intermediate part, we will learn about different SQL functions, wild cards, and playing with dates. We will also learn about SQL joins, case statement, DDL, DCL, and DTL concepts.

In the advanced part, we will go through SQL stored procedures, triggers, views and transactions, SQL keys, indexes, injection and constraints. SSRS, SSIS, cloud database (Azure), SQL hosting, and JSON Support. We will also learn about the new features of SQL 2016, 2017, CTP-2019, and SQL performance improvement tips. We will finally end with some fuzzy interview questions and answers.

Chapter 1, Database and SQL Basics, talks about the basics of the database, which includes what is a database, types of databases, why to use it, etc. SQL basic, SQL tables, and SQL advantages.

Chapter 2, DDMS SQL Statements and Clauses, describes SQL statements that are used to define and manipulate database and data, and the clauses that are used to filter and arrange data. It also describes the different SQL statements and clauses with examples.

Chapter 3, SQL Operators, Keywords, and Datatypes, talks about the different SQL operators, SQL keywords, and clauses.

Chapter 4, SQL Operators, discusses SQL operators like comparison, logical, assignment, bitwise, and set operators.

Chapter 5, SQL Functions, Wildcards, and Dates, describes multiple functions of SQL, including dates function to select, manipulate, and arrange data. Additionally, SQL has a magical search technique where we can search with specific wild cards that match any characters and get the result. This chapter also talks about the different SQL functions, wildcards, and dates.

Chapter 6, SQL Joins and CASE Statement, talks about how to get records from multiple tables with different selection criteria. It also talks about how we can use SQL Joins on them. It describes the various SQL Joins, their usage and SQL Case statements is used for the conditional executiona.

Chapter 7, SQL DDL, DCL, and DTL Statements, discusses how to alter table or data structure or to delete any column, table or database. We need to use data definition statements. This chapter also talks about the different SQL DDL, DCL, and DTL statements.

Chapter 8, SQL Stored Procedures, Triggers, Views, and Transactions, describes how to run some group of SQL statements again and again. It also describes stored procedures, and if you want to automatically fire/execute some group of SQL statements depending on the database changes, you can use Triggers. It talks about SQL views and transactions.

Chapter 9, SQL Keys, Indexes, Injections, and Constraints, focuses on how to fetch/get or store data to/from a table. SQL uses different keys and in this chapter, we will review all SQL keys ad indexes. Additionally, we will learn about SQL injection and SQL constraints.

Chapter 10, SSRS, SSIS, SQL Cloud database (Azure), and JSON Support, talks about how SQL can connect to JSON and interchange data. We will learn more about SQL and JSON connection, SQL reporting and integration services. We will also learn how to host your SQL to cloud server (Azure).

Chapter 11, New features of SQL 2016, 2017, and 2019, walks you through the new features of SQL 2016, 2017, and 2019.

Chapter 12, Fuzzy Interview Questions and SQL Performance Tips, gives an overview of some interview breaking fuzzy interview questions and SQL performance tips that will help you to boost the SQL query performance.

Errata

We take immense pride in our work at BPB Publications and follow best practices to ensure the accuracy of our content to provide with an indulging reading experience to our subscribers. Our readers are our mirrors, and we use their inputs to reflect and improve upon human errors if any, occurred during the publishing processes involved. To let us maintain the quality and help us reach out to any readers who might be having difficulties due to any unforeseen errors, please write to us at :

errata@bpbonline.com

Your support, suggestions and feedbacks are highly appreciated by the BPB Publications' Family.

Table of Contents

CHAPTER 1
Database and SQL Basics

Introduction

Welcome to the world of database. This chapter is a gateway to the database world, where you will learn what is database, what is DBMS, types of database, their usage, advantages, disadvantages, SQL Query execution plan, SQL table structure and how to play with them. Databases have been in use widely since last many decades (early 60's). Databases are not only used to store data but to also help us make it more secure and manageable. By encryption and standard hashing techniques, databases are becoming more powerful to fight against data theft and cyber-attacks.

To follow this chapter, you do not need any prior knowledge of database (Yes, the only thing you should have is interest in learning database). The best thing about this chapter, rather this book, is that we have amazing sections like *Rapid fire questions and answers* and *Do you know (lights on fact?)* which will give you a different experience of subject knowledge as well as quick interview questions and answers for rapid revision.

After studying this chapter, you will learn the following points:
- Data, database, and DBMS
- Usage of database
- What are the different types of DBMS?

- Structured Query Language (SQL)
- Usage of SQL
- SQL Query execution plan
- SQL tables
- Advantages and disadvantages of SQL
- Rapid fire questions and answers
- Conclusion
- Do you know (lights on fact?)

So, let's begin.

Data, database, and DBMS

First let's understand what is data? Now, data is a simple object, it may be a living or a non-living thing. The following example will clear your doubts.

Let's take an example, your name, address, blood group is *data* that is related to you (or we can say it represents you), so the data can be in any form, like text, image, files, binary, date, number, and may more.

Now we can move to the concept of database.

As the name suggests, database is the *base of data*. It's a collection of data or arrangement of data at a central point, and it is arranged in such a manner that it can be easily managed. Earlier, data-base was maintained in the form of dossier (number of papers, hard-copies) but with time, we have gradually moved to a digitalized world where we store our data in electronic forms, and this is what the data-base in current world.

To manage (fetch, add, remove, or alter) all these stored data, we need some system. This is where **Database management system (DBMS)** is introduced. DBMS is a system which helps you define, modify, remove, and retrieve data. It also monitors data, apply security policy, observe performance, maintain data integrity, and more. DBMS mainly comprises of software that acts as a bridge between the user and the database. DBMS also provides a way to figure out a way as how data is going to be stored in a database and which structure to follow in doing so.

Now let's walk through the features of database:

- **Well organized data:** Due to this feature, the data base concept is widely used; database keeps your data well organized.
- **Security:** Due to encryption like technique, database keeps your data secure and hidden from attackers.

- **ACID:** Database provides atomic, consistent, isolated and durable data transaction.
- Relation between the different entities and data across multiple database tables.
- Due to tabular representation and data storing technique and it is very easier to store and fetch data in database.

Usage of database

To answer that question, Database keeps the data well-organized so that it can be controlled easily.

We need database for the following things:

- The first and the very basic answer is we need a database to store data; database is a centralized place where we can find our data.
- As the data is centralized, it is easy to manage (add, remove, or alter),
- To enforce data security.
- To maintain large/huge data.
- To maintain data integrity. (Data integrity is nothing but consistency and accuracy of data).
- To simplify data fetching.
- To create and maintain relationship between data (this is a very important function of database).
- To increase the efficiency of the end user.
- To avoid duplication and redundancy.

Different types of DBMS

Database management system (DBMS) divides databases into different types. So, let's see the different types of DBMS.

The database management system is not new, and over the years DBMS has improved a lot in its processes, and the way it handles data. Here are the types of DBMS.

- Navigational DBMS (Hierarchical DBMS)
- Network DBMS
- Relational DBMS (RDBMS)
- Object-oriented Database Management (OODBMS)
- Object-relational database management system (ORDBMS)
- No-SQL Database

Let's trace them one by one in the following sections.

Navigational DBMS (Hierarchical DBMS)

Hierarchical database was invented in the 1960's and it is a simple form of data storage. This database uses tree-like structure to store data. The structure looks simple but is difficult to manage as larger tree has many branches which make it more complex to handle large amount of data. Imagine a big tree with a lot of branches, can you count the number of branches or trace any specific branch easily? The answer is a NO. The perfect example of Hierarchical DBMS is Windows registry. Have you ever seen Windows registry? It has a lot of branch-like structure with roots and child combination. These databases are popular for their rapid data access, as each root is defined through a specific parent. In one to one relationship child and parent is only one, so the relationship is weak than that of one-to-many or many-to-many. Data is mostly linked in this database depending upon the how the linking flexibility data is grouped.

We can say **IMS (Information Management System** was developed by IBM), Windows registry and the RDM Mobile are examples of a hierarchical database.

We can define its structure as follows:

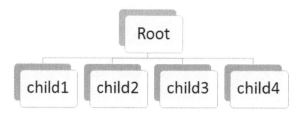

Figure 1.1: Logical data storing structure of Hierarchical DBMS

Network DBMS

This is a part of navigational database as we are navigating from one node to another and so on. We have seen in Hierarchical DBMS that it is difficult to maintain too many relations, and to overcome this limitation, Network DBMS was introduced in the late 1960's. In this structure, any node can connect to any other node. So, each record has multiple parent and child (basically this forms a graph-like structure rather than a tree). We can define its structure as follows:

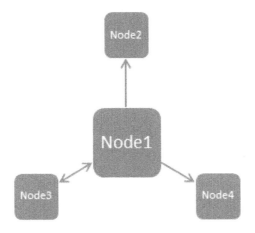

Figure 1.2: Logical data storing structure of Network DBMS

Relational DBMS (RDBMS)

This database management system brought a big revolution in the database world, where binding of data relation through tabular data format was made possible. This database management system uses tabular structure to store data (combination of rows and columns form a table which is then used to store data). The column has specific datatype to store data. This database does not directly have too many relationships, but it forms specific datatypes and integrity keys that can support any number of relationships. The concept of Relational database was founded in early 1970's but it was truly implemented by dBase database in the 1980's, when it had arranged data with relational mappings for the first time. Relational databases take up the minimum memory as they are storing only the linkages to related database instead of the whole table. These databases use Query language to manage data, see the below example to understand this:

I have 2 tables, one is `Emp` records and the other is `Emp` salary records. Here I am going to show the relation between two tables.

Sample table A (Emp)				Sample table B (Salary)	
Emp No	**Emp Name**	**Address**		**Emp No**	**Sal**
1	ABC	MUMBAI		1	10000
2	XYZ	DELHI		2	15000
3	PQR	CHENNAI		3	9000

In the above table we can see only `Emp No` column from **table A** is linked to **table B** with the help of *key* (we will learn about this concept in coming chapters), so to fetch column `Emp Name` and **Sal** from **table A** and **table B**, I can use `Emp No` as linking. It also helps me to minimize column redundancy / duplication.

This is the most popular and most-used database management system. The popular example of this database management is Microsoft SQL, MySQL, Oracle, DB2, among others.

Object-oriented database management (OODBMS)

This DBMS treats each data value as a separate object and query on the database accordingly. This DBMS is developed by blending database abilities and programming abilities together. Here, a developer can program a database and develop software directly as both database and programming language uses the same representation model. Gbase, Wakanda, Realm are some of the popular examples of object-oriented database. These databases are also known as object databases.

Object-relational database management system (ORDBMS)

This is the next generation of Relational database management system where Relational database and Object database are mixed to get advantages of both objects and relation mapping. In this database management system, all object related concepts (like abstract, classes, inheritance, encapsulation) can be directly supported in query language. Today's popular databases like MS-SQL, DB2, Oracle, and MySQL support these DBMS. These databases are well known for following ACID property (where A-Atomicity, C-Consistency, I-Isolation, D-Durability).

No-SQL databases

These databases are often called as Non-SQL databases, means no query language support is available to these databases, in short, and these databases are not using tabular structure to store data. No-SQL uses key-value pair, document, and graph-like data structure to store data, which is quite different from relational databases. No SQL follows CAP property where C - Consistency, A – Availability and P - Partition tolerance.

We can categorize this database in the following ways:

- **Key-value supported databases:** These databases use key-value pair to store data and fetch values accordingly. ArangoDB, Apache Ignite, Dynamo, No-SQL Database, developed by Oracle, are the popular databases in this series.

- **Graph databases:** These databases are specially designed to store data that are more convenient to show in a graphical module. These databases are widely used in road or territory maps, social network, and many more. AllegroGraph, OrientDB, Apache Graph, and MarkLogic are some popular example of Graph DB.
- **Document databases:** As the name suggests, these databases are used to store documents, basically the document is encapsulated and encrypted using XML, JSON, and binary formats. The database column has a unique key which identifies the document and can be retrieved. MangoDB and Couch DB are popular examples of document databases.

Besides these categories, we have search engines which are also a type of No-SQL database, typically used for text search, streaming, grouping, and distributed search.

For example: Elasticsearch and Splunk.

Here are some advantages of No-SQL:

- Basically, these databases are developed to handle big data, so these are capable of handling volumes of structured and unstructured data
- It is quick in response to modern technologies like Agile, Sprint and frequent patch releases
- Cheaper and easier in implementation
- Support multiple data structures

Here are some disadvantages of No-SQL:

- Table mapping and JOINS is complex in No-SQL.
- As of now, No-SQL is trying to be more secure, but some challenges need to be addressed.
- Most of the No-SQL does not support ACID and BASE (will learn about ACID and BASE in the coming chapters).

Structured Query Language (SQL)

In simple words, it's a **Structured Query Language (SQL)** as the name suggests, it is a structured language with some set of pre-defined syntax. Some people called it *si-que-el*. It's a query language that help us manage relational databases like MS-SQL, MySQL, Oracle, MonetDB, PostgreSQL, SQL Lite, MS-Access, SAP databases, and many more. According to American National Standards Institute, SQL is a standard with pre-defined set of statements and syntax, and is followed by all relational databases. Although it is a standard, but each database has still made some customized changes in it. SQL has changed a lot over the last few years, and now it supports all the latest technologies, including XML and JSON. SQL supports the table structure to store data. Each column and row uniquely identifies data value.

Further, SQL can be divided into 4 sub languages or we can say it's a standard:

- **Data Definition Language (DDL)**
- **Data Manipulation language (DML)**
- **Data Control Language (DCL)**
- **Transaction Control Language (TCL)**

Let's check them out one by one in the next sections.

Data Definition Language (DDL)

To define database, tables, and columns we can use this language. It comes with four commands/statements,which are as follows:

- CREATE: This statement is used to create database, tables, store procedures, SQL keys, triggers, view, and constraints.
- DROP: This statement is used to delete/drop tables from database.
- ALTER: This statement is used to modify database or the table structure, the stored procedures, SQL keys, triggers, view, constraints.
- TRUNCATE: This statement is used to clear all records from a table, where the table structure, constraints and indexes remain the same. Only the identity seed is reset to its default value.
- MODIFY: This statement is not a statement, but it is a keyword that is used with the ALTER statement and can be used to modify the table or database design.

Data Manipulation Language (DML)

DML is one of the sub languages of SQL, used to select and manipulate data from/to database for data manipulation language. The commands of this language deal with actual stored data. It comes with four commands/statements, which are as follows:

- SELECT: This statement is used to fetch values from database tables. Depending on the query condition, it fetches data in rows format, where original data remains unchanged. (This is read only command).
- INSERT: This statement is used to insert values in database table.
- UPDATE: This statement is used to alter/edit values in database table.
- DELETE: This statement is used to delete records from database tables.

Data Control Language (DCL)

DCL is one of the sub languages of SQL. As the name suggests, commands of these language are used for data control, in short, these commands deal with permission, rights of the datable tables. It comes with two commands/statements, which are as follows:

- GRANT: This statement is used to give (grant) user permission to access database.
- REVOKE: This statement is used to block the access or remove user access given by GRANT command.

Transaction Control Language (TCL)

TCL is one of the sub languages of SQL. These commands are used in transaction scope (transaction is nothing but a group of task or execution queries that must be executed in a single point of time) It comes with two commands/statements, which are as follows:

- SET TRANSACTION: This command is used to initiate or start an SQL transaction.
- COMMIT: This command is used to save/reflect the changes in database done by transaction queries.
- ROLLBACK: This command is used to undo the changes of transaction that have not yet reflected on the database
- SAVEPOINT: This command is used to create a rollback point in transaction where you can rollback transaction up to that point only. (So, no need to rollback the whole transaction.)
- RELEASE SAVEPOINT: This command is used to remove/delete save point that you created with SAVEPOINT command.

Usage of SQL

As we know, SQL is the bridge between the user and actual data store. We can do following things with SQL:

- SQL can interact with the database to manage it.
- SQL can create databases, tables, and may more.
- SQL can insert, update, and delete records to/from tables.
- SQL can alter database structure.
- SQL can do administrative task like user creation, deletion, define access permission on tables, procedures, and views.
- SQL can do performance monitoring and load balance of database.
- SQL can encrypt and hide data.
- SQL can support ACID and transaction-based executions.
- SQL can relate and map multiple tables that help to store data separately and fetch it with ease, to relate tables with each other we need keys and constraints.

SQL Query execution plan

This is the most frequently-asked interview question. SQL has Query execution in two parts:

- Estimated plan
- Actual plan

As the name suggests, estimated plan delivers work estimation, including syntax verification, query binding, query optimization, while actual plan delivers when actual query is fired on database.This plan is a runtime plan, which may contain actual resource utilization. Look at the flow chart below, which will clarify your doubts about SQL query execution:

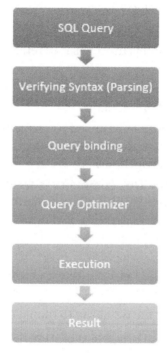

Figure 1.3: SQL Query execution plan

When we execute any SQL query then SQL parser analyzes the query and verifies all the syntax according to the SQL standard. Later, if the syntax is correct then Query binding process is run, which resolves all the names, conflicts, and then that query is passed to the optimizer engine. This engine helps create *best plan to execute* based on low cost plan technique, where calculating plan memory and CPU consumption play vital roles. Finally, the query pass to actual execution plan where the actual Query is fired on the database and the result is passed to the result pane. In short, we can say whatever command is fired by the user, first it is sent to SQL syntax and after successful compilation, it will be sent to execution engine and then it executes on actual data.

SQL tables

SQL uses tabular structure to store data. SQL table is a combination of rows and columns. Each column and row is combination of a cell in which we can store data. See the SQL table structure below:

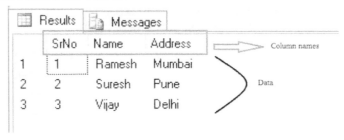

Figure 1.4

In above structure, we have a SQL table with 3 rows and 3 columns. First row is the column header (contains column name by which columns are get identified) and rest of the rows are actual data.

Depending on column datatype SQL stored data in cell, in above example first column datatype is numeric (which store numbers only) so we have store only number in it, rest of the column datatype is varchar (in SQL there is `varchar` datatype us used to store `char` and `string` values), in later chapters we will see in details about datatypes of SQL. The SQL table has specified number of columns but any number of rows.

Advantages and disadvantages of SQL

The following are the advantages of SQL:

- **Easy to learn:** It is easy to learn as all syntax are made with high-level language, so it is easily readable and recognizable
- **Portability:** Now a days, database is not limited to desktop and server machines only, it has spanned across laptops, smart devices, tabs, mobile phones, and many more. SQL has a wide range of support for all these modern technologies,and it supports all devices. SQL is portable and flexible enough to support all devices. Linux and all its variants are now supported by SQL 2017.
- **Performance:** SQL performs well while dealing with large amount of data so you can fetch, insert, and update data with ease and a better speed.
- **Uniform syntax:** SQL is a standard adopted by **ANSI (American National Standards Institute)** and ISO standard, which makes it uniform in all SQL supported database, like MS-SQL, MySQL, SQL-Lite, and Oracle.

- **Enforced safety:** SQL has improved a lot over the last few years. With standard encryption algorithms, SQL provides better data safety and security. SQL also offers different types of access permissions, security audits and log files to trace issues.

- **Backup and Recovery facility:** SQL has good backup and recovery plan, where you can schedule your hot backup (**Hot backup:** No need to de-attach database while backup). SQL has good recovery plan in case of data-loss or data corruption. SQL backup facility is also supported by many 3rd party backup software

- **SQL support:** SQL has a wide range of support from the community, MSDN and supporters.

The following are the disadvantages of SQL:

- **Cost:** As SQL is an enterprise-level database management system, the cost of implementation and licensing is a bit costlier than other alternative databases.

- **Customized syntax:** Although SQL follows ANSI standard but still,syntax varies from one database to another. So, we need to keep track of those changes when connecting different databases.

Rapid fire questions and answers

1. **What is DBMS?**

   It is a database management system that is used to manage data stored in the database so; it's a bridge between the user and the actual data stored. Data can be managed with the help of different database queries

2. **Which type of data can we store in SQL database?**

   SQL Database is capable of handling and storing any type of data, including text, images, graphics, audio, video files, and binary data.

3. **What are the advantages of SQL over No-SQL database?**

   The following are the advantages of SQL over No-SQL database:

   - SQL follows ACID (Atomicity, Consistency, Isolation and Durability) properties for every transaction execution, where as in No-SQL, there is no ACID yet.

   - SQL has good production support from all database providers, whereas for No-SQL there is no such strong support. We can say No-SQL community is not well defined yet.

   - SQL is used since the last 4-5 decades and now the product is more stable and secure, No-SQL is new and an emerging technology compared to SQL and it needs more stability.

- SQL has table structure to store data and it is easier to read and alter, whereas No-SQL uses key-value pair, document, graph-based structure-based database structure, which makes it complex to edit records.
- No-SQL has not much good reporting tools No-SQL reporting tools are not friendly as compared with SQL, whereas SQL is well known for its reporting services.
- SQL is well known for its inbuilt functions (for mathematical calculations, date functions, and more), easily-understandable syntax, but No-SQL is a bit complex compared to SQL.

Conclusion

- Database is used to store data and DBMS is used to manage and maintain that data.
- Database gives us flexibility notonly to store data but to also manage them in secure ways.
- There are different types of DBMS;each one is differed from another with regards to data storing technique and relation.
- SQL is a kind of DBMS, which supports RDBMS and ORDBMS structure
- SQL uses tabular format to store data.

Do you know (lights on fact?)

- As database and DBMS are related, both are casually referred as database (so when you ask people, what is SQL they always say it's a database but if you notice it's a database management system).
- DBMS concept was first implemented in the 1960's, when they used to have disk-drums to store data and manage it.
- In 1962, a California-based company usedthe word 'data-base' as a technical term for the first time.
- The cylindrical shape is used to show the database sign.
- Hierarchical database was invented in the 9060's, but it became a hybrid in 1990s with Relation database, and now it is widely used in tele-communications industry.
- The No-SQL term was first used in 1998.
- Hadoop is not a database but a framework system that supports and uses No-SQL database to store data and documents.
- SQL was originally developed by IBM in early 1970's.

CHAPTER 2

SQL Statements, Keywords, and Datatype

We know database is important not only to store data but also to secure it and manage it. SQL keeps data storage very clear and simple with its different datatypes. The datatypes are also very simple and user-friendly. It helps to arrange, store data separately, and speed up the data searching as well. According to data operations, SQL is further divided into different sublanguages like DDL, DML, DCL, and DTL. In this chapter we will see the different SQL datatypes, SQL statements, and SQL keywords.

Prerequisite for this chapter

Form this chapter onwards, we will also concentrate on SQL practical, and so you should have a laptop/desktop with SQL server installed on it. There is no specific knowledge required to learn this chapter, just start reading this with interest in database concepts.

Structure

After studying this chapter, you will learn the following points:

- SQL keywords
- SQL datatypes

       o   Numerical SQL datatypes
- ♦ Exact numeric
- ♦ Approximate numeric

       o   The string and char SQL datatypes
- ♦ Character string
- ♦ Unicode string
- ♦ Binary string

       o   Date and time SQL datatypes

       o   Miscellaneous SQL datatypes

- Different types of SQL statements
- DDL statements
- DML statements
- Conclusion
- Rapid fire questions and answers
- Do you know (lights on fact?)

So, let's begin

SQL keywords

Every programming language has its own set of reserved words that are used by its compiler to perform various operations. Similarly, in SQL, we have a set of reserved words and it is recommended to not use those reserved words as table name, column, and identifiers. If you want to use them, then enclose them in square braces [ ], these words are known as keywords. Basically, database uses this keyword for definition, manipulation, and accessing data.

SQL has a very large list of keywords, but here I am picking up some important keywords for you:

ADD	PROCEDURE	BEGIN
ALL	PUBLIC	BETWEEN
ALTER	FILE	REVERT
AND	REFERENCES	REVOKE
ANY	FOR	RIGHT
AS	FROM	ROLLBACK
ASC	RESTORE	ROWCOUNT
BREAK	GROUP	IDENTITY

BY	HAVING	CHECKPOINT
IF	CASE	IN
SELECT	CLOSE	SET
COMMIT	SCHEMA	SETUSER
COMPUTE	INTERSECT	SHUTDOWN
CONSTRAINT	IS	DROP
CONTAINS	JOIN	ELSE
CONTAINSTABLE	KEY	UNION
CONTINUE	LEFT	UNIQUE
CONVERT	LIKE	UPDATE
CREATE	NOT	TO
CURRENT	NULL	TOP
CURSOR	TRANSACTION	UPDATETEXT
DATABASE	TRIGGER	ON
DBCC	TRUNCATE	DELETE
DEFAULT	TABLE	DESC
DISTINCT	DISK	OR

Table 2.1: Important SQL keywords

SQL datatypes

SQL database has different datatypes. As the name suggests, datatypes show/denote what type of data a column can store. In short, a column is restricted to store data according to its datatypes. Going forward, SQL datatypes are divided into the following; depending upon the type of data they can hold:

- Numerical SQL datatypes
  - o Exact numeric
  - o Approximate numeric
- The string and char SQL datatypes
  - o Character string
  - o Unicode string
  - o Binary string
- Date and time SQL datatypes
- Miscellaneous SQL datatypes

Let's discuss them one by one.

Numerical SQL datatypes

As the name suggests, these datatypes contain numerical data. Further, these datatypes have two sub types:

- Exact numeric
- Approximate numeric

Exact numeric

Exact numeric datatypes contain only numbers; there is no precision or floating point. Depending upon the size limitation, these numeric datatypes are organized in the following types:

- `tinyint`: As the name suggests, this data type stores integer values ranging from 0 to 255, and takes 1 byte of storage space; this is more useful when we need to store numeric data between 0 to 255.

  Real-time example: Number of minutes in hour is 60, so it is always between 0 to 255; here we can use `tinyint` to store hour data. Another example would a person's age where it will not go beyond 255, and hence we can use `tinyint` here.

- `smallint`: Small integer datatype stores integer values between -32,768 to 32,767 and takes 2 byte of storage space.

  Real-time example: You can use this data type whenever you want to store numeric data ranging between -32768 to 32768. Say, I want to store daily temperature of Antarctica then it would be ranging from -60 Celsius to 10 Celsius. Here we can use `smallint` datatype.

- `int`: This is widely used in many applications, where you want to store numerical values ranging between -2,147,483,648 and 2,147,483,647. It takes 4 byte of storage space.

  Real -time example: Say I want to store the numerical data whose values are in millions, for example, to store yearly population of my city, I can use this datatype.

- `bigint`: To store very large-scale numbers, we can use this datatype, which ranges from -9,223,372,036,854,775,808 to 9,223,372,036,854,775,807 and takes 8 byte of storage space

  Real-time example: The example is very subjective here (but still we will try). To store the earth age in years we can use this database. Or to store, how much water does Amazon River puts into the sea each year, we can use this datatype.

- `numeric`: This datatype is used to store huge volumes of numbers, ranging from $- 10^{38} +1$ through $10^{38} - 1$. This datatype is also called as decimal.

- `bit:` To store Boolean value, we can use thisdatatype. `True` value is stored as 1 and `False` value is stored as 0, and it takes 1 byte of storage space.

  Real-time example: To store the answer of a multiple choice question, we can use this datatype, for example, the answer of a question like *The earth is the fourth planet from the sun*, and we can store the value as `true` or `false`.

- `money:` To store currency and money value we need this datatype. This datatype supports most of the currencies. It takes 4 to 8 byte of storage space. It will take 4 bytes for `smallmoney` datatype, and 8 bytes for money datatype, The range of the `smallmoney` datatype is in between - 214,748.3648 and 214,748.3647.

  Real-time example: Store flight ticket when flying from US to Canada, if the flight tickets are in US dollars then we can use that currency, or we can use Canadian dollar currency.

  Money datatype supports many commonly used currencies like Dollar, Cent, Pound, Yen, Euro, Lira, Rupee, among others.

Approximate numeric

As the name suggests, this datatype does not only contain pure numbers but also decimal values and precision. The value of these numbers is not exact but floating and approximate to complete numbers (say `3.94` which is nearly equal to 4) these numeric datatypes are organized in the following sub types:

- `real:` To store value up to 7 digit of precision we can use this data type. Here the 7 digit means the digit laying right of the decimal point. Here numbers ranging from - 3.40E + 38 to -1.18E - 38, 0 and 1.18E - 38 to 3.40E + 38. It takes 4 byte of storage space.

  Real-time example: To store the value of PI we can use this datatype. (PI = π = 3.14159).

- `float:` To store value of up to 15 digits of precision, we can use this datatype. Here the 15 digit means the digit laying right of the decimal point. Here numbers ranging from - 1.79E+308 to -2.23E-308, 0 and 2.23E-308 to 1.79E+308. It takes 8 byte of storage space.

  Real-time example: If you divide 10 by 3 then the answer would be 3.3333333333. To store such results we can use float datatype.

The string and char SQL datatypes

As the name suggests, these datatypes contains textual data. Numbers can also be a part of this character/string datatype but they will not hold any numeric value, the numbers are also considered as text. Further, this datatype are divided in to three -sub types:

- Character string
- Unicode string
- Binary string

Character string

Character string datatypes contain textual/character data. Depending upon the size they can hold, these character strings are organized as the following types:

- char: This is the fixed length data type; the value ranges from 1 char to 4000 char. The storage size is defined as per the string length. This datatype also stores multi-byte encoding character set like Asian languages (Chinese, Japanese, Korean, and many more).

  When the size of data is consistent and fixed, then we can use this datatype

  Real-time example: If you want to store exam result as F for fail and P for pass, then you can use char datatype, here the length of char is fixed (either F or P).

- varchar: As the name suggests, varchar is variable length character, but the storage capacity of this datatype is more than char datatype. The value ranges from 1 char to 8000 or use varchar(max) where the max indicates the storage size up to 2 GB. For single byte encoding, it takes 1-byte storage space and for multi-byte encoding it takes 2bytes.

  When the size of data is not fixed or vary according to a condition, then we can use this datatype.

  Real-time example: If you want to store a user feedback of any software, then you can use this datatype as you cannot predict the exact length of the text.

- text: If you want to store only non-Unicode then you can use this datatype, the value ranges from 1 to 2,147,483,647 bytes.

  When you want to store only non-Unicode text but have variable length, then you can use this datatype.

Unicode string

- nchar: These are the fixed length datatypes with Unicode support, where the value ranges from 1 char to 4000 char. The storage size is defined as per the string length. Basically, these data types are used to store the full range of Unicode character data and use the UTF-16-character encoding.

  When the size of data is consistent, fixed with the support for UTF-8 and UTF-16 Unicode, then we can use this datatype.

- nvarchar: As the name suggests, nvarchar is used to store variable length character, but the storage capacity of this datatype is more than char datatype.

The value ranges from 1 char to 8000 or use `varchar(max)` where the `max` indicates the storage size up to 2 GB.

When the size of data is not fixed or vary according to condition then we can use this datatype with the support for UTF-8 and UTF-16 Unicode

* `ntext:` As the name suggests, `ntext` is used to store variable length character but it is also capable of storing Unicode data, it does store the size up to `2^30 - 1 (1,073,741,823)` bytes, it is exactly 2 times greater than that of string datatype.

Binary string

* `binary:` This datatype is used to store binary data having fixed length With Unicode support, the value ranges from 1 char to 8000 bytes or use `varchar(max)` means up to 2GB, when the binary data length is not defined then it takes the default length as 1.

When the size of data is consistent or fixed, then you can use this datatype.

* `varbinary:` As the name suggests, `varbinary` is used to store variable length binary data where the value ranges from 1 char to 8000 bytes.

When the size of binary data is not consistent or not fixed, then you can use this datatype.

* `varbinary(max):` This datatype is same as `varbinary`, which is used to store variable length binary data. The only difference is that the storage capacity of `varbinary(max)` is more than `varbinary`.

When the size of binary data is not consistent or not fixed and exceeds 8000 bytes, then you can use this datatype.

* `image:` The `image` datatype is used to store binary data only which can be of variable length type, that ranges from 0 to 2^31-1 (2,147,483,647) bytes.

Date and time SQL datatypes

To store date and time values, SQL has different datatypes as the following:

* `date`
* `time`
* `datetime`

Date

As the name suggests, this datatype is used to store date SQL. The default date format of SQL storage is YYYY-MM-DD. The date range ranges between 0001-01-01 and 9999-12-31.

- **YYYY** is the year and it has a range from 0001 to 9999.
- **MM** is the month and it has a range from 1 to 12 (from January to December).
- **DD** is the day and it has a range from 1 to 31.

Basically, date is stored as string with the max value is 10 characters (**YYYY-MM-DD**). The storage capacity for date storage is fixed, which is 3 bytes, if you leave this field empty then the default value is 1900-01-01. SQL has date range limited to 1582-10-15 (October 15, 1582 CE) to 9999-12-31 (December 31, 9999 CE).

When you want to store only date in database then you can use this datatype.

Real-timeexample: If you want to store DOB of all employees, then you can define a column with date datatype.

Time

As the name suggests, this datatype is used to store time. SQL does not follow any specific time zone; it always stores time in 24-hour clock format. Default time format of SQL storage is hh: mm: ss. nnnn. The time ranges from 00-00-00 to 23-59-59.

- hh is the hour unit and it ranges between 00 and 23.
- mm is the minute unit and it ranges between 00 and 59.
- ss is the seconds and it ranges between 00 and 59.
- nn is the nano-seconds and it ranges between 00 and 999.

Basically, time is stored as string, where the max value is 8 characters **(hh:mm:ss)** The storage capacity for time datatype is fixed, which is 5 bytes, and if you leave this field empty then the default value is 00:00:00. It does supports different time formats.

When you want to store only time value in database then you can use this datatype

Real-time example: If you want to store time lapse of racing game, then you can define a column with time datatype.

Datetime

As the name suggests, this datatype is used to store datetime in a single column. Here date and time are combined with 24-hour. Default datetime format of SQL storage is YYYY-MM-DD hh:mm:ss:nnnn. The date ranges between 0001-01-01 and 9999-12-31, and the time ranges between 00-00-00 and 23-59-59.

- **YYYY** is the year and it ranges from 0001 to 9999.
- **MM** is the month and it ranges from 1 to 12 (from January to December).
- **DD** is the day and it ranges from 1 to 31.
- **hh** is the hour unit and it ranges between 00 and 23.

- **mm** is the minute unit and it ranges between 00 and 59.
- **ss** is the seconds and it ranges between 00 and 59.
- **nn** is the nano-seconds and it ranges between 00 and 999.

Basically, time is stored as string,where the max value is 19-23 characters **(YYYY-MM-DD hh:mm: ss)** The storage capacity for time datatype is fixed, which is 8 bytes, and if you leave this field empty, then the default value is 1900-01-01 00:00:00.

When you want to store both date and time value in a single column, then you can use this datatype.

Real-time example: If you want to store student's birthday with date and time, then you can define a column with `datetime` datatype.

If you want more options in seconds precision the you can use `datetimeoffset` datatype and to support different time zones, you can use `datetimeoffset`.

Miscellaneous SQL datatypes

The previous sections of datatypes covered most of the type of datatypes used to store in SQL, but apart from that we also have a few more datatypes that can be used to store different values. Go through the following datatypes for more details:

- `xml`: This datatype was introduced in version SQL 2008, and as the name suggests, this datatype is used to store xml instance in column. The data size of the XML should not be more than 2 GB. Here XML datatype has some rule while storing data:
  - o There should be one or more nodes
  - o There must be only one root element
  - o You can create optional schema if needed
  - o You can store contents or document as XML

  When you want to store XML data in the form of document or contents then you can use this datatype.

  Real-time example: XML is very good for storing and describing data, if we put employee information like name, address, gender, and department in XML then we can store that data in database with `xml` datatype.

- `uniqueidentifier`: As name suggests, this datatype is used to store unique identifier that is **GUID (Global unique identifier)**. This unique identifier can be created using `NewID ( )` function (`NewID( )` is inbuilt function in SQL, and it is used to create new GUID per call). GUID is made up of 36 characters string with the combination of alphabets and numbers with 4 hyphen (dash) as a separator. (for example, 706b30a8-1893-4c5f-bb41-37d406331bf5).

  When you want to store unique identifier then you can use this datatype.

Real-time example: If you want to generate serial numbers and assign to your factory products, then you can use `uniqueidentifier` data type. Alternatively, you can use it in applications like Stock Keeping Unit, Organizations global employee identification number.

- `table`: If you need to process any data and got some results from it, then to store that result for processing at a later time, we can use this datatype. We can say it is temporary storage which returns the output in tabular format. When we define any `table` datatype, we can give its column name, datatypes and different constraints (constraints are nothing but the set of rules that are applied on table and its columns. In later chapters, we will walk through these concepts)

  When you want to store return result executed by SQL functions and stored procedures then we can use this datatype.

  Real-time example: If you want to fetch sales records of a company for a given financial and then want to use it for further graphical reports, then you can use this datatype and store first level results in it.

- `sql_variant`: This datatype is same as object datatype in programming language, where you can store anything in it and later on if you want to use them you need to convert them to original base type. This data type can store all SQL supported datatypes. Say, if I create one column with `sql_variant` as datatype then you can store string, numbers and float values in it. This datatype can store up to 8000 byte.

  When you want to return some value from SQL function or stored procedure, but you are not sure of its datatype then you can use `sql_variant`.

  Real-time example: If you want to store result of 2 number divisions but the input is coming from user, then in this case you can use `sql_variant` datatype as it stores numeric as well as float or real value.

- `geography`: This is longitudinal database which is used to store round-earth coordinate system, meaning, GPS latitude and longitude coordinates. This datatype represent co-ordinates.

- `geometry`: This type can hold data in a Euclidean (flat) coordinate system; SQL server has some inbuilt methods that support this datatype. These methods are as per **Open Geospatial Consortium (OGC)** standard.

SQL statements

We know SQL is a query language and further it has been divided in sublanguages as per the nature of data handling and manipulation. These sublanguages are also known as SQL statements. We have the following sublanguages:

- **Data Definition Language (DDL)**

- **Data Manipulation Language (DML)**
- **Data Control Language (DCL)**
- **Transaction Control Language (TCL)**

DDL statement

As the name suggests, **Data Definition Language (DDL)** statements are used to define data in SQL database. Here define means, we can create, change, delete, and rename database objects like table, column datatypes, view, stored procedure, database with the help of DDL statement. DDL statement gives us the following command to manage and create database objects:

- CREATE
- ALTER
- DROP
- TRUNCATE

Let's discuss them one-by-one.

Create

With the help of CREATE command, we can create different database objects like table, column datatypes, view, stored procedure, and database. The typical syntax (syntax is nothing but a standard way of writing command/query/statement) as follows:

CREATE [database object] [object name] ([column definitions])

- database object: It's a database object that you want to create. Suppose if you want to create new database, then you need DATABASE keyword, to create table you need TABLE keyword.
- object name: CREATE command is used to create database, table, function, view stored procedure, so the object name is the object you want to create.
- column definition: If you want to create table then column definitions contains the following:
  - o List of the column that table should contain.
  - o Datatypes of those columns.
  - o Size of that column (storage capacity).

Whenever you want to create new database, table, column, function, view, or stored procedure, you can use this command.

Let's create database in SQL by following the below steps:

1. Open SQL Server.
2. Connect database engine (local/remote).

3. Open SQL analyzer and execute the following query:

`CREATE DATABASE testdb`

Here `CREATE` is the DDL command, `DATABASE` is the keyword that will instruct SQL engine to create `testdb` database.

See the following screenshot:

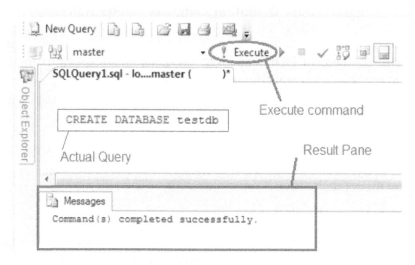

In preceding screenshot, we can see SQL query analyzer with **Actual Query** and **Result Pane**. When I click on `Execute` command (in exclamatory sign) then actual query is send to SQL engine and the result will be displayed in `Result Pane`.

Now if you click on `Object Explorer` (left side of the snap) you can see the database is created successfully. See the following screenshot:

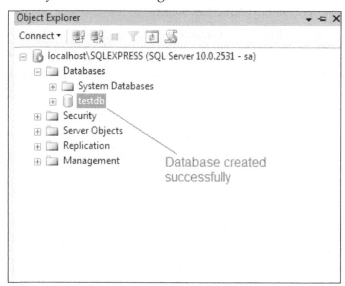

Let's take another example. This time we will create TABLE in our just created database testdb, follow same steps as given below:

1. Right click on testdb.
2. Click on NewQuery.
3. Put create TABLE command and execute the following query:

```
CREATE TABLE [EmpMaster]
(
    [SrNo] [int] NULL,
    [Name] [varchar](50)NULL,
    [Address] [varchar](50)NULL,
    [Dept] [varchar](50)NULL
)
ON [PRIMARY]
```

The previous query is a bit interesting, where we have added 4 columns in table with different columns and its datatypes. Here EmpMaster is the table name SrNo, Name, Address, and Dept are the column names with int (this columns holds numeric values) and varchar (this columns holds textual values) as datatypes. You can see, for varchar we have kept the string limit up to 50. When I execute the query, we will get the following output:

Message is output pane `command completed successfully` indicates the activity has executed successfully. Refer to the following screenshot:

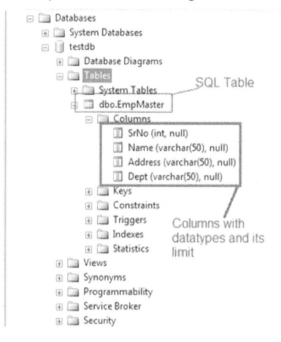

Alter

Alter is used to change or modify database, table, and column definition. We can rename database and table name with this command, alternatively we can add and drop columns from the existing table. We can also change column datatype too. The typical syntax is as follows:

```
ALTER [database object] [object name] [ALTER] [MODIFY] [ADD] ([specify
database/table/column name])
```

- `database object`: It's a database object that you want to create. Suppose if you want to create new database then you need `DATABASE` keyword. To create table you need `TABLE` keyword.

- `object name`: `ALTER` command is used to modify definition of database, table, function, view stored procedure, so the object name is the object you want to create.

- If you want to modify database/table name or add/drop/rename any column or change its datatype then we can specify size of that column here.

This command has a very big scope. It is used to modify database, table, and column definition, including column-related operations like add, drop, rename, or change its datatype. In short, all database, table column design changes can be done with this command.

Let's rename database in SQL by following the below steps:

1. We have already created database `testdb`, now we will rename it. Use the following query:

    `ALTER DATABASE testdb MODIFY NAME = renameddb;`

2. If you fire above query, you will get the following result (`database is successfully renamed`):

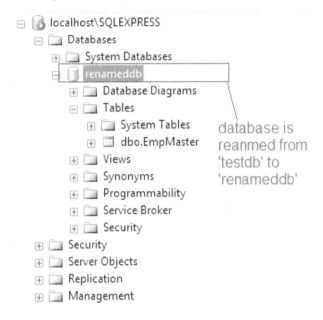

Now, take another example, where we change column datatype size. We have name column with size 50, now if we want to increase it to 100. Use the following query:

`ALTER TABLE empmaster ALTER COLUMN name varchar(100)`

Now if you see the output, you will find the following result:

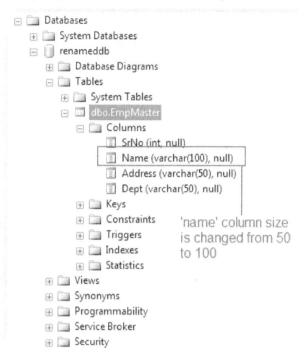

Take another example where we want to add an additional column in table, check below query, which will helps us to add column in table

```
ALTER TABLE empmaster add city varchar(50)
```

In the preceding query we have added column city with the size limitation of 50.

Drop

Drop command is used to delete database, table, column, view, stored procedure. In short, to delete anything from the database structure, we can use this command. The typical syntax is as follows:

```
DROP objecttypeobjectname
```

- **objecttype:** It's a database object which can be database, table, stored procedure, view, and more.
- **objectname:** Name of the database, table, stored procedure, view that you want to delete.

When you want to remove entire database, table or any database object like stored procedure or view, then you use this command, if we fire this command on table and if that table has already data (records) in it, then all table with data gets destroyed.

Let's drop our existing SQL table `empmaster`. Use the following query:

```
DROP TABLE empmaster
```

In the preceding query `DROP` and `TABLE` are reserved and mandatory keywords as per the syntax and `empmaster` is the table name, if you fire this query `empmaster` table will get deleted from database.

Truncate

This command is used to delete all rows (records) from table in one go. This command is quick in action, as it will not delete records row by row. Here one thing to note is, `TRUNCATE` deletes only records not table but `TRUNCATE` resets the sequence for `IDENTITY` column types. (In coming chapters we will learn about `IDENTITY` column types) so the increment seed will be reset to default value. `TRUNCATE` command does not have `WHERE` clause. This command will only fire on SQL table. The typical syntax is as follows:

`TRUNCATE TABLE objectname`

* `objectname:` Name of the table you want to truncate.

This command is useful when you have a volume data in your SQL table, and you want to delete all records as well as reset any identity column.

Let's `TRUNCATE` our existing SQL table `empmaster`. Use the following query:

```
TRUNCATE TABLE empmaster
```

In preceding query `TRUNCATE` and `TABLE` are reserved and mandatory keywords as per the syntax and `empmaster` is the table name, if you fire this query on `empmaster` then all the records gets removed from table. We don't have any identity column set on our table so it will not show any effect related to it

DML statement

As the name suggests, DML statements are used to manipulate data stored in SQL tables. Here manipulation means, we can insert, change, delete, fetch/select data from table. DML statement gives us following command to manage data:

* `INSERT`
* `UPDATE`
* `DELETE`
* `SELECT`

Insert

As the name suggests, this command is used to insert record in SQL table, we need to insert data as per the column datatype. With this command we can insert one or more records in single execution. The typical syntax is as follows:

`INSERT INTO tablename [columnnames] VALUES [column values]`

- `tablename:` name of the SQL table in which we need to insert values.
- `columnnames:` name of the SQL table column in which we need to insert values, this is optional part if we do not specify column name then we need to insert values in each column
- `column values:` Here we need to provide actual data/values that we need to insert in SQL column as per the datatype (which means we cannot insert numbers in `varchar (string)` column)

This command is useful when you need to insert records in SQL table; you can use same command for bulk (multiple records) insertion also.

Let's insert some records in our `empmaster` table. Check out the following query:

`INSERT INTO [EmpMaster]`

`([SrNo],[Name],[Address],[Dept])`

`VALUES`

`(10,'Manavya','Pune','Development')`

Now checkout above query, compare it with syntax `INSERT INTO` is the mandatory keyword then we have given all column name in angular braces, after that `VALUES` is again mandatory keyword and then we have pass actual data.

Have you observed one thing here? For numeric value 10 we have not given single quotes otherwise all `varchar` (Now onwards I will call string values as `varchar`) values are enclosed in single quotes. Yes, all non-numerical datatypes need to be enclosed in single quotes. (Now, what happed if want to insert 100 to `varchar` column? Then, I need to enclose 100 in single quotes. As the datatype is non-numeric).

If we execute our insert query, we will get the following output:

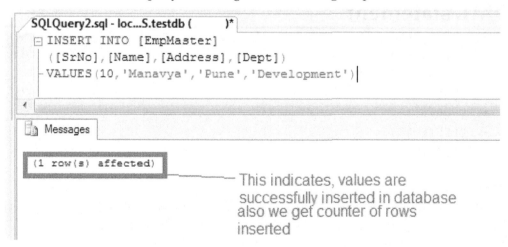

This indicates, values are successfully inserted in database also we get counter of rows inserted

And if open `EmpMaster` table we can see, data is successfully inserted in table. See the following screenshot:

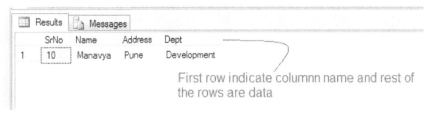

First row indicate columnn name and rest of the rows are data

Insert multiple values example:

We can insert multiple values in single query; we just need to separate each record with a comma. See the following query:

```
INSERT INTO EmpMaster VALUES
(20,'PK','Pune','Testing'),(30,'Pankaj','Mumbai','Testing')
```

In preceding query, we have not pass column name as we need to insert values in each column. When we fire the above query, we will get the following output:

```
SQLQuery3.sql - loc...S.testdb (      )*
    /****** Script for SelectTopNRows command from SSMS ******/
  INSERT INTO EmpMaster
  VALUES (20, 'PK', 'Pune', 'Testing'), (30, 'Pankaj', 'Mumbai', 'Testing')

  Messages
  (2 row(s) affected)            2 Rows are inserted
```

Insert values in columns with different order with example:

Do you know we can change the order of column while inserting records in tables, here we have written same query but despite changing the arrangement of columns, we still ran the query successfully, see the following query:

```
INSERT INTO [EmpMaster]

([Dept], [SrNo], [Address], [Name])

VALUES('Development', 10,'Pune','Manavya')
```

Here, we have shifted `SrNo`, `Dept` columns.

If there is any identity column (auto incremented column) then do not consider that column in `INSERT` statement.

Update

As the name suggests, this command is used to update record in SQL table. With the help of this command, we can set new values to column by replacing old values. The typical syntax is as follows:

`UPDATE tablename SET column name = value [WHERE Condition]`

- `tablename`: It is the name of the SQL table in which we need to insert values.
- `column names`: It is the name of the SQL table column which we want to change.
- `value`: New value of the column.
- `Condition`: This is the state which returns either Boolean value or evaluates an expression, if the Boolean value is `TRUE` then `UPDATE` command will fire or if there is an expression then update command will fire as per the expression

This command is useful when you need to change existing column values. Additionally, you can do it on specific condition.

Let's update some records in our `Empmaster` table. Check out the following query:

`UPDATE EmpMaster SET Address='Delhi'`

Here `UPDATE` is the reserved keyword, `EmpMaster` is our table name and `SET` is again a reserved keyword and the `Address` is the column name and `Delhi` is the new record/value of column address. Now check out the output of the following query:

If we open table and check records, then we got the following result:

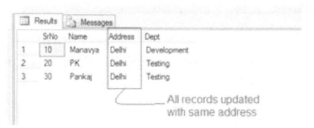

In the preceding screenshot, we can see all rows are updated as there is no WHERE condition, here we can restrict the column changes with the help of WHERE clause (in our coming chapter we will see WHERE condition in details).

Update multiple columns with single query:

In the previous example, we have checked how to update one column, now we will check how to update multiple columns with a single query. Suppose we want to update Address and Dept column using a single query, then we can use the following query:

```
UPDATE EmpMaster SET Address='Pune', Dept='Cust Support'
```

The above example shows we can update multiple columns in a single query. We need to use comma to separate these columns.

Delete

As the name suggests, this command is used to DELETE records from SQL table. With the help of this command, we can delete one or more records but delete command deletes record one by one. The typical syntax is as follows

```
DELETE FROM tablename   [WHERE Condition]
```

- **tablename:** It is the name of the SQL table in which we need to insert values.
- **Condition:** This is the state which returns either Boolean value or evaluates an expression, if the Boolean value is TRUE then delete command will fire or as per the expression.

This command is useful when you need to delete records from table.

Let's delete some records from Empmaster table. Check out the following query:

```
DELETE FROM EmpMaster
```

Here DELETE and FROM are mandatory keywords and EmpMaster is the table name.

If we execute the above query, then all rows from table will get removed as there is no WHERE clause in the query. See the following screenshot:

With the help of `WHERE` clause we can limit the number of rows deleted.

Suppose if we want to delete any particular row, then we do it using `WHERE` clause (we will learn this clause in deep in the coming chapters)

`DELETE FROM empmaster WHERE name = 'xyz'`

In the preceding query, we have used `WHERE` clause to delete rows whose name column contains value `xyz`.

Select

As the name suggests, this command is used to fetch records from SQL table.With the help of this command we can fetch one or more records. The typical syntax is as follows:

`SELECT * [columnnames] FROM tablename [WHERE Condition]`

- `columnnames:` Name of the column that we need to fetch from SQL tables.
- `tablename:` Name of the SQL table in which we need to insert values
- `Condition:` This is the state which returns either Boolean value or an expression, if the Boolean value is `TRUE` then delete command will fire or if there is an expression then delete command will fire as per the expression

This command is useful when you need to fetch records from table.

Let's fetch some records from `Empmaster` table. Check out the following query:

`SELECT * FROM EmpMaster`

In the above query, `SELECT` and `FROM` are mandatory keywords and `EmpMaster` is the table name and here * means all columns, check out the following output:

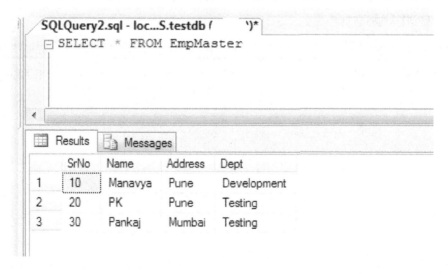

Instead of * we can select limited columns also. Check out the following query:

```
SELECT Name,address FROM EmpMaster
```

If we execute the above query, we will get the following output:

Have you noticed the difference? Yes, we can select a limited number of columns in SELECT query.

If you want to select a particular record, then you can use WHERE clause with SELECT statement. See the below query:

```
SELECT FROM empmaster WHERE name = 'xyz'
```

If we run the above query then SELECT query will display only those rows that have the name column values as xyz.

Conclusion

In this chapter we have seen that SQL engine uses some reserved words to execute queries that are known as keywords. SQL stores data in columns according to its datatype. SQL has different datatype as per the nature of the data including different datatypes for textual, encrypted, binary and numeric data. SQL also stores date and time as separate datatypes. To define and create database and its object we use DDL in SQL. DDL offers us different commands to define data, the command is CREATE, ALTER, DROP, and TRUNCATE. To manipulate and manage data in SQL tables, we use DML in SQL. DML offers us different commands to define data, the commands are INSERT, UPDATE, DELETE, and SELECT.

Rapid fire questions and answers

1. **What are SQL keywords?**

    SQL keywords are reserved words that are used by SQL engine for query execution.

2. **Which datatype is used to store number in SQL?**

SQL server has its different inbuilt datatypes to store numerical values; SQL can store values with or without precision point. We can use `tinyint`, `smallint`, `int`, `bigint`, `numeric`, `real`, and `float` datatypes for string numbers.

3. **Which datatype is used to store alphanumeric values SQL?**

There are a number of different datatypes in SQL depending on the storing capacity. You can use `char`, `varchar`, `text`, `ntext`, `nvarchar`, `nchar`, and many more.

4. **Which datatype is used to store only date value?**

We can use `date` datatype to store only date value.

5. **Which datatype is used to store only time value?**

We can use `timedatatype` to store only time value.

6. **Which datatype is used to store date and time together?**

We can use `datetime` datatype to store `datetime` value.

7. **Can I store file in database? If yes, then which datatype should I use to store it?**

To store file in database, we can use `binary`, `varbinary`, `varbinary(max)` datatype to store file. First we need to convert that file in binary data and then insert that binary data in column.

8. **What is DDL?**

It is a Data Definition Language used to define database and its object. With the help of this language we can create database, tables, columns, views, and stored procedures. The commands offered by DDL are `CREATE`, `ALTER`, `DROP`, and `TRUNCATE`.

9. **What is DDL?**

DDL is a Data Manipulation Language used to manipulate original data. With the help of this language we can create insert, change, remove, or fetch values from SQL tables. The commands offered by DML are `INSERT`, `UPDATE`, `DELETE`, and `SELECT`.

10. **What is the difference between `TRUNCATE` and `DELETE`?**

This is the most asked interview question. Basically, both are used to delete rows from database table, but `TRUNCATE` is faster than `DELETE` as it clears data in one go where as `DELETE` removes data row by row. There is one more difference, which is `TRUNCATE` resets database table identity keys but `DELETE` will not do any such activity. `TRUNCATE` is DDL command where `DELETE` is DML command.

Do you know (lights on fact?)

- SQL has released future keywords list that may be reserved by SQL in coming builds.

- You can also define your own data types in SQL.

- Numeric and decimal datatypes are basically the same; they are synonyms and can be referred with different names by different vendor.

- String and char SQL datatypes not only store textual data but also can store numbers, but numbers will be considered/treated as text only. These numbers do not contain any value.

- Single byte encoding characters are defined in ASCII character set (mainly all European languages) and multi-byte encoding characters are not from ASCII character set (mainly other than European languages like Japanese, Chinese, and many more)

- SQL date datatype follows Gregorian calendar.

- Date can also be stored in string datatype column, but it will lose its original value and will not contain any DATE value, hence to store date always use date datatype.

- A table can contain multiple or all `sql_variant` columns.

- System databases, table and column cannot be renamed or `altered` using `ALTER` command.

- If you want to change size of any column and if that column has data already stored in it then the new size should not be less than the existing data size limit.

- Column rename activity can be allowed in SQL 2016 version and above using special inbuilt stored procedure.

- SQL queries are not case sensitive, so no needs to take extra care while executing queries.

- Auto identity column does not accept data from query; it has its own incremented value.

CHAPTER 3
SQL Statements and Clauses

Introduction

We have seen how different datatypes are used by SQL to store data depending upon its type. We have also checked how SQL defines and creates database, table and its columns, and how SQL manipulates data using different sub languages, like DDL, DML. In this chapter, we will see more about Data control statements and Data transaction statements. In addition to that we can also learn about the different operators and clauses offered by SQL.

Prerequisite for this chapter: Before walk through this chapter, you should have knowledge of DDL and DML statements. With a laptop/desktop with SQL server installed, just start reading this with interest in database concepts.

Structure

After studying this chapter, you will learn the following points:

- **Data Control Language (DCL)** statement
- **Transaction Control Language (TCL)** statement
- Where clause
- From clause

- Distinct clause
- Order by clause
- Group by clause
- Having clause
- Conclusion
- Rapid fire questions and answers
- Do you know (lights on fact?)

Objective

So the objective of the chapter is to learn about Data control and Transaction control statements, and different clauses that help us filter and arrange records. Finally we have some popular, frequently-asked interview questions and their answers.

So, let's begin.

Data Control Language (DCL) statement

As the name suggests, DCL statements are used to control data access with various data control commands. In short, these commands give different privileges to the user to control database objects like database, table, stored procedure, view. DCL statement gives us the following command to manage and create database objects:

- GRANT command
- REVOKE command

GRANT command

This command is used to set different access permissions on different database objects. We can allow specific privileges to specific roles; that role may be database user, application roll, Windows user, or asymmetric key. The typical syntax is as follows:

```
GRANT <Privilege Name>

ON <Database Object>

TO <User/Role Name>
```

SQL syntax is always easy to understand. In the above syntax, we can just grant access of some database to some user, here is its explanation:

- Privilege Name: Privilege name is the name of access permission that we want to grant access to different database object. These privileges are nothing but different permissions, like ALTER, CONTROL, DELETE, EXECUTE, INSERT, RECEIVE, REFERENCES, SELECT, TAKE OWNERSHIP, and UPDATE.

- **Database Object:** Database object name is the SQL object to which we need to grant permission. Those objects maybe SQL database, SQL table, stored procedure, scalar function, aggregate function service queue, or SQL view.

    o   If the SQL object is database then GRANT command works for BACKUP DATABASE, BACKUP LOG, CREATE DATABASE, CREATE DEFAULT, CREATE FUNCTION, CREATE PROCEDURE, CREATE TABLE, CREATE RULE, and CREATE VIEW commands.

    o   If SQL object is SQL table then GRANT command works for DELETE, INSERT, UPDATE, and SELECT command.

    o   If SQL object is function, then GRANT command works for EXECUTE command.

    o   If SQL object is stored procedure, then GRANT command works for EXECUTE command.

    o   If SQL object is view, then GRANT command works for DELETE, INSERT, REFERENCES, SELECT, and UPDATE commands. (In our coming chapters we will learn more about stored procedures, views, and functions)

- **User/Role Name:** Role name is the database username.

Whenever we need to set access permission to any database object then we can use this command.

Let's **GRANT** some access to the database table, perform the following steps:

1. Open SQL Server.
2. Connect database engine (local/remote).
3. Open SQL analyzer.
4. Execute the following query:

    GRANT SELECT ON testdb.empmaster TO TestUser

5. If we run previous query, we will get the following output:

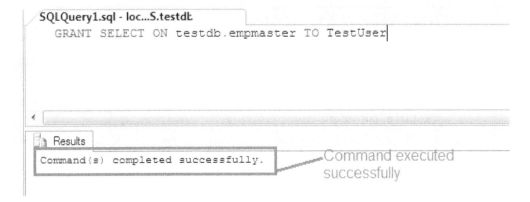

Here, GRANT is the DCL command, SELECT is the privilege that we need to give; ON is the reserved keyword as per syntax, `testdb.empmaster` SQL table full name (SQL full name can be given with the `databasename.table` name), TO is the reserved keyword as per syntax, and `TestUser` is the database user to which we have granted permission to fire SELECT query on database table.

REVOKE command

This command is used to remove previously granted access permissions. In short it works like rollback of permissions. Revoke command is also worksfor DDL and DML statements, including SELECT, INSERT, UPDATE, DELETE, CREATE, and EXECUTE commands. The syntax is quite similar to GRANT command; the typical syntax is as follows

```
REVOKE <Privilege Name>

ON <Database Object>

TO <User/Role Name>
```

In the preceding syntax, we can just revoke access using REVOKE keyword on some database to some user, here is the explanation:

- Privilege Name: Privilege name is the name of access permission that we want to remove or withdraw access to different database objects. These privileges are nothing but different permissions, like ALTER, CONTROL, DELETE, EXECUTE, INSERT, RECEIVE, REFERENCES, SELECT, TAKE OWNERSHIP, and UPDATE.
- Database Object: Database object name is the SQL object to which we need to remove permission from. That object maybe SQL database, SQL table, stored procedure, scalar function, aggregate function service queue, or SQL view.
  - o If the SQL object is database then REVOKE command works for BACKUPDATABASE, BACKUP LOG, CREATE DATABASE, CREATE DEFAULT, CREATE FUNCTION, CREATE PROCEDURE, CREATE TABLE, CREATE RULE, and CREATE VIEW commands.
  - o If SQL object is SQL table then REVOKE command works for DELETE, INSERT, UPDATE, and SELECT command.
  - o If SQL object is function, then REVOKE command works for EXECUTE command.
  - o If SQL object is stored procedure, then REVOKE command works for EXECUTE command.
  - o If SQL object is view, then REVOKE command works for DELETE, INSERT, REFERENCES, SELECT, and UPDATE commands.
- User/Role Name: Role name is the database username.

Whenever we need to withdraw or delete/remove access permission (remove rights) from any database object, which is earlier given by GRANT command, then we can use this command.

Let's REVOKE some access to the database table. Perform the followingsteps:

1. Open SQL Server.
2. Connect database engine (local/remote).
3. Open SQL analyzer.
4. Execute the following query:

   REVOKE SELECT ON testdb.empmaster TO TestUser

5. If we run the previous query, we will get the following output:

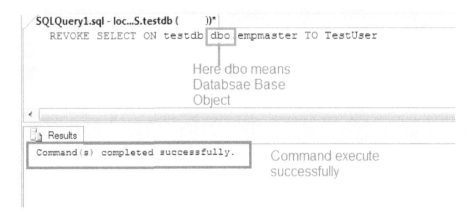

Here, REVOKE is the DCL command, SELECT is the privilege that we need to remove; ON is the reserved keyword as per syntax, testdb.dbo.empmaster SQL table full name (SQL full name can be given with the databasename.table name), TO is the reserved keyword as per syntax and TestUser is the database user to which we have removed permission to fire SELECT query on database table.

Transaction Control Language (TCL) statement

As the name suggests, TCL statements are used to control data transactions between two or more databases or database tables. Transaction is a set of SQL operational queries that are logical in order and fire for a specific work flow. Transaction is important because certain database operations need to execute in given logical sequence and complete without fail. If any linked operation fails, then all operations should fail too. Transaction follows ACID properties, where these properties give us a surety that our set of operations are safe and executed as per the expectation.

In ACID property, A stands for Atomicity, C stands for Consistency, I stands for Isolation, and D stands for Durability. So ACID gives us surety that either the transaction is successful or gets rolled back. TCL statement gives us the following command to manage SQL database transaction:

- COMMIT command
- ROLLBACK command
- SAVE command

COMMIT command

This command marks the successful end of a set of query execution and marks all database operations as permanent and part of database. The typical syntax is as follows:

```
BEGIN TRANSACTION;
SQL Query 1
SQL Query 2
SQL Query 3
SQL Query N
COMMIT TRANSACTION;
```

In the previous syntax, we have enclosed all SQL queries in BEGIN and COMMIT transaction, here is the explanation:

- **BEGIN TRANSACTION:** It is the starting point of the transaction, which starts with BEGIN TRANSACTION keyword, it is the reserved keyword.
- **SQL Query 1...N:** Set of the SQL queries that need to execute in a set as a single operation.
- **COMMIT TRANSACTION:** It is the end point of the transaction where all the database changes are treated as permanent, it is the reserved keyword.

Whenever we use SQL transaction, we need to use this scope to and put all our SQL statement in it.

Let's fire some set of queries on database and COMMIT them:

```
BEGIN TRANSACTION;

DELETE FROM EmpMaster WHERE SrNo = 30;

COMMIT TRANSACTION;
```

If we run previous query, we will get the following output:

Here COMMIT is the DCL command, BEGIN TRANSACTION is the starting point of the transaction;

ROLLBACK command

As the name suggests, it reverts/rolls back all transactions within the scope. Its rollback transaction up to BEGIN keyword.In short, you can rub out all data changes and modifications made from the start of the transaction. The typical syntax is as follows:

BEGIN TRANSACTION;

SQL Query 1

SQL Query 2

SQL Query 3

SQL Query N

ROLLBACK TRANSACTION;

In the previous syntax, we have enclosed all SQL queries in BEGIN and ROLLBACK transaction, here is the explanation:

- BEGIN TRANSACTION: It is the starting point of the transaction which starts with BEGIN TRANSACTION keyword, it is the reserved keyword.
- SQL Query 1...N: Set of the SQL queries that needs to execute in set as a single operation.

- **ROLLBACK TRANSACTION:** From this point, all our database operation gets rolled back to **BEGIN** statement, **TRANSACTION** is reserved keyword.

Whenever we use SQL transaction, we need to use this command to make all these changes permanently in database. Use this for each transaction. It is good to use this command as it gives us assurance of completeness of transaction

Let's fire some set of queries on database and rollback them:

```
BEGIN TRANSACTION;

DELETE FROM EmpMaster WHERE SrNo = 20;

ROLLBACK TRANSACTION;
```

If we run the previous query, we will get the following output:

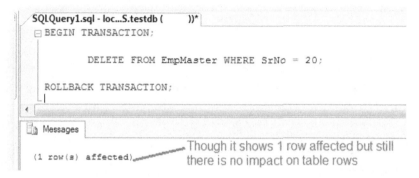

Here, **ROLLBACK** is the DCL command, **BEGIN TRANSACTION** is the starting point of the transaction; proceed by the query. Result snap says' **1 row(s) affected**. But still there is no impact on table rows, after this query; if we try to check number of rows then we can see that not even a single row is affected. See the following screenshot:

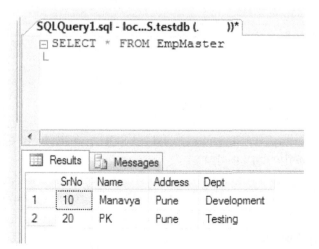

SAVE command

As the name suggests, it sets a save point in transaction. In some SQL vendors, SAVE command is also known as **save point**, basically it is the location to which we can roll back the transaction. So if you have transaction with SAVE TRANSACTION command then you can rollback your transaction to that point only. When we have multiple save points, then the transaction is rolled back to the most recent save point. The typical syntax is as follows:

```
BEGIN TRANSACTION;

SQL Query 1

SQL Query 2

SQL Query 3

SQL Query N

SAVE TRANSACTION transaction name;

SQL Query 1

SQL Query 2

COMMIT TRANSACTION;
```

In the previous syntax, we have enclosed all SQL queries in BEGIN, SAVE, and COMMIT transaction that will help us to complete the transaction, here is the explanation:

- BEGIN TRANSACTION: It is the starting point of the transaction which starts with BEGIN TRANSACTION keyword, it is the reserved keyword.
- SQL Query 1…N: Set of the SQL queries that needs to execute in set as a single operation.
- SAVE TRANSACTION: Up to this point, all our database operation can be rolled back.
- transaction name: It is the name of the save point to identify for rollback.
- COMMIT TRANSACTION: It is the end point of the transaction where all the database changes are treated as permanent, it is the reserved keyword.

SAVE TRANSACTION is used for step-by-step execution so that if somewhere any transaction gets failed, you can rollback your database operations up to the SAVE transaction point. It is recommended to use this in large transactions.

Let's fire some set of queries on database and create save point:

```
BEGIN TRANSACTION;
UPDATE EmpMaster SET Name='MN' WHERE SrNo = 20;
SAVE TRANSACTION sp1
```

```
UPDATE EmpMaster SET Name='MN-Test' WHERE SrNo = 20;
COMMIT TRANSACTION;
```

In preceding example, `BEGIN TRANSACTION` is the starting point of the transaction, `SAVE TRANSACTION` is the save point, `sp1` is the save point name, `COMMIT TRANSACTION` is the end of the transaction.

WHERE clause

The `WHERE clause` is mostly used in data manipulation language (popular as DML). However, it is not mandatory in DML statements. Basically, it is used to restrict the number of rows that are affected by DML queries so that only particular rows can be get altered. The `WHERE` is the simple conditional statement used to filter records. The typical syntax is as follows:

```
DML Query WHERE condition
```

In the previous syntax we have attached `WHERE` condition with DML query, here is the explanation:

The syntax is easy to understand as we know `WHERE` clause is used with DML quires (like `INSERT`, `UPDATE`, `DELETE`, and `SELECT`).

- condition: It is the condition that is meant for the rows to be affected. Here, conditional operators are used to fetch the condition. The below conditional operators can be used.

Sr No	Operator	Description
1	=	Equal to
2	>	Greater Than
3	<	Less Than
4	<=	Less Than Equal to
5	>=	Greater Than Equal to
6	BETWEEN	Used to filter between values
7	LIKE	Used to filter records fit in LIKE case
8	IN	Used to search in given scope
9	<>	Not Equal to

We use this when we need to filter some rows, depending upon some condition for a specific operation including `SELECT`, `INSERT`, `UPDATE`, and `DELETE`.

Let's select some records using `WHERE` condition:

```
SELECT * FROM EmpMaster WHERE SrNo = 20
```

In the above sample, `SELECT` is the DML command concatenate with the `WHERE` clause, which checks the condition to fetch records having `SrNo` column value as `20` We get the following output when we fire this query.

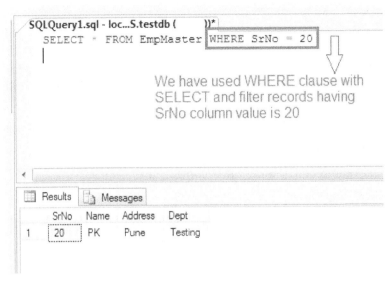

We can also check multiple condition in `WHERE` clause, see the example below:

`SELECT * FROM EmpMaster WHERE SrNo = 10 AND Name='Manavya'`

In the previous sample, we are fetching all the records having `SrNo` column value as `10` and `Name` column value as `Manavya`. If we fire the above query, we will get the following output:

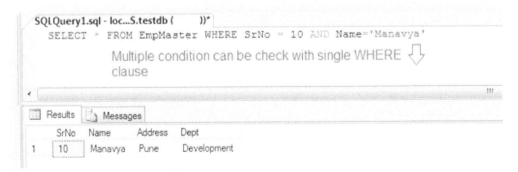

In the same way, we can use any conditional operator in `WHERE` clause.

FROM clause

It used to specify the database object name used in DML queries. This clause helps us to retrieve records from database objects like table, view, joined tables used in `SELECT`, `UPDATE`, `INSERT`, and `DELETE` commands. The typical syntax is as follows:

`DML Query FROM Database Object`

In the preceding syntax, we have attached `FROM` clause with DML query, here is the explanation:

In the earlier syntax,

- `DML Query`: Data manipulation query (select, insert, update or delete).
- `FROM`: it is a table selection operator. The syntax is easy to understand as we know `FROM` clause is used with DML queries (like `DELETE` and `SELECT`), here database object is SQL tables or joined tables or view.

When we need to select/fetch records from SQL table, joined tables or View at that time we need `FROM` clause.

Let's `SELECT` some records using `FROM` condition:

`SELECT * FROM EmpMaster`

In the above sample, we have used `FROM` clause with SQL table. If we fire the above query, the output will be as follows:

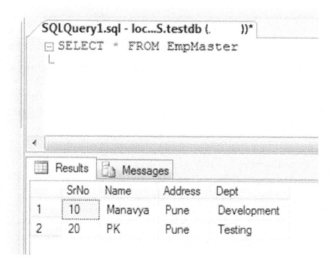

We can use multiple tables with `FROM` clause.

DISTINCT clause

The `DISTINCT` keyword is used to fetch unique values from column. Basically to remove duplicate rows from result set, we can use this clause. This clause is used with `SELECT` command only. The typical syntax is as follows:

`SELECT DISTINCT (columnName) FROM tablename`

In the preceding syntax, we have attached DISTINCT clause on specific column that helps us to retrieve unique values, here is the explanation:

- columnName: Name of the column from which we have to select unique values
- tablename: Table name is the SQL table from which we need to fetch unique values

When we need to avoid duplicate records from any particular column then we can use this DISTINCT clause.

Let's fetch some unique records using DISTINCT condition.

Before that, I have inserted some records in our EmpMaster table, see the following snapshot:

SrNo	Name	Address	Dept
10	Manavya	Pune	Development
20	PK	Pune	Testing
30	Vijay	Delhi	Marketing
40	Sujay	Chennai	Testing
50	Anand	Delhi	Testing
60	Mayur	Mumbai	Development
NULL	NULL	NULL	NULL

- dbo.EmpMaster

We do have duplicate records in 'Address' columns

Now, in above snap, we can see we have duplicate values in Address column. Now we will fire DISTINCT query on database. See the following query:

```
SELECT DISTINCT (Address) from EmpMaster
```

In above sample, SELECT and DISTINCT are the reserved keywords Address is the column name from which we have to select unique values, and EmpMaster is the table, DISTINCT command can be fired on multiple columns. If we fire previous query, then the output will be as follows:

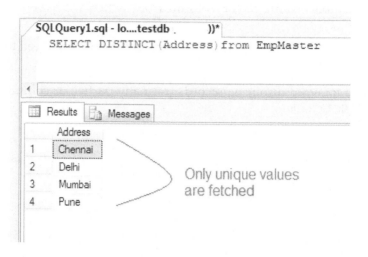

ORDER BY clause

The ORDER BY clause is the sorting clause used to sort result set that we have fetched from database. The sorting may be ascending or descending, used to fetch unique values from column. This clause is used with SELECT command only. You can also specify the column with ORDER BY even if it is not enlisted in SELECT query. You need to use word ASC for ascending arrangement and DESC for descending arrangement, respectively. There is no limit on the number of columns to be put with ORDER BY clause. You can even use ASC (ascending) and DESC (descending) order in same query for different columns. The typical syntax is as follows:

```
SELECT column names FROM tablename ORDER BY Column1, Column2…Column N
ASC/ DESC
```

In the preceding syntax, we have selected different columns and arranged them in ascending or descending order. As best practice, avoid integers in ORDER BY clause. Whenever we use TOP in SELECT statement then always use order by clause, here is the explanation:

- column names: Name of the columns that we need to fetch from table with SELECT query.
- tablename: Table name is the SQL table from which we need to fetch values.
- Column1, Column2: Name of the columns that we need to make ORDER BY.

When we need some sorted result, either ascending or descending, we use ORDER BY clause.

Let's fetch some records using ORDER BY clause, with ascending and descending order:

```
SELECT * from EmpMaster order by Name ASC
```

Here we have fetched all columns (using *) from table EmpMaster, sorting on Name column in ascending order. (Here ASC is the optional keyword as the default sorting is ascending only).

So, we can write the same in the following format also:

```
SELECT * from EmpMaster order by Name
```

If we run the previous query, the output would be as follows:

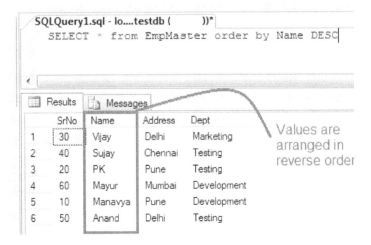

If we want sort value in descending order, then we can use the following query:

```
SELECT * from EmpMaster order by Name DESC
```

If we fire the previous query, the output will be as follows:

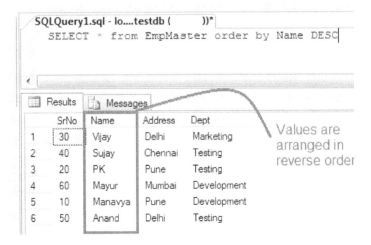

We can also give multiple columns with ORDER BY clause:

```
SELECT * from EmpMaster order by Name, Address
```

GROUP BY clause

The GROUP BY clause is also one of the sorting clauses used with the SELECT statement and aggregate functions.(Aggregate are the mathematical functions that are used to calculate sum, minimum, maximum values from numerical columns. We will learn about these functions in the coming chapters).This clause is used to divide the result in the number of groups as per the column values. In simple terms, it is used to group the result set as per the column values. In GROUP BY clause, one row per group is returned by SELECT statement. The typical syntax is as follows:

```
SELECTcolumn_names FROMtable_name WHEREcondition GROUPBYcolumn_names
```

In the previous syntax, we have selected different columns and used GROUP BY clause to filter the results, here is the explanation:

- column_names: Name of the columns that we need to fetch from table with SELECT query.
- table_name: Table name is the SQL table from which we need to fetch values.
- condition: It is the WHERE condition to filter values.
- column_names: Name of the column by which we need to make a group of result set.

When we need some group-wise result; this could be effective when we need to analyze group-wise data. Always keep in mind that GROUP BY clause will never sort the result set, you need to use ORDER BY for it.

Let's fetch some records using GROUP BY clause.

I have added Salary column in EmpMaster, see the following screenshot:

SrNo	Name	Address	Dept	Salary
10	Manavya	Pune	Development	1000
20	PK	Pune	Testing	500
30	Vijay	Delhi	Marketing	800
40	Sujay	Chennai	Testing	600
50	Anand	Delhi	Testing	500
60	Mayur	Mumbai	Development	900
NULL	NULL	NULL	NULL	NULL

Now fire the following query on `EmpMaster` table:

```
SELECT Address, count(salary) from EmpMaster group by Address
```

Here we have fetched `Address` column and used `COUNT` (which is internal aggregate function) as inbuilt function and fired `GROUP  BY` clause to divide result address-wise. Check the following sample:

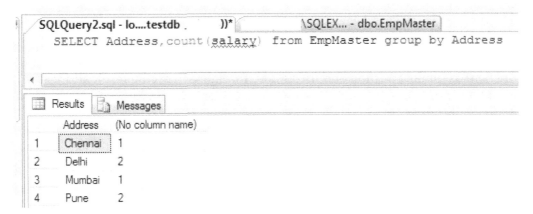

Now, in the preceding screenshot,, we can see that `Salary` has been grouped as per the location—for `Pune,  Delhi` we have 2 entries, so it shows count as 2. For `Chennai` and `Mumbai`, we have only 1 entry, so it shows count as 1.

HAVING clause

The `HAVING` clause is also used to specify the search conditions and filter the rows, and it is mostly similar to `WHERE` clause. But it was introduced in SQL because `WHERE` could not be used to aggregate functions. The `HAVING` clause can be used as a simple `WHERE` clause or can be used with `GROUP  BY` clause too. `HAVING` clause is mostly used for filtering; the typical syntax is as follows:

```
SELECT column names FROM Tablename WHERE condition GROUPBY column_name
HAVING condition
```

In the previous syntax, we have selected different columns and used `GROUP  BY` and `HAVING` clause to filter the results, here is the explanation:

- `column names:` Name of the columns that we need to fetch from table with `SELECT` query.
- `Tablename:` Table name is the SQL table from which we need to fetch values.
- `condition:` It is the `WHERE` condition to filter values.
- `column_name:` Name of the column by which we need to make a group of result set.

- `condition:` It is the `HAVING` condition to filter values.

When we need group-wise result along with the filtration facility then we can use the `HAVING` clause.

Let's fetch some records using the combination of `WHERE`, `HAVING`, and `GROUP BY` clause. See the following query:

```
SELECT Address,count(salary) from EmpMaster group by Address having count(salary) > 1
```

Here, we have fetched `Address` column and used `COUNT` (which is internal aggregate function) as inbuilt function and fire `GROUP BY` clause to divide result address-wise but the `Salary` count should be greater than 2. When we fire this query, we get the following output:

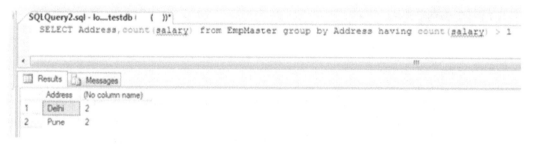

Conclusion

In this chapter, we have seen how we can restrict a user from accessing the database and its objects using DCL. With the help of TCL and different commands of SQL transaction, we can successfully complete any complex and interdependent database operations. With the help of ACID property, we can make consistency and durability in SQL transactions

There are different clauses introduced by SQL to filter and fetch records from datatables; with the help of `GROUP BY` clause we can divide our result in group. We have also learned that SQL has different operators to perform specific operations and these operators are categorized into multiple types depending upon its workings and nature. We have learned about addition, subtraction, multiplication, division, and modulo-like operators.

In the coming chapters, we will learn more about the remaining SQL operators, the various string and math functions, and the different wildcards, with examples. we will also learn about the different date functions that allow us to play with dates. So stay tuned.

Rapid-fire questions and answers

1. **What is DCL?**

   DCL is a Data Control language used to control and restrict data access using different access permissions, such as GRANT and REVOKE commands.

2. **What is TCL?**

   TCL is a Transaction Control language used to make complex SQL operations safe and secure. These transaction control commands allow users to roll back an operation if the operation gets failed.

3. **What is ACID in SQL?**

   ACID is the property of transaction command where A stands for Atomicity, C stands for Consistency, I stands for Isolation, and D for Durability.

4. **What is WHERE clause?**

   WHERE clause is used to put condition while fetching results from database. This clause is used to restrict and filter row results.

5. **What is HAVING clause?**

   HAVING clause is also used to put condition while fetching results from database, and is used to filter rows. But this clause can also be used with aggregate functions like SUM, AVG, COUNT, and others.

6. **What is Arithmetic operator?**

   We do the arithmetic operations with this, and the signs are the same as general mathematics sign, and we can use them in SQL query.

7. **What is the use of modulo % operator?**

   This operator is used to return reminder of the division of two numbers.

8. **What are the different operators that exist in SQL?**

   SQL has a number of different operators, that are categorized depending upon their nature. The list of the operator is as follows:

   - Arithmetic operators
   - Comparison operators
   - Logical operators
   - Assignment operator
   - Scope resolution operator
   - Bitwise operators
   - Set operators
   - String concatenation operator
   - Compound operators

- Unary operators

Do you know (lights on fact?)

- SQL LITE version will not have any access permission as it has file level access.
- If you write two or more SQL queries in a row, then they must be separated with a semicolon (;) sign. Semicolon indicates the termination of an SQL query statement.
- After execution of COMMIT TRANSACTION command, the transaction cannot be rolled back.
- Query performance may get hampered with lots of tables with FROM clause.
- There is no limit on the column name you put for ORDER BY clause, but the total size of all columns should not be more than 8060 bytes.
- You cannot use ORDER BY clause on next, image like binary columns.
- We can use ADD operator on string column (varchar, char) also. As a result, it will just concatenate those two column values.

CHAPTER 4
SQL Operators

Introduction

Till now, we have seen how we can control data access using different control commands that are provided by DCL. In the same way we can control SQL transactions, which allow us to fire multiple SQL queries in single set of batches. We have also seen how we can use `FROM, DISTINCT, WHERE, ORDER BY,` and `GROUP BY` clause to filter and arrange records that we have fetched using `SELECT` query. Let's move ahead. In this chapter we will see more about SQL operators, the different SQL functions, and wildcards.

Prerequisite for this chapter: Before we walk through this chapter you should have knowledge of DDL, DML, DCL, TCL statements with simple SQL clauses like `WHERE, ORDER BY, FROM` and a laptop/desktop with SQL server installed.

Structure

After studying this chapter, you will learn the following points:

- Types of operators
- Arithmetic operators
- Comparison operators
- Logical operators

- Assignment operators
- Bitwise operators
- Set operators
- String concatenation Operator
- Conclusion
- Rapid fire questions and answers
- Do you know (lights on fact?)

Objective

So, the objective of this chapter is to learn about the different SQL operators, including Arithmetic, comparison, logical, bitwise, set, and compound operator. Additionally, we will go through the concept of SQL functions, its types, and how to work with them. In this chapter, we will also learn about the SQL wildcards and their usage with example.

So, let's begin

Types of operators

An operator is a symbol or a sign, which is linked to some specific action. In SQL, we will look at different types of operators which are categorized according to their nature of work and behavior. See the list of available SQL operators below:

- Arithmetic operators
- Comparison operators
- Logical operators
- Assignment operator
- Scope resolution operator
- Bitwise operators
- Set operators
- String concatenation operator
- Compound operators
- Unary operators

Arithmetic operators

The arithmetic operators are meant for arithmetic operations. These operators are used for mathematical operations only and these operations include addition, subtraction, multiplication, and division. In SQL, we have the following types of arithmetical operators:

- + (for addition)
- - (for subtraction)
- * (for multiplication)
- / (for division)
- % (Modulo: it returns the reminder of the division)

Let's go through them one by one.

+ (for addition)

This operator is used to add two numbers, it also useful to add two different dates, days, among other values. Here is the syntax for the same:

```
SELECT Column1 + Column2 / value as columnname FROM Tablename
```

In the previous syntax we have used + operator to add two columns, here is the explanation:

- `Column1:` Name of the first column that we need to add to.
- `Column2 / value:` Name of the second column that we need to add to. We can add constant value or expression also.
- `columnname:` Name of the result column. This column is autocreated by SQL.

You can also add `WHERE` condition, which is non-mandatory.

When you want to add two columns or some value in a particular column, then you can use this operator.

Let's use `ADD` operator in our `salary` column. In the following query, we have added `10` values to our `salary` column and named the result column as `addition`:

```
SELECT *, salary + 10 as addition from EmpMaster
```

If we run preceding query, we will get the following output:

- (for subtraction)

This operator is used to subtract two numbers. It is also useful to subtract two different dates, days, among other values. Here is the syntax for the same:

```
SELECT Column1 - Column 2 / value as columnname FROM Tablename
```

In the previous syntax we have used - operator to subtract two columns. Here is the explanation:

- **Column1:** Name of the first column that we need to subtract from.
- **Column2 / value:** Name of the second column that we need to subtract from, or we can subtract constant value or expression as well.
- **columnname:** Name of the result column. This column is auto-created by SQL.

You can also add WHERE condition, which is non-mandatory

When you want to subtract two columns or some value in a particular column, then you can use this operator.

Let's use subtract operator in our **salary** column. In the following query we have subtracted **20** values from our **salary** column and named the result column as **subtraction:**

```
SELECT *, salary - 10 as subtraction from EmpMaster
```

If we run the preceding query, we will get the following output:

SQLQuery2.sql - lo....testdb (SA (53))*

```
SELECT *, salary - 10 as substraction  from EmpMaster
```

◀

▦ Results | ▤ Messages

	SrNo	Name	Address	Dept	Salary	substraction
1	10	Manavya	Pune	Development	1000	990
2	20	PK	Pune	Testing	500	490
3	30	Vijay	Delhi	Marketing	800	790
4	40	Sujay	Chennai	Testing	600	590
5	50	Anand	Delhi	Testing	500	490
6	60	Mayur	Mumbai	Development	900	890

New column is added with values from salary columns substracted by 10

* (for multiplication)

This operator is used to multiply two numbers. In SQL, multiplication sign is denoted with an asterisk (*). Here is the syntax for the same:

```
SELECT Column1 * Column 2 / value as columnname FROM Tablename
```

In the preceding syntax, we have used * operator to multiply two columns. Here is the explanation:

- Column1: Name of the first column that we need to multiply to.

- Column2 / value: Name of the second column that we need to multiply to, or we can multiply constant value or expression as well.

- columnname: Name of the result column. This column is auto-created by SQL.

You can also add WHERE condition, which is non-mandatory.

When you want to multiply two columns or some value in a particular column then you can use this operator.

Let's use multiply operator in our salary column. In the following query, we have multiplied 2 values to our salary column and named the result column as Multiply:

```
SELECT *, salary * 2 as Multiply from EmpMaster
```

If we run the preceding query, we will get the following output:

```
SQLQuery2.sql - lo....testdb (        ))*
    SELECT *, salary * 2 as Multiply from EmpMaster |
```

	SrNo	Name	Address	Dept	Salary	Multiply
1	10	Manavya	Pune	Development	1000	2000
2	20	PK	Pune	Testing	500	1000
3	30	Vijay	Delhi	Marketing	800	1600
4	40	Sujay	Chennai	Testing	600	1200
5	50	Anand	Delhi	Testing	500	1000
6	60	Mayur	Mumbai	Development	900	1800

Newly created column with Salary column value multiplied by 2 using Multiply operator

* (for division)

This operator is used to divide two numbers. In SQL, division sign is denoted with forward slash sign (/). Here is the syntax for the same:

```
SELECT Column1 / Column 2 / value as columnname FROM Tablename
```

In the above syntax, we have used / operator for division of two columns. Here is the explanation:

- **Column1:** Name of the first column that we need to divide to.

- **Column2 / value:** Name of the second column that we need to divide to, or we can divide constant value or expression also.

- **columnname:** Name of the result column. This column is auto-created by SQL.

You can also add WHERE condition, which is non-mandatory

When you want to divide two columns or some value in a particular column, then you can use this operator.

Let's use divide operator in our salary column. In the following query we have divided 2 values to our salary column and named the result column as Divide:

```
SELECT *, salary / 2 as Divide from EmpMaster
```

If we run the above query, we will get the following output:

```
SQLQuery2.sql - lo....testdb (        ))*
    SELECT *, salary / 2 as Divide from EmpMaster
```

	SrNo	Name	Address	Dept	Salary	Divide
1	10	Manavya	Pune	Development	1000	500.000000
2	20	PK	Pune	Testing	500	250.000000
3	30	Vijay	Delhi	Marketing	800	400.000000
4	40	Sujay	Chennai	Testing	600	300.000000
5	50	Anand	Delhi	Testing	500	250.000000
6	60	Mayur	Mumbai	Development	900	450.000000

New column created with division result of salary column by 2

% (for modulo)

This operator is used to return reminder of division between two numbers. In SQL, modulo sign is denoted with the percentage sign (%). Here is the syntax for the same:

```
SELECT Column1 % Column 2 / value as columnname FROM Tablename
```

In the above syntax, we have used %(modulo) operator to get reminder of division of two columns. Below is the explanation:

- `Column1:` Name of the first column that we need to divide to.
- `Column2 / value:` Name of the second column that we need to divide to, or we can divide constant value or expression as well.
- `columnname:` Name of the result column. This column is auto-created by SQL.

You can also add `WHERE` condition, which is non-mandatory.

When you want reminder of the division between two columns or some value in particular column then you can use this operator.

Let's use modulo operator in our `salary` column. In the following query we have divided 2 values to our `salary` column and return modulo, the result column name is `Modulo`:

```
SELECT *, salary % 2 as Modulo from EmpMaster
```

If we run the above query, we will get the following output:

```
SQLQuery2.sql - lo....testdb |        )*
    SELECT *, salary % 2 as Modulo from EmpMaster
```

	SrNo	Name	Address	Dept	Salary	Modulo
1	10	Manavya	Pune	Development	1000	0
2	20	PK	Pune	Testing	500	0
3	30	Vijay	Delhi	Marketing	800	0
4	40	Sujay	Chennai	Testing	600	0
5	50	Anand	Delhi	Testing	500	0
6	60	Mayur	Mumbai	Development	900	0

Here the result of the modulo is 0, if we divide Salary column by 2 then the remider would be 0

Comparison operators

As the name suggests, these operators are meant to be created for comparison of different values or expression. Comparison operator gives us the following signs:

Sign	Description
=	Equals
>	Greater than
<	Less than
>=	Greater than or equal to
<=	Less than or equal to
<>	Not equal to
!=	Not equal to
!<	Not less than
!>	Not greater than
SOME	SOME operator
ANY	ANY operator

Please note that the comparison operators will not work with text, ntext and image datatypes.

Let's trace them one by one.

= (Equals)

It is a simple comparison operator, denoted with = sign, and used to compare two expression or values. The syntax is as follows:

```
Any DML query where expression/value = expression/value
```

In the above syntax we have used =(equals) operator to compare two expressions or values. Here is its explanation:

- **Any DML query:** Any DML query, including insert/update/delete. (for `INSERT` query `WHERE` will not be used).
- **expression/value:** expression or value that we need to compare.

When you want to compare two expressions or values, then you can use this operator.

Let's compare address column value using comparison operator = (equals) and fetch records of employees. Check out the following query:

```
SELECT * FROM EmpMaster WHERE Address = 'Pune'
```

In the above query we have fetched `Address` column whose value is equal to 'Pune' and for that we have used equal to (=) operator. If we run the above query, we will get the following output:

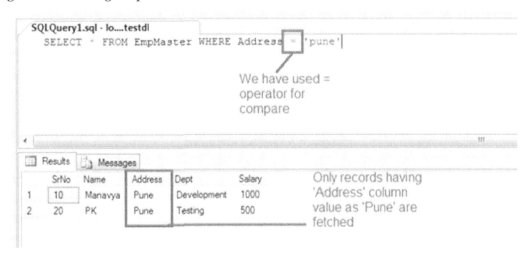

With this operator you can compare null and non-null values as well.

> (Greater than)

It is a simple comparisonoperator denoted with > sign, and used to compare two expression or values. This will return `TRUE` if value of the left side expression is greater than right side expression, else it returns `FALSE`, it also returns record set if the result is `TRUE`. The syntax is as follows:

```
Any DML query where expression/value > expression/value
```

In the above syntax we have used > (greater than) operator to compare two expressions or values, here is the explanation:

- `Any DML query`: Any DML query including insert/update/delete. (for `INSERT` query `WHERE` will not use).
- `expression/value`: expression or value that we need to compare.

When you want to compare/fetch values and check if left side expression is greater than right side expression then you use this operator.

Let's compare salaries using comparison operator > (greater than) and fetch records of employees. Check out the following query

```
SELECT * FROM EmpMaster WHERE Salary > 600
```

In the above query, we have fetched all employee records where salary is greater than `600`, and for that we have used greater than (>) comparison operator. If we run the above query, we will get the following output:

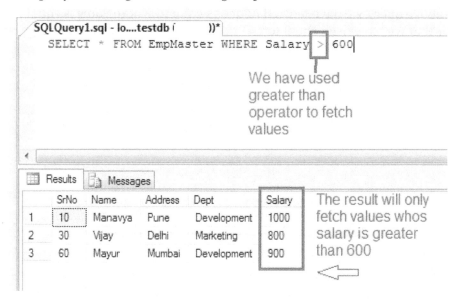

You can compare not only values but variables as well with this operator.

< (Less than)

It is a simple comparison operator denoted with < sign, and is used to compare two expressions or values. This will return `TRUE` if the value of the left side expression is less than right side expression, else it returns `FALSE`, it also returns record set if the result is `TRUE`. The syntax is as follows:

```
Any DML query where expression/value < expression/value
```

In the above syntax, we have used < (less than) operator to compare two expressions or values, here is the explanation:

- **Any DML query:** Any DML query including insert/update/delete. (for INSERT query WHERE will not use).
- **expression/value:** Expression or value that we need to compare.

When you want to compare/fetch values and check if left side expression is less than right side expression, then use this operator.

Let's take same example but reverse the condition, fetch salary using comparison operator < (less than) and fetch records of employees. Check out the following query:

```
SELECT * FROM EmpMaster WHERE Salary < 600
```

In the above query, we have fetched all employee records whose salary is less than 600, and for that we have used less than (<) comparison operator. If we run the above query, we will get the following output:

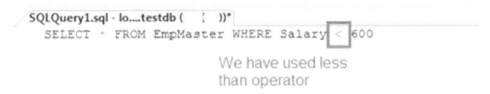

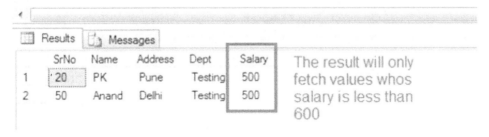

You can compare not just values but variables as well with this operator.

>= (Greater than or equal to)

It is a simple comparison operator denoted with >= sign, and is used to compare two expressions or values. This will return TRUE if value of the left side expression has greater or equal value than right side expression, else it returns FALSE, it also returns record set if the result is TRUE. The syntax is as follows:

```
Any DML query where expression/value >= expression/value
```

In the above syntax we have used >= (greater than or equal to) operator to compare two expression or values, here is the explanation:

- `Any DML query:` Any DML query including insert/update/delete. (for `INSERT` query `WHERE` will not use).
- `expression/value:` Expression or value that we need to compare.

When you want to compare/fetch values and check if left side expression has greater or equal value than right side expression, then you use this operator.

Let's take the same example and fetch salary using comparison operator >= (greater than or equal to) and fetch records of employees. Check out the following query:

```
SELECT * FROM EmpMaster WHERE Salary >= 600
```

In the above query, we have fetched all employee records whose salary is greater than or equal to 600, and for that we have used greater than or equal to (>=) comparison operator. If we run the above query, we will get the following output:

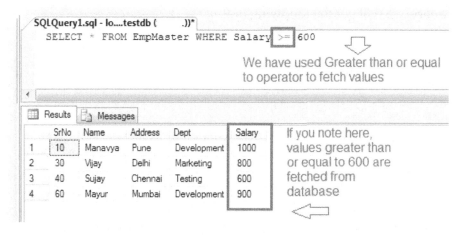

You can compare not only values but variables as well with this operator.

>= (Less than or equal to)

It is a simple comparison operator denoted with <= sign, and is used to compare two expression or values. This will return TRUE if value of the left side expression has less or equal value than right side expression, else it returns FALSE, it also returns record set if the result is TRUE. The syntax is as follows:

```
Any DML query where expression/value <= expression/value
```

In the above syntax, we have used <= (less than or equal to) operator to compare two expression or values, here is its explanation

- `Any DML query:` Any DML query including insert/update/delete. (for `INSERT` query `WHERE` will not use).

- `expression/value`: Expression or value that we need to compare.

You use this operator when you want to compare/fetch values and check if left side expression has less or equal value than right side expression

Let's take the same example and fetch salary using comparison operator <= (less than or equal to) and fetch records of employees. Check out the following query

`SELECT * FROM EmpMaster WHERE Salary <= 600`

In the above query, we have fetched all employee records whose salary is less than or equal to `600`, and for that we have used less than or equal to (<=) comparison operator. If we run the above query, we will get the following output:

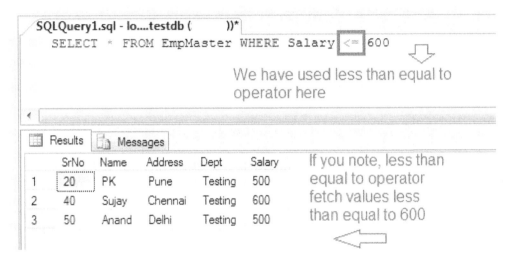

You can compare not only values but variables as well with this operator.

<> (Not equal to)

It is a simple comparison operator denoted with <> sign, and is used to compare two expression or values; this will return `TRUE` if value of the left side expression and right-side expression are not equal, else it returns `FALSE`, it also returns record set if the result is `TRUE`. The syntax is as follows:

`Any DML query where expression/value <> expression/value`

In the above syntax we have used <> (not equal to) operator to compare two expression or values, here is the explanation:

- `Any DML query`: Any DML query including insert/update/delete. (for `INSERT` query `WHERE` will not use)
- `expression/value`: Expression or value that we need to compare.

You use this operator when you want to compare/fetch values and check if left side expression and right-side expressions are not equal.

Let's take the same example and fetch salary using comparison operator <> (not equal to) and fetch records of employees. Check out the following query:

```
SELECT * FROM EmpMaster WHERE Salary <> 600
```

In the above query, we have fetched all employee records whose salary is not equal to 600, and for that we have used not equal to (<>) comparison operator. If we run the above query, we will get the following output:

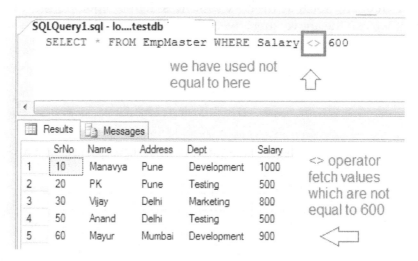

You can compare not only values but variables as well with this operator.

If both the operands are NULL, meaning if both the values are NULL, then the result will return as per the ANSI_NULL settings. Now to know more about ANSI_NULL concept, see the below explanation.

ANSI_NULL

It is an ISO compliant standard that is used when both the operands are NULL. When we set ANSI_NULL value as ON then the column = NULL condition returns 0 rows if there are NULL values in the column name. It will return 0 even if it is NULL, see the below chart of when both the values are NULL and ANSI_NULL is set to ON and OFF

Expression	When SET_ANSI is ON	When SET_ANSI is OFF
NULL = NULL	UNKNOWN	TRUE
NULL <> NULL	UNKNOWN	FALSE
NULL > NULL	UNKNOWN	UNKNOWN

NULL IS NULL	TRUE	TRUE
NULL IS NOT NULL	FALSE	FALSE

SOME

SOME operator compares expression or a scalar value with a set of columns or values. In simple words, it compares the value with the set of given values. The syntax is as follows:

`Expression or value [Any comparison operator]query or set of values`

Let's understand the syntax

Expression: Is the scalar value that needs to compare with the set of values

Any comparison operator: Is the comparison operator that will compare scalar value with set of value (these operator could be anything between = | <> | != | > | >= | !> | < | <= | !<)

Query or set of values: A query that produces a set of values for comparison

This operator returns TRUE if the left side value is found or compares to the set of right side values.

Take an example: I have a table (`temp`) with 1 numeric column (name as id) and values as (1,2,3,4,5,6,7,8,9). Now let's fire the below query:

`IF 6< SOME (SELECT ID FROM temp)`

`PRINT 'TRUE'`

`ELSE`

`PRINT 'FALSE';`

If I fire the above query, the output would be TRUE, as less than 6 values are present in our value set.

`ANY` operator would be the same as `SOME` operator.

Logical operators

These operators are same as comparison operators, which will return Booleanm value, but these are not made up of symbols, these operators are SQL reserved keywords; see the following list of logical operators. Go through the following table, which will gives you an idea of SQL logical operators. I have given one line description of each logical operator:

Logical operators	Description
AND	AND operator is used to compare values, but it will also return TRUE if left and right-side value/expression are TRUE
OR	OR operator is used to compare between two value/expression
BETWEEN	BETWEEN operator is used to check if the value is falling between a range
IN	IN operator is used to check if the value is falling within range
ALL	ALL operator is used to compare expression/values in a set
ANY	ANY operator is also used to compare expression/values in a set but returns TRUE if any of the expression is TRUE
EXISTS	EXISTS operator checks if the value is existing in row
NOT	Used to reverse the condition of Boolean expression

Let's trace them one by one.

AND operator

This logical operator is used to compare two expressions/values and returns Boolean value. This will return TRUE, if both the left side and right-side expressions are TRUE, else it returns FALSE and fetches results according to it. The syntax is as follows:

```
Any DML query where expression/value AND expression/value
```

In the above syntax we have used AND operator to compare two expression or values, here is the explanation:

- **Any DML query:** Any DML query including insert/update/delete. (for INSERT query WHERE will not use)
- **expression/value:** expression or value that we need to compare.

When you want to compare/fetch two values and check if left side expression AND right-side expression are TRUE then you can use this operator.

Let's take the same example and fetch employee details using comparison operator AND. Check out the following query:

```
SELECT * FROM EmpMaster WHERE Name = 'Manavya' and Salary=1000
```

In the above query, we have fetched all employee records whose Salary is 1000 and Name column value is Manavya. If we run the above query, we will get the following output:

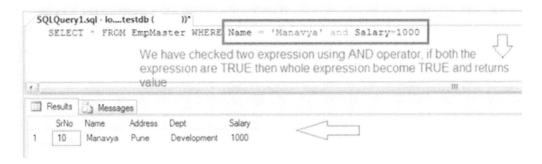

See below a chart where we can see what happens when left and right side expressions are true or false.

Expression	Description	Outcome
True AND True	When both the expressions are true	TRUE
True AND False	When one of the expression is true	FALSE
False AND True	When one of the expression is true	FALSE
False AND False	When both expressions are true	FALSE

OR operator

This logical operator is used to compare two expressions/values and returns Boolean value, this will return TRUE, if any of the side (either left or right side) expressions are TRUE else it returns FALSE and fetches results according to it. The syntax is as follows:

```
Any DML query where expression/value OR expression/value
```

In the above syntax we have used OR operator to compare two expression or values, here is the explanation:

- **Any DML query:** Any DML query including insert/update/delete. (for INSERT query WHERE will not use)
- **expression/value:** Expression or value that we need to compare.

When you want to compare/fetch two values and check if any of the side (left side or right side) expression is TRUE, then you can use this operator.

Let's take the same example and fetch employee details using comparison operator OR. Check out the following query:

```
SELECT * FROM EmpMaster WHERE Name = 'Manavya' OR Salary=800
```

In the above query, we have fetched all employee records whose `Salary` is `800` or `Name` column value is `Manavya`. If we run the above query, we will get the following output:

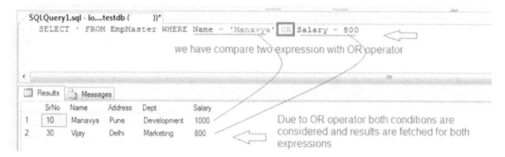

See the below chart where we can see what happens when left and right side expressions are true or false.

Expression	Description	Outcome
True OR True	When both the expressions are true	TRUE
True OR False	When one of the expression is true	TRUE
False OR True	When one of the expression is true	TRUE
False OR False	When both expressions are true	FALSE

BETWEEN operator

This logical operator is used to get the values between a range, and this operator is used in combination with **AND** operator. **AND** operator is used to specify the range, the syntax is as follows:

`Any DML query where column name BETWEEN expression/value AND expression/value`

In the above syntax, we have used `BETWEEN` operator to specify the range, here is the explanation:

- `Any DML query`: Any DML query including insert/update/delete. (for `INSERT` query `WHERE` will not use)
- `column name`: Name of the column for which we have to check range.
- `expression/value`: Expression or value that we need to compare.

When you want to check if the specified column values are fall between specified ranges, then you can use this operator.

Let's take the same example and fetch employee details using comparison operator `BETWEEN`. Check out the following query:

```
SELECT * FROM EmpMaster WHERE Salary BETWEEN 800 AND 1000
```

In the above query, we have fetched all employee records whose `Salary` is in between `800` and `1000`. If we run the above query, we will get the following output:

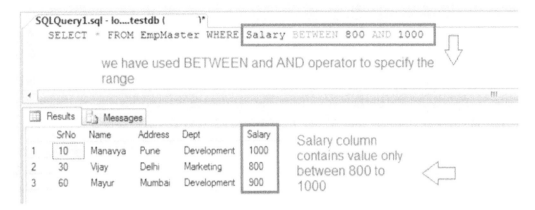

For larger range, always use less than and greater than, because if there is NULL values in `BETWEEN` clause, then it would return NULL.

IN operator

This logical operator is also used to check the range, and it returns `TRUE` if the specified value falls within the range, the syntax is as follows:

```
Any DML query where column name IN (expression1/value1, expression2/
value2...N)
```

In the above syntax we have used `IN` operator to check if the given column name contains given value, here is the explanation:

- `Any DML query`: Any DML query including insert/update/delete. (for `INSERT` query `WHERE` will not use)
- `column name`: Name of the column for which we have to check range.
- `expression/value`: Expression or value that we need to compare.

When you want to check if the specified column name has the values in specified range, then you can use this operator.

Let's take the same example and fetch employee details using `IN` operator. Check out the following query:

```
SELECT * FROM EmpMaster WHERE Salary IN (800, 1000)
```

In the above query, we have fetched all employee records whose `Salary` is in `800` and `1000`. If we run the above query, we will get the following output:

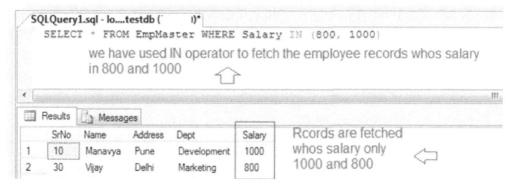

If you passlarger number of parameters to `IN` clause then it may throw error 8623 to 8632. To avoid this, try to use `SELECT` clause with subquery rather than passing direct values in `IN` clause

ALL operator

This logical operator is also used to compare a set of columns to a single value, this operator is used with subquery, (now first learn what is subquery).

- Subquery: It is a nested query which is query within query. Sample query is as follows:

  `SELECT * FROM EmpMaster WHERE Salary = (select Salary from EmpMaster where Salary=800)`

Now we can see there are two queries in the above sample, but which query will run first? See the following steps of execution:

1. The query which is inside the bracket (inner query) will execute first.
2. Then the outer query will execute.
3. The result of inner query will pass to outer query.
4. Then the final result gets produced.

If I run the above query, the output will be as follows:

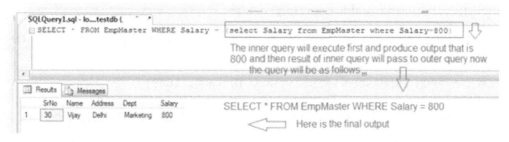

Now let's continue to ALL operator. As we discussed, ALL operator is used with subquery and produces the result, the syntax is as follows:

```
Any DML query where column name scalar value ALL (Subquery)
```

In the above syntax we have used ALL operator to compare and check value, here is the explanation:

- Any DML query: Any DML query including insert/update/delete. (for INSERT query WHERE will not use)
- column name: Name of the column for which we have to check range.
- scalar value: Scalar values may contain comparison operator like (=, <>, =, >, >=,>, <, <=, <)
- Subquery: inner query.

When you want to compare a set of columns to a single value then you can use this operator.

Let's take the same example and fetch employee details using ALL operator. Check out the following query:

```
SELECT * FROM EmpMaster WHERE Salary > ALL (select Salary from EmpMaster
WHERE Salary=800)
```

In the above query, first the inner query will execute and then pass that result to the outer query. So, the result of inner query that is 800 will pass to outer query and the outer query will fetch the records having salary column value greater than 800. If we run the above query, we will get the following output:

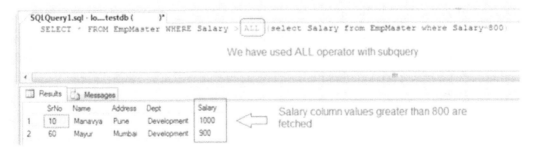

ANY operator

This logical operator is also used to compare a set of columns to a single value like ALL operator, but the difference is, ALL is used to check every value returned by the subquery and need every value's specifiedrange and ANY is used to check each value returned by the subquery, but does not expect every value in specified range. This operator is also used with subquery, the syntax is as follows:

```
Any DML query where column name scalar value ANY (Subquery)
```

In the above syntax, we have used ANY operator to compare and check value, here is the explanation:

- Any DML query: Any DML query including insert/update/delete. (for INSERT query WHERE will not use)
- column name: Name of the column for which we have to check range.
- scalar value: Scalar values may contain comparison operator like (=, <>, =, >, >=,>, <, <=, <)
- Subquery: inner query.

When you want to compare set of columns to a single value then you can use this operator.

EXISTS operator

This logical operator will return Boolean value and execute with the help of subquery, the complete query will execute only if the subquery returns TRUE. The syntax is as follows:

```
Any DML query where EXISTS (Subquery)
```

In the above syntax we have used EXISTS operator which returns Boolean value and according to that, the outer query will execute, here is the explanation:

- Any DML query: Any DML query including insert/update/delete. (for INSERT query WHERE will not use)
- Subquery: Inner query.

When you want to execute any query but want to check some condition to return TRUE then you can use this operator.

Let's take the same example and fetch employee details using EXISTS operator. Check out the following query:

```
SELECT * FROM EmpMaster WHERE EXISTS (SELECT salary FROM EmpMasterWHERE
Salary=1500)
```

In the above query, we have fetched all employee records but for that inner query value should returned TRUE. According to our table if we have Salary column value as 1500 only then the complete query gets executed. If we run the above query, we will get the following output:

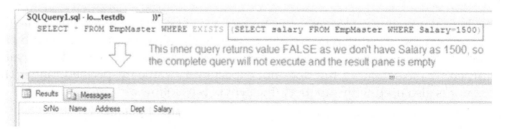

NOT operator

This logical operator will do the reserve of the Boolean value, which means it will make the result FALSE if it's TRUE (bit confusing right !!). Let's make it simple, the syntax is as follows:

```
Any DML query where NOT expression
```

In the above syntax, we have used NOT operator with the expression, so whatever value is returned, the expression will reverse it, here is the explanation:

- Any DML query: Any DML query including insert/update/delete. (for INSERT query WHERE will not use)
- expression: Any condition/value.

When you want to fetch the exact reverse result of the actual result then you can use this. The following example makes it clear.

Let's take the same example and fetch employee details using NOT operator. Check out the following query

```
SELECT * FROM EmpMaster WHERE NOT salary > 800
```

In the above query, we fetch values having salary greater than 800, so the expected output is 900 and above, but due to the NOT operator, it will fetch values less than 800, thus we will get the following output:

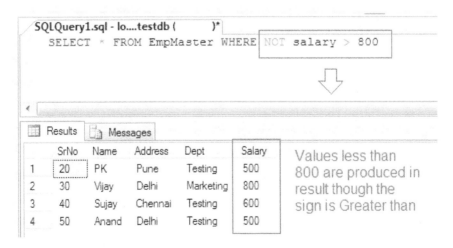

Assignment operators

Assignment operators are used to assign values in SQL. Only one assignment operator exists. Equal to (=) operator is used as assignment operator in SQL. The syntax is as follows:

```
Variable Name = value/expression
```

In the above syntax, we have used = as assignment operator, in which right side value is assigned to left side variable, here is the explanation:

- `Variable Name`: Any identification name excluding SQL reserved keywords.
- `value/expression`: The value that you need to assign to variable.

When you want to assign some value to variable name then you can use this operator.

Let's take the same example and assign some value to variable and add that in `salary` column. Check out the following query:

```
DECLARE @testVar INT;

SET @testVar = 1;

SELECT Name, Address, Dept, Salary + @testVar AS salary FROM EmpMaster
```

In the above query, declare a variablenamed **@testVar** with **INT** datatype (we have learned SQL datatypes in previous chapter) and then assign value **1** using assign operator, and finally after we have added that variable value to **salary** column, we will get the following output:

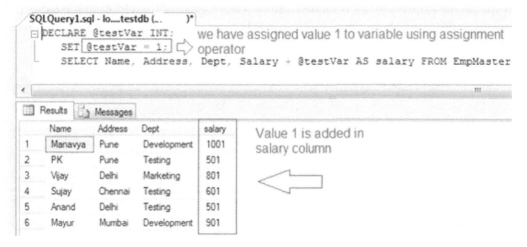

Bitwise operators

These are the one of the least used operators. Bitwise operators are mostly used on bitwise math for manipulation of bit between two expressions or values; here are the bitwise operators and their description:

Bitwise operators	Description
& (Bitwise AND)	Used to perform logical bitwise AND operations between two values.

| (Bitwise OR)	Used to perform logical bitwise OR operations between two values.
^ (Bitwise XOR)	Used to perform logical bitwise XOR operations between two values, it is also known as exclusive OR.
~ (Bitwise NOT)	Used to perform logical bitwise NOT operations between two values.
&= (Bitwise AND assignment)	Used to perform logical bitwise AND operations between two values.
|= (Bitwise OR assignment)	Used to perform logical bitwise OR operations between two values.
^= (Bitwise XOR assignment)	Used to perform logical bitwise XOR operations between two values.

Set operator

These operators are used to return values, either including result set of multiple queries or excluding the result of multiple queries, depending on the condition we have passed. We have the following types of `Set` operators:

- `EXCEPT`
- `INTERSECT`
- `UNION`

Let's trace them one by one:

EXCEPT

This operator is used to fetch the unique values from two queries, in which the values returned by the first query should not be present in the output returned by the second query. Syntax is as follows:

`Query1 EXCEPT Query2`

In the above syntax, we have used `EXCEPT` operator that will fetch the distinct rows from output first query that do not exist in output of second query, here is the explanation:

- `Query1:` A simple select query.
- `Query2:` A simple select query.

When you want to select a query result from 2 different queries whose result is distinct and not present in second query then you can use this operator.

Let's take the same example, and select some records using EXCEPT. Check out the following query:

```
SELECT name FROM EmpMaster EXCEPT SELECT name FROM EmpMaster where Name = 'manavya'
```

In the above query, we have fetched all values of name column and in second query we have only selected record having name column value is manavya, but we have joined both queries with EXCEPT operator, now imagine what could be the output? Yes, the records without manavya entry will be fetched; we will get the following output:

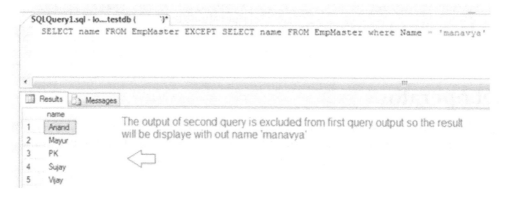

This operator is as good as EXCEPT method.

INTERSECT

This operator is used to fetch the common but unique values from two queries, so the output of both the queries is present here. Syntax is as follows:

```
Query1 INTERSECT Query2
```

In the above syntax, we have used INTERSECT operator that will fetch the common distinct rows from output of first query and second query, here is the explanation:

- Query1: A simple select query.
- Query2: A simple select query.

When you want to select common distinct records from two different queries' output then you can use this operator.

Let's take the same example and select some records using INTERSECT. Check out the following query:

```
SELECT name FROM EmpMaster INTERSECT SELECT name FROM EmpMaster where Name = 'manavya'
```

In the above query, name column from two different queries. As we know both queries will produce output as **manavya** the result will also show the common and distinct name. If you run the above query, we will get the following output:

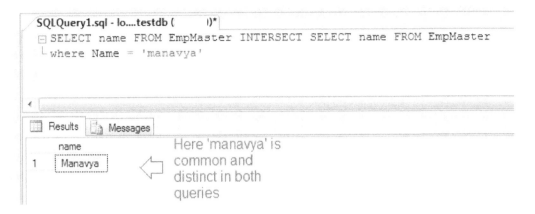

UNION

This operator is used to combine results of two or more different queries. Syntax is as follows:

`Query1 UNION Query2`

In the above syntax, we have used `UNION` operator that will fetch the combined rows from output of first query and second query, here is the explanation:

- **Query1:** A simple select query.
- **Query2:** A simple select query.

When you want to combine the result set of multiple queries then you can use this operator.

Let's take the same example and select some records using `UNION`. Check out the following query:

```
SELECT name FROM EmpMaster UNION SELECT name FROM EmpMaster where Name =
'manavya'
```

In the above query, we have fired two different queries, it will recordboth the queries' output. If you run the above query, we will get the following output:

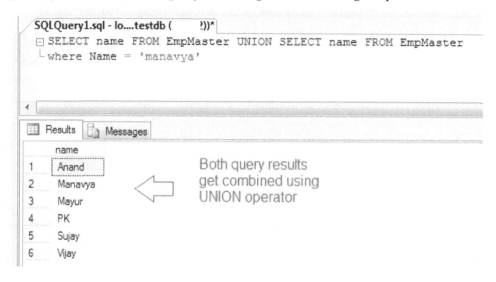

This operator is equivalent to `UNION(MDX)` method.

String concatenation operator

String concatenation operators are used to concatenate two or multiple string or columns. We can concatenate values of columns using string concatenate operator. + (plus) operator is used as string concatenate operator. The syntax is as follows:

```
Expression/value/column name 1 + Expression/value/column 2
```

In the above syntax, we have used one or more expressions and have concatenated them with + plus operator, here is the explanation:

- `Expression1`: A simple expression or column name or a value.
- `Expression 2`: A simple expression or column name or a value.

When you want to concatenate or combine two or more expression/column values then you can use this operator.

Let's take the same example and select some records using + (plus) concatenate operator. Check out the following query:

```
SELECT name + address FROM EmpMaster
```

In the above query, we have concatenated two column values using + operator. If you run above query, we will get the following output:

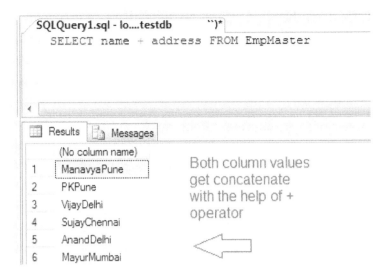

Conclusion

In this chapter we have seen how we can use different SQL operators for specific purposes. There are arithmetic operators which can be used with the help of sign, and we can do popular mathematical operations like addition, subtraction, multiplication and division, moreover we can use comparison operator that are used for filtration of the records, we can use those operators on textual as well numerical data. Logical and assignment operators are also helpful when we want to fetch data from multiple tables or databases, we can divide the data logically with the help of AND and OR like operators.

We have also seen how set operators are helpful in finding out duplicate and unique data and how we can use them to get common, distinct, and combined data from multiple queries. Finally we have seen more about the string concatenation likeoperators, which are helpful in concatenation of two or more different strings, columns values or constant values.

In the upcoming chapters, we will learn more about the remaining SQL operators, like compound and unary operators, LIKE operator, with the help of different wildcards and how to use them. We will also learn how wildcards are more useful in string concatenation. We will learn about the different date functions that allow us to play with dates.So, stay tuned.

Rapid fire questions and answers

1. **What arecomparison operators?**

   Comparison operators are used to compare one or more values or expressions. We have different comparison operators, like equals (=), greater than (>), less than (<), greater than or equal to (>=), less than or equal to (<=), not equal to not equal to (<> and !=), not less than (!<), not greater than (!>).

2. **What are logical operators?**

These operators are similar to comparison operators, but these are not made up of symbols. These operators are SQL reserved keywords.

3. **What is the use of assignment operators?**

As the name suggests, these operators are used for assignment of a value to a variable in SQL.

4. **What are set operators?**

These operators are used to filter database values. When we want distinct, common or combined values then we can use operators like INTERSECT, UNION.

5. **What are string concatenation operators?**

String concatenation operators are used to combine two or multiple values or column names; we can use + plus operator for it.

Do you know (lights on fact?)

- Comparison operators are compatible with all expressions except text, ntext, or image datatypes.

- In SQL, for not equal to operator you can use two signs <> and !=. Both will produce the same result.

- Like less than (<) operator, we can use not greater than (!>) operator and it can produce the same result as less than.

- Like greaterthan (>) operator, we can use not lessthan (!<) operator and it can produce the same result as greater than.

- The difference between BETWEEN and IN operatorsis that the former refers to the range to fetch records from, whereas IN is used to fetch records only from IN query.

- In ALL, ANY, EXISTS operators, the subquery should contain only SELECT query.

CHAPTER 5

SQL Functions and Wildcards

Till now, we have seen the different SQL operators, like comparison operator to compare two values or expression, logical operator to filter data logically, assignment operator to assign value to variable, bitwise operator for bitwise operations. In this chapter we will learn SQL functions, its types and usage. In addition to that, we will also learn about the LIKE operator and different SQL wildcards.

Prerequisite for this chapter: Before we walk through this chapter, you should have knowledge of SQL Operators, SQL clauses and SQL table structure. You should also have a laptop/desktop with SQL server installed.

Structure

After studying this chapter, you will learn the following points:

- SQL functions
- LIKE operator using wildcard
- Conclusion
- Rapid fire questions and answers
- Do you know (lights on fact?)

Objective

So, the objective of the chapter is to learn about the different SQL functions, including configuration function, conversion functions, cursor functions, date and time datatypes and functions, JSON functions, logical functions, mathematical functions, metadata functions, security functions, string functions, system functions, system statistical functions, text and image functions, and many more. We will also learn about the SQL wildcards and their usage with examples.

So, let's begin.

SQL functions

Like other programming languages, SQL Server also has its own built-in functions, (function is a standard set of code that can be reused, and it helps us to remove code redundancy). SQL allows you to create/customize your own function. SQL built-in functions can be categorized as follows:

Function category	Description
Configuration functions	Functions of these categories are used to return information about the current configuration.
Conversion functions	Functions of these categories are used for casting and converting of support datatype.
Cursor functions	Functions of these categories are used to return cursor information.
Aggregate functions	Functions of these categories are used to perform calculation of a set of values
Date and time datatypes and functions	Functions related to date and time belong to this category
JSON functions	These functions are used to validate JSON data.
Logical functions	Functions of these categories are used to perform logical operations.
Mathematical functions	These functions are used to perform logical functions.
Metadata functions	The information about the database and database objects can be retrieved with these functions.
Security functions	Functions of these categories are used to fetch all the information related to users, and their roles can be retrieved using this function.
String functions	Functions of these categories are used to play with string and its different operations.

System functions	Functions of these categories are used to perform operations related to an instance of SQL Server.
System statistical functions	Functions of these categories are used to fetch statistical information of system.
Text and image functions	Operations like image processing can be carried out by these functions.

Let's trace them one by one.

Configuration functions

As discussed earlier, functions belonging to this category are used to fetch current configuration settings. This category has the following inbuilt functions, these functions are also called as non-deterministic functions or variable functions as their output is not the same every time when we call them, not even when the same set of input are passed to them. This category contains functions that are explained in the next sections

SET DATE FIRST

This function is used to set the first day of week to a number (number starts from 0 to 7).

The syntax is simple; we just need to pass the number of the day (the day that we want to set as the first day of week. Bydefault, the first day is Sunday, which means number 7. Following is the syntax:

```
SET DATEFIRST number;
```

Here,the number ranges from 0 to 7 for each day

Let us take an example,

```
SET DATEFIRST 7;
```

Now, if I fire the above query, then the first day would be Sunday.

@@DATEFIRST

This function is used to return a value set by `SET_DATEFIRST` method (`SET_DATEFIRST` function is used to set the first day of week to number 1, which means `Monday` is 1, `Tuesday` is 2 and so on). Basically, here the syntax is nearly equal to the example, so we can directly jump on the sample; it will help us to clear our doubts.

When you want to return a value set by `SET_DATEFIRST` method, and then you can use this method/function.

Let take an example, check out the following query:

```
SET DATEFIRST 3;

GO

SELECT @@DATEFIRST; -- 3 (3 is for Wednesday)

GO
```

In the above query, we have used @@DATEFIRST function, if we run the above query, we will get the following output:

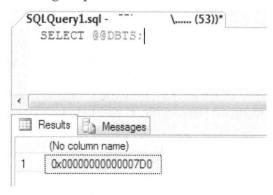

@@DBTS

This function is used to retrieve current database time stamp in encrypted format.

When you want to retrieve current database time stamp, then you can use this method/function.

Let's take an example, check out the following query:

```
SELECT @@DBTS;
```

In the above query, we have used @@DBTS function. If we run the above query, we will get the following output:

@@LANGUAGE

This function returns the database's current language.

When you want to retrieve current database language name, then you can use this method/function.

Let's take an example, check out the following query:

```
SELECT @@LANGUAGE as 'lang name'
```

In the above query, we have used **@@LANGUAGE** function. Here `lang name` is the temporary name of the column. If we run the above query, we will get the following output:

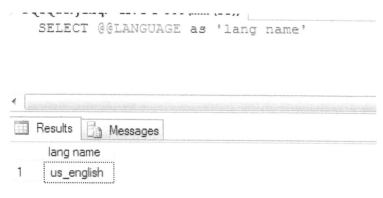

In the above screenshot, we got `us_english` as database language.

@@LANGID

This functions returns database current language ID. Basically, it returns an integer value.

When you want to retrieve current database language ID, then you can use this method/function.

Let's take an example, check out the following query:

```
SELECT @@LANGID as 'lang ID'
```

In the above query, we have used **@@LANGID** function. Here lang ID is the temporary name of the column, if we run the above query; we will get the following output:

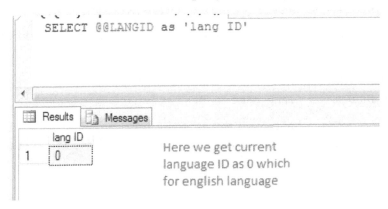

@@MAX_CONNECTIONS

This function returns the maximum allowed simultaneous concurrent database connection per SQL instance.

When you want to retrieve the maximum allowed simultaneous concurrent database connection per SQL instance, then you can use this method/function.

Let's take an example, check out the following query:

SELECT @@MAX_CONNECTIONS as 'maxCon'

In the above query, we have used **@@MAX_CONNECTION** function. Here, maxCon is the temporary name of the column. If we run the above query, we will get the following output:

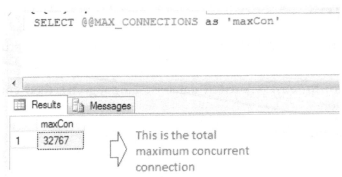

@@LOCK_TIMEOUT

This function returns lock time out in milliseconds. Here time out means the maximum time for a query to wait to release a resource (if it is blocked somewhere).

When you want to retrieve lock timeout of a query, then you can use this method/function.

Let's take an example, check out the following query:

`SELECT @@LOCK_TIMEOUT as 'LockTime'`

In the above query, we have used `@@LOCK_TIMEOUT` function. Here `LockTime` is the temporary name of the column. If we run the above query, we will get the following output (-1 is the default timeout):

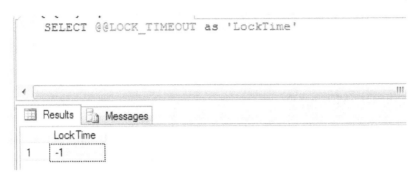

@@MAX_PRECISION

This function returns the maximum precision level used by integer and numeric datatypes set by the current database.

When you want to retrieve the maximum precision level used by integer and numeric datatypes, then you can use this method/function.

Let's take an example, check out the following query:

`SELECT @@MAX_PRECISION`

In the above query, we have used `@@MAX_PRECISION` function. If we run the above query, we will get the following output. The default value is 38:

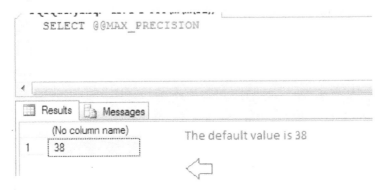

@@REMSERVER

This function is used to retrieve name of the remote SQL server as per the login record.

When you want to retrieve name of the remote SQL server, then you can use this method/function.

Let's take an example, check out the following query:

```
SELECT @@REMSERVER as 'Name'
```

In the above query, we have used @@REMSERVER function. Here Name is the temporary name of the column, if you are not connected to the remote SQL server then the return value should be null.

@@SERVERNAME

This function is used to retrieve name of the local SQL server as per the login record.

When you want to retrieve name of the local SQL server, then you can use this method/function.

Let's take an example, check out the following query:

```
SELECT @@SERVERNAME as 'Name'
```

In the above query, we have used @@SERVERNAME function. Here Name is the temporary name of the column. If you are not connected to the local SQL server then the return value should be null. If we run the above query, we will get the following output:

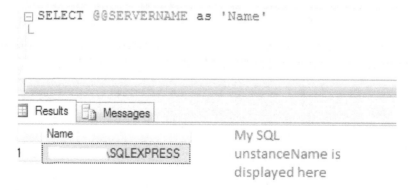

@@ SERVICENAME

This function is used to retrieve name of the registry as a current SQL server instance name, like MS SQL Server or SQL EXPRESS Edition.

When you want to retrieve SQL service name from registry, then you can use this method/function.

Let's take an example, check out the following query:

`SELECT @@SERVICENAME as 'Name'`

In the above query, we have used @@SERVICENAME function. Here Name is the temporary name of the column. If we run the above query, we will get the following output:

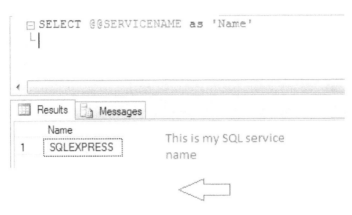

@@VERSION

This function returns the database and system information of the current SQL server.

When you want to retrieve database and system information of the current SQL server, then you can use this method/function.

Let's take an example, check out the following query:

`SELECT @@VERSION as 'Name'`

In the above query, we have used @@VERSION function. Here Name is the temporary name of the column. If we run the above query, we will get the following output:

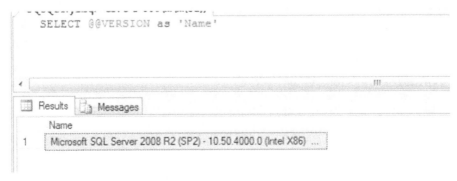

@@TEXTSIZE

This function is used to return current value of textsize option (here textsize means the maximum size of text that SQL can store).

When you want to retrieve current value of textsize option, then you can use this method/function.

Let's take an example, check out the following query:

```
SELECT @@TEXTSIZE as 'Size'
```

In the above query, we have used **@@TEXRSIZE** function. Here `Size` is the temporary name of the column. If we run the above query, we will get the following output:

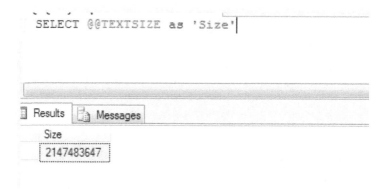

In the above sample we can say SQL can store up to the size of 2147483647 characters

Conversion functions

Many times we need to convert some data from its datatype to another datatype and at that time we can use these functions. These functions are used for conversion of one datatype to another, and this concept is also known as **casting**. This category contains functions that are explained in the next section.

CAST

This function is used to convert value/expression from one datatype to another;the typical syntax is as follows:

```
CAST (value/expression AS DATATYPE)
```

In the above syntax, value or expression can be converted into the given datatype:

- `CAST:` It is the name of the function.
- `value/expression:` A value or expression that we need to convert to.
- `DATATYPE:` The name of the new datatype that we need to cast to.

When you want to convert any value or expression from one datatype to another, then you can use this method/function.

Let's take an example, check out the following query:

```
SELECT CAST (1.5 AS int)
```

In the above query, we have used CAST function and we are trying to convert **1.5** to integer. If we run the above query, we will get the following output:

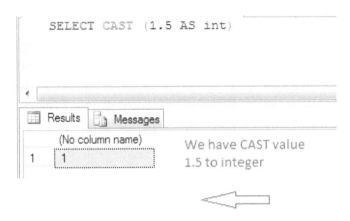

Here we can say that value 1.5 has been converted into integer and it has become 1.

CONVERT

This function is used to convert the value/expression from one datatype to another; the typical syntax is as follows:

```
CONVERT (DATATYPE, value/expression)
```

In the above syntax, value or expression can be converted into the given datatype:

- CONVERT: It is the name of the function.
- value/expression: A value or expression that we need to convert into.
- DATATYPE: The name of the new datatype that we need to convert to.

When you want to convert any value or expression from one datatype to another, then you can use this method/function.

Let's take an example, check out the following query:

```
SELECT CONVERT(int, 9.5)
```

In the above query, we have used `CONVERT` function and we are trying to convert `9.5` to integer. If we run the above query, we will get the following output:

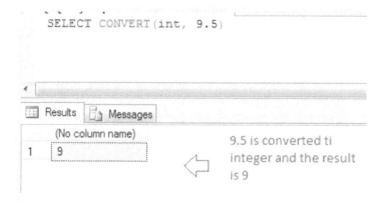

TRY_CAST

This function is also used to convert value/expression from one datatype to another, but if the conversion fails, then this will return a null value. The typical syntax is as follows:

```
TRY_CAST (value/expression AS DATATYPE)
```

In the above syntax, value or expression can be converted in given datatype. If the conversion fails, then null value is returned.

- `CAST:` It is the name of the function.
- `value/expression:` A value or expression that we need to convert to.
- `DATATYPE:` The name of the new datatype that we need to assign to value.

When you want to convert any value or expression from one datatype to anotherbut you are not sure of the type of data, then you can use this method/function.

Let's take an example, check out the following query:

```
SELECT TRY_CAST(1.5 AS int)
```

In the above query, we have used `CAST` function, and we are trying to convert `1.5` to integer. Here it will produce the output as `1`.

Cursor functions

These functions are non-deterministic functions, which mean that the output cannot be predicted. They do not produce the same output each time even if we pass the same input. These are scalar functions and return information about `CURSOR` (A cursor is a temporary work area of SQL created with the `SELECT` statements. We will learn more about cursor and cursor related functions in the coming chapters).

Logical functions

In SQL, logical operators are more popular than logical functions. So, most of the time logical functions are hidden from user. These functions return Boolean value and perform a logical operation on object, the famous function of this category is `IsEmpty()` (this method/function is used to check if a given expression or value is null).

Mathematical functions

The most commonly used SQL functions are mathematical functions. These functions are deterministic functions as the outputs of these functions are always/anytime same when we pass same input to them. The following sections describethe functions used under this category.

ABS

This function is used to return absolute value of an expression or a value, the typical syntaxis as follows

```
ABS(number)
```

`number` is the numeric value which is input to our function

When you want to return the absolute value (positive value) of an expression or a value, then you can use this method/function.

Let's take an example, check out the following query:

```
SELECT ABS(-1.0)
```

In the above query, we have used `ABS` function, and we are trying to return absolute value of `-1.0`. Here it will produce the output as `1.0`.

CEILING

This function is used to return the smallest integer that would be greater than or equal to the value. The syntax is as follows

```
CEILING(number)
```

`number` is the numeric value which is input to our function

When you want return the smallest integer that would be greater than or equal to the value, then you can use this method/function.

Let's take an example, check out the following query:

```
SELECT CEILING(4.4)
```

In the above query, we have used `CEILING` function, and we are trying to return the smallest integer that would be greater than the current value. Here we pass `4.4`, so the answer would be 5.

COS

This function is used to return trigonometric cosine value of expression or value.The syntax is as follows

`COS(number)`

`number` is the numeric value which is input to our function

When you want return cosine value of expression or value, then you can use this method/function.

Let's take an example, check out the following query:

`SELECT COS(3.2)`

In the above query, we have used `COS` function, and we are trying to return cosine value of `3.2`. If we run the above query, the answer would be `-0.998294775794753`.

COT

This function is used to return trigonometric cotangentvalue of expression or value.

The syntax is as follows

`COT(number)`

`number` is the numeric value which is input to our function

When you want to return trigonometric cotangent value of expression or value, then you can use this method/function.

Let's take an example, check out the following query:

`SELECT COT(9.1)`

In the above query, we have used `COT` function, and we are trying to return trigonometric cotangent value of `9.1`. If we run the above query, the answer would be `-2.9699983263892`.

EXP

This function is used to return exponential value of expression or value.

The syntax is as follows:

`EXP(number)`

number is the numeric value which is input to our function

When you want return the exponential value of expression or value, then you can use this method/function.

Let's take an example, check out the following query:

`SELECT EXP(10)`

In the above query, we have used `EXP` function, and we are trying to return the exponential value of `10`. If we run the above query, the answer would be `1.54235104535692`.

FLOOR

This function is used to return the largest integer that would be less than or equal to the value of expression or value.The syntax is as follows:

`FLOOR(number)`

number is the numeric value which is input to our function

When you want return the largest integer that would be less than or equal to the value of expression or value, then you can use this method/function.

Let's take an example, check out the following query:

`SELECT FLOOR(5.6)`

In the above query, we have used `FLOOR` function, and we are trying to return the largest integer that would be less than or equal to the value of `5.6`. If we run the above query, the answer would be 5.

LOG

This function is used to return natural logarithmic value of expression or value.

The syntax is as follows:

`LOG(number)`

number is the numeric value which is input to our function

When you want return natural logarithmic value of expression or value, then you can use this method/function.

Let's take an example, check out the following query:

`SELECT LOG(2)`

In the above query, we have used `LOG` function, and we are trying to return natural logarithmic value of 2. If we run the above query, the answer would be `0.693147180559945`.

LOG10

This function is used to return base-10 logarithmic value of expression or value.

The syntax is as follows:

`LOG10(number)`

`number` is the numeric value which is input to our function

When you want return base-10 logarithmic value of expression or value, then you can use this method/function.

Let's take an example, check out the following query:

`SELECT LOG10(2)`

In the above query, we have used `LOG10` function, and we are trying to return base-10 logarithmic value of 2. If we run the above query, the answer would be `0.301029995663981`.

POWER

This function is used to return power of specified value of expression or value.

The syntax is as follows:

`POWER(number)`

`number` is the numeric value which is input to our function

When you want return power of specified value of expression or value, then you can use this method/function.

Let's take an example, check out the following query:

`SELECT POWER(2,2)`

In the above query, we have used `POWER` function, and we are trying to return power of 2. If we run the above query, the answer would be 4.

RAND

This function is used to return random values between 0 and 1. The output of this function is float value and it comes under non-deterministic category.

The syntax is as follows:

`RAND()`

This function does not require any input parameter.

When you want return random value between 0 to 1, then you can use this method/function.

Let's take an example, check out the following query:

```
SELECT RAND()
```

In the above query, we have used RAND function, and we are trying to return random float value output. If we run the above query, the answer would be 0.28769876521071.

ROUND

This function is used to return rounded value of expression or value. If the input value is negative then it always returns null value. This function takes 2 parameters. The first parameter is for the input value and other is for the precision level.

The syntax is as follows:

```
ROUND(number, precision)
```

- number is the numeric value which is input to our function
- precision is the valueupto which we need to set the precision point.

When you want return rounded value of expression or value, then you can use this method/function.

Let's take an example, check out the following query:

```
SELECT ROUND(4.5656,2)
```

In the above query, we have used ROUND function, and we are trying to return value of 4.5656 with the precision 2. If we run the above query, the answer would be 4.57.

SQUARE

This function is used to return square value of the input value.

The syntax is as follows:

```
SQUARE(number)
```

number is the numeric value which is input to our function

When you want return square value of the input value, then you can use this method/function.

Let's take an example, check out the following query:

```
SELECT SQUARE(4)
```

In the above query, we have used SQUARE function, and we are trying to return square of value 4. If we run the above query, the answer would be 16.

SQRT

This function is used to return square root value of the input value.

The syntax is as follows:

```
SQRT(number)
```

`number` is the numeric value which is input to our function

When you want return square root value of the input value, then you can use this method / function.

Let's take an example, check out the following query:

```
SELECT SQRT(16)
```

In the above query, we have used `SQRT` function, and we are trying to return square of value `16`. If we run the above query, the answer would be 4.

TAN

This function is used to return tangent value of expression or value.

The syntax is as follows:

```
TAN(number)
```

`number` is the numeric value which is input to our function

When you want to return tangent value of expression or value, then you can use this method / function.

Let's take an example, check out the following query:

```
SELECT TAN(2)
```

In the above query, we have used `TAN` function, and we are trying to return tangent value of 2. If we run the above query, the answer would be `-2.18503986326152`.

Aggregate functions

Aggregate functions are deterministic functions, and these are used to perform calculations on a set of values. Most of the times, it returns a single value as a result. These functions are mostly used with `HAVING`, `GROUPBY`, or `SELECT` clause. There are a lot of aggregate functions that exist in SQL, but we have picked up the most popular one's for you, and explained them with samples. Let us go through the following functions.

AVG

This function is used to calculate the average of the given series of values. Basically, it ignores the NULL values,

The syntax is as follows:

AVG(number)

number is the numeric value which is input to our function

When you want to calculate the average of the given series of values, then you can use this method/function.

Let's take an example. Now back to our EmpMaster table and calculate average salary of all employees. Check out the following query:

SELECT AVG(salary) FROM EmpMaster

In the above query, we have used AVG function to calculate the average of a specified salary column. If we run the above query, we will get the following output:

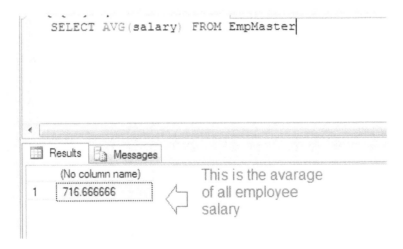

COUNT

This function is used to count number of records that exist in a column or an expression. This function always returns numeric value.

The syntax is as follows:

COUNT(number)

number is the numeric value which is input to our function

When you want to count number of rows/records that exist in a column or an expression, and then you can use this method/function.

Let's calculate count employee in an `EmpMaster table`, check out the following query:

```
SELECT COUNT(Name) FROM EmpMaster
```

In the above query, we have used `COUNT` function to calculate the total number of employee of a specified column. If we run the above query, we will get the following output:

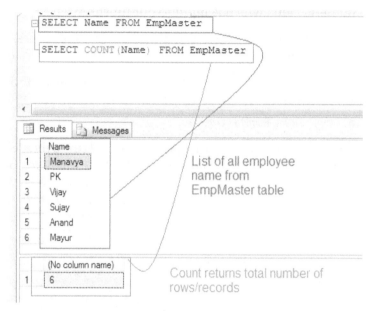

In above screenshot, we have first selected all employee lists and then used `COUNT` method to get total number rows/records.

MAX

This function is used to retrieve the max value of the collection/set of values or an expression.

The syntax is as follows:

```
MAX(collection/set of values or an expression/column name)
```

`collection/set` of values or an expression, column name: is the input of values, column name from which we need to fetch the maximum value

When you want to retrieve the max value of the collection/set of values or an expression, then you can use this method/function.

Let's fetch the max salary from set of all employee salaries in an `EmpMaster` table, check out the following query:

```
SELECT MAX(Salary) FROM EmpMaster
```

In the above query, we have used **MAX** function to find the maximum salary from the list of employees. If we run the above query, we will get the following output:

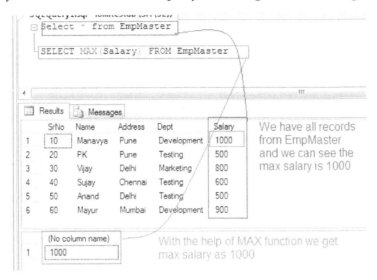

In above screenshot, we have first selected all the employee records and then fired **MAX** function query to get the desired output.

MIN

This function is used to retrieve the minimum value from the collection/set of values or an expression.

The syntax is as follows:

```
MIN(collection/set of values or an expression/column name)
```

`collection/set` of values or an expression, column name: is the input of values, column name from which we need to fetch the minimum value

When you want to retrieve the minimum value of the collection/set of values or an expression, then you can use this method/function.

Let's fetch the minimum salary from the set of all employee salaries in an **EmpMaster** table, check out the following query:

```
SELECT MIN(Salary) FROM EmpMaster
```

In the above query, we have used `MIN` function and fetched the minimum salary from the list of employees. If we run the above query, we will get the following output:

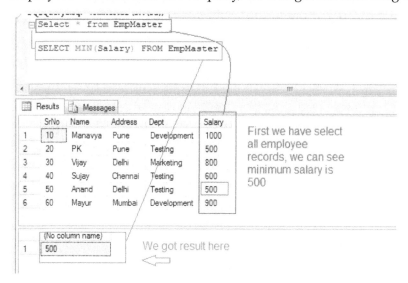

In the above screenshot, we have first selected all the employee records and then fired `MIN` function query to get the desired output.

SUM

This function is used to retrieve the summation of all values from the collection/set of values or an expression.

The syntax is as follows:

```
SUM(collection/set of values or an expression/column name)
```

`collection/set` of values or an expression, column name: is the input of values, column name for which we need to fetch the summation value

When you want to retrieve summation of the collection/set of values or an expression, then you can use this method/function.

Let's fetch the sum of all salaries from set of all employee salaries in an `EmpMaster` table, check out the following query:

```
SELECT SUM(Salary) FROM EmpMaster
```

In the above query, we have used `SUM` function and fetched summation of all salaries from the list of employees. If we run the above query, we will get the following output:

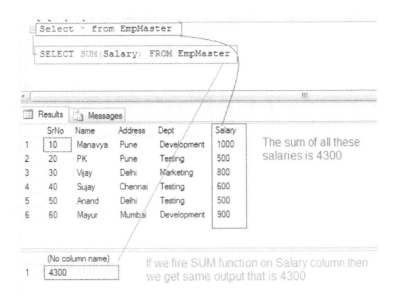

In above screenshot, we have first selected all employee records and then fired SUM function query to get the desired output.

Metadata functions

As the name suggest, these functions are mostly used for the metadata information of SQL database and its object. There are multiple metabase functions that exist in SQL server but we will cover the most-used functions from among them. So let's start.

COL_LENGTH

This function is used to retrieve length of the specified column. We need to pass table name and column name to the function (table is used to avoid the conflicts between tables, as same name column can be present in table).

The syntax is as follows:

```
COL_LENGTH(table name, column name)
```

- `table name` is the name of the table for which we need fetch the column length
- `column name` is the name of the column whose length we need to calculate

When you want to retrieve length of the specified column, then you can use this method/function.

Let's fetch the length of name column from our `EmpMaster` database, check out the following query:

```
SELECT COL_LENGTH('EmpMaster','Name') FROM EmpMaster
```

In the above query, we have used `COL_LENGTH` function and fetched length of the column. If we run the above query, we will get the following output:

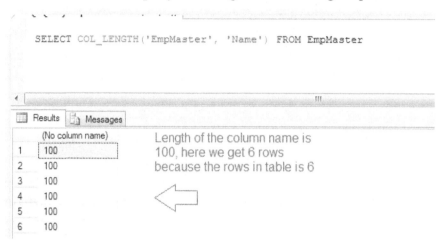

APP_NAME()

This function is used to retrieve current application name, where we have run queries. It returns the name of the application that is responsible for executing queries for current session.

The syntax is as follows:

```
APP_NAME()
```

This function does not accept anyinput.

When you want to retrieve current application name where we have run queries, then you can use this method/function.

Let's fetch the application name, check out the following query:

```
SELECT APP_NAME()
```

In the above query, we have used `APP_NAME` function and fetched application name. If we run the above query, we will get the following output:

DB_NAME()

This function is used to retrieve current database name on which you are executing queries.

The syntax is as follows:

```
DB_NAME()
```

This function does not accept any input.

When you want to retrieve current database name, then you can use this method/function.

Let's fetch the database name, check out the following query:

```
SELECT DB_NAME()
```

In the preceding query, we have used **DB_NAME** function and fetched database name. If we run the above query, we will get the following output:

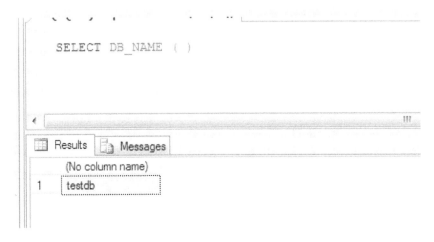

Security functions

As the name suggests, these functions are used to fetch security-related information of database. The following list shows the functions under this category. So let's start.

CURRENT_USER

This function is used to retrieve the name of the current database user, this function is the same as the USER_NAME () function.

The syntax is as follows:

```
CURRENT_USER()
```

This function does not accept any input.

When you want to retrieve length of the specified column, then you can use this method/function.

Let's fetch the name of the current database user, check out the following query:

```
SELECT CURRENT_USER
```

In the above query, we have used CURRENT_USER function and fetched the name of the user. If we run the above query, we will get the following output:

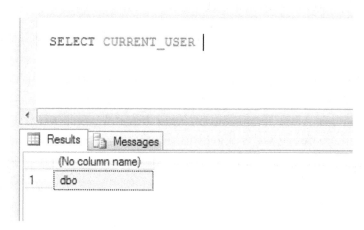

HAS_DBACCESS

This function is used to check if the current user has database access or not. If the current user has database access then it returns 1, otherwise it returns 0. We need to pass the database user name to the function.

The syntax is as follows:

```
HAS_DBACESS(USERNAME)
```

USERNAME is the name of the database user

When you want to check if the current user has database access or not, then you can use this method/function.

Let's check if our user having access of testdb database, check out the following query:

```
SELECT HAS_DBACCESS('testdb')
```

In the above query, we have used HAS_DBACCESS function and fetched the access details of the current user. If we run the above query, we will get the following output:

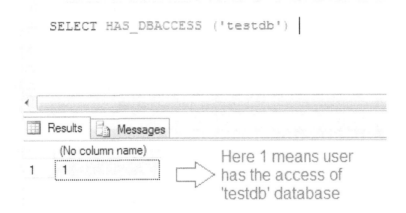

IS_MEMBER

This function is used to check if the current user is a member of specified SQL role. This function accepts parameter as the role name, and it will return 1 if the user has role access, otherwise it will return 0.

The syntax is as follows:

```
IS_MEMBER(databaserole)
```

databaserole is the name of the database role. When you want to check if the current user is a member of specified SQL role, then you can use this method/function.

Let's check if the current user has db_ownerrole access, check out the following query:

```
SELECT IS_MEMBER('db_owner')
```

In the above query, we have used IS_MEMBER function and checked if the current has db_owner role access. If we run the above query, we will get the following output:

Here 1 indicates that a user is the owner of the testdb database.

String functions

As the name suggests, these functions are the most popularfunctions in SQL. They may return string or numeric value as output. There are many functions that come under this category, but we will pick up only the poplar ones. So let's start.

ASCII

This function is used to return ASCII (American Standard Code for Information Interchange) value of the expression.

The syntax is as follows:

```
ASCII(char)
```

charis the character for which we need to retrieve to ASCII code. When you want to retrieve ASCII value of any expression then you can use this method/function.

Let's fetch the ASCII value of any random char, check out the following query:

```
SELECT ASCII('a')
```

In the above query we have used ASCII function and fetched the ASCII value of character a. If we run the above query, we will get the following output:

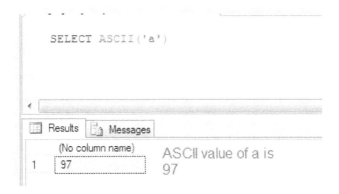

LEFT

This function is used to fetch the left part of the string, up to a specified length. This function returns string value.

The syntax is as follows:

```
LEFT(value/column, length)
```

- `value/column` is the value or column name for which we need to fetch the left part.
- `length` is the specified length up to which we need to fetch the left part of the string.

When you want to retrieve the left part of a string up to a specified length, then you can use this method/function.

Let'suse the `LEFT` function and fetch the value from `EmpMaster` table, check out the following query:

```
SELECT LEFT(Name, 2) from EmpMaster
```

In the above query, we have used `LEFT` function and fetched the left part of the `Name` column up to 2 chars. If we run the above query, we will get the following output:

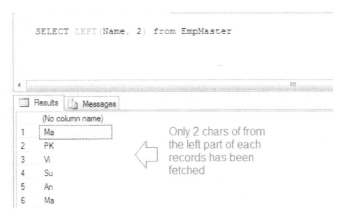

LEN

This function is used to return the number of characters of a string/expression or a specified column. This function returns numeric value.

The syntax is as follows:

`LEN(value/column)`

`value/column` is the input parameter.

When you want to retrieve the number of characters of a string, then you can use this method/function.

Let's use the `LEN` function and fetch the number of characters from `EmpMaster` table, check out the following query:

`SELECT LEN(Name) from EmpMaster`

In the above query, we have used `LEN` function and fetched the length of each record. If we run the above query, we will get the following output:

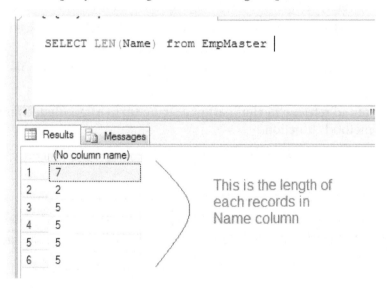

LOWER

This function is used to return the values by converting them in a lower case.

The syntax is as follows:

`LOWER(value/column)`

`value/column` is the input and it will convert the input value to lower case. When you want to return the values by converting them in a lower case, then you can use this method/function.

Let's use the LOWER function and fetch the number of characters from EmpMaster table, check out the following query:

SELECT LOWER(Name) from EmpMaster

In the above query, we have used LOWER function and made all Name records in lower case. If we run the above query, we will get the following output:

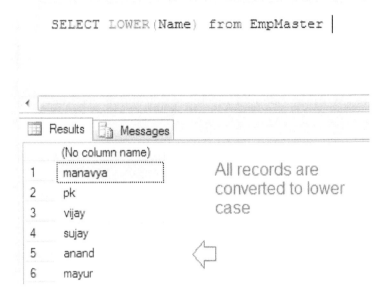

Wildcards in SQL

Wildcards are nothing but a substitute to any characters. These cards are used with the LIKE operator in SQL, and they will check if any string matches the given pattern. If it does then it will fetch that matched record from the database. Now that pattern can include wild or regular characters. Now first let's see how wildcards are used with LIKE operator.

In SQL, we use 4 different characters that are explained in the following table:

Sr No	Wildcards	Usage
1	%	This character is used to denote one or more characters in the string or an expression.
2	_	This underscore character is used to denote one character at particular position.
3	[]	This square braces are used to denote single character with specified range.

Let's trace them one by one.

% **character**

If the LIKE operator is followed by the % character, then rows with all matching pattern is retrieved.

When you retrieve the value as per the pattern then you can use this method/ function.

Let's use the LIKE function and %wild character to match the pattern, check out the following query:

```
SELECT * from EmpMaster where Name like 'Mana%'
```

In the above query, we have used LIKE function with % character. It will fetch the values that start with the Mana string. If we run the above query, we will get the following output:

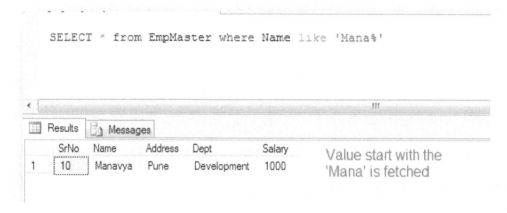

In the same way, we can use % wild character at start position, which will help us start the string with any character, see the following sample.

Let's use the LIKE function and % wild character and will now put that character at start of the pattern, check out the following query:

```
SELECT * from EmpMaster where Name like'%Man'
```

In the above query, we have used LIKE function with % character, where it will fetch the values that start with the any characters but end with the Man. Here we will get the NULL result as we don't have any rows that end with Man.

Another way to use the % wild character is by putting that character multiple times in string so that matching result will collect the rows as per the pattern. See the following sample.

Let's use the LIKE function and % wild character, and will now put that character at multiple locations in string, check out the following query:

```
SELECT * from EmpMaster where Name like 'Ma%n%'
```

In the above query, we have used LIKE function with % character, and it will fetch the values that start with letter Maand followed by any character, but it should contain n letter in between. This is how we can use wildcards. If we run the above query then we will get the same result with one row as name = manavya.

_ character

If the LIKE operator is followed by the _ character, then rows with all matching pattern is retrieved, but here _ (underscore) can be replaced with only one character.

When you retrieve the value as per the pattern, then you can use this method/function.

Let's use the LIKE function and _wild character to match the pattern, check out the following query:

```
SELECT * from EmpMaster where Name like 'Manavy_'
```

In the above query, we have used LIKE function with _ character. Now it will fetch the values that start with the Manavy string and last underscore wildcards can be replaced with only one character

If we run this query, then we will get the result that contains 1 record with name =manavya.

Same way, we can put _ wildcard anywhere or multiple times in a string.

[] character

If the LIKE operator is followed by the [] character, then rows with all matching pattern is retrieved, but here we need to specify the [range].

When you retrieve the value as per the pattern, then you can use this method/function.

Let's use the LIKE function and [ ] wild character to match the pattern, heck out the following query:

```
SELECT * from EmpMaster where Name like 'Man[a-c]vya'
```

In the above query, we have used LIKE function with [] character with the range as a-c. Now it will fetch the values that start with the letters Man and contain letters ranging from a to c, and string end with vya letters. If we execute this query, then we will get the same records with 1 row and name = manaya

Same way, we can put [] wildcard anywhere and multiple times in a string.

Conclusion

In this chapter, we have seen the different SQL functions--configuration functions will help us to return information about the current configuration, conversion functions will help us in casting and converting of support datatypes, aggregate functions will help us to perform calculation of a set of values, mathematical functions will help us to perform logical functions, metadata functions will help us to get information about database objects, security functions will help us to fetch all the information related to users and their roles can be retrieved with this function. String functions will help us to play with string and its different operations.

Additionally, we have learnedthe different SQL wildcards that can be used to fetch the rows as per the applicable pattern.

In the upcoming chapters, we will learn more about the remaining SQL functions likedate related functions, `text_images` functions, and some remaining SQL operators, like compound and unary operators. Additionally, we will have a deep dive through different SQL `JOINS` and SQL `CASE` statements. So, stay tuned.

Rapid fire questions and answers

1. **What is SQL function?**

   SQL function is a standard set of code that can be reused and it helps us to remove code redundancy.

2. **What different types of SQL functions exist?**

   The following types of SQL functions exist. Configuration functions, conversion functions, cursor functions, aggregate functions, JSON functions, logical functions, mathematical functions, metadata functions, security functions, string functions, system functions, and system statistical functions.

3. **What is aggregate function?**

   Aggregate functions are used to perform calculation on a set of values; they either return float or integer value. These functions are mostly used with `GROUP BY`, and `SELECT` clauses. The examples of these functions are `SUM`, `AVG`, and more.

4. **What is the usage of configuration function?**

   These functions are used to return information about the current configuration. The examples of these functions are `@@DATE_FIRST`, `@@DBTS`, `@@LANGUAGE`, and many more.

5. **What are wildcards in SQL?**

   Wildcards are a substitute to any character. These cards are used with the LIKE operator in SQL, and are used to check if any string matches the given pattern. If it does, then it will fetch that matched records from the database. SQL has the following wildcards--%, _(underscore), [] (range).

Do you know (lights on facts?)

- @@ means this function will return some value.

- FROM SQL 2012, we can also PARSE function for conversion of data from one datatype to another.

- Aggregate functions are different from mathematical functions as they are run on set of values and used with SELECT and HAVING like clauses.

- If you want to count all rows in a column, then you can use * for it (for example, SELECT COUNT(*) from tbl1).

- MAX function returns NULL if no records exist in table.

CHAPTER 6

SQL Dates, Joins and Case

Introduction

Till now we have seen the different types of SQL functions and their usage. We have also learnt about wildcards in SQL and how to use them. In this chapter we will learn SQL date related functions, `text_image` related functions, `JOINS` in SQL, and how SQL uses `CASE` statement.

Prerequisite for this chapter: Before walking through this chapter you should have knowledge of SQL functions, SQL operators and clauses. You should also have a laptop/desktop with SQL server installed.

Structure

After studying this chapter, you will learn the following points:

- SQL date related functions
- SQL `JOIN`
- SQL `CASE` statement
- Conclusion
- Rapid fire questions and answers
- Do you know (lights on fact?)

Objective

So, the objective of this chapter is to learn about the various SQL functions related to dates, including different date format supported by SQL, system date, date difference in days, months or years, or even in terms of hours, minutes or seconds.

Additionally, we will also learn about SQL joins including inner join, cross join, left and right outer join, self-join, with example. We will also learn about SQL CASE statement.

So, let's begin.

SQL date related functions

We have seen SQL has date and time related datatype (Do you remember the earlier chapters?), lets brush up on them. In SQL, we have the following date time related datatypes that are used to store date and time value separately. Go through the following table:

Date type	Date/time store format
Date	MM/dd/yyyy
Time	HH:MM:SS
Smalldatetime	MM/dd/yyyy hh:mm:ss
Datetime	MM/dd/yyyy hh:mm:ss[nnn]
Datetime2	MM/dd/yyyy hh:mm:ss[nnnnnn]

Now we will see the different SQL functions that are used to support date and time related operations.

SYSDATETIME

This function is used to return currentdate time value in YYYY-MM-DD hh:mm:ss:nnn format, where YYYY represents year value, MM represents month value, DD represents day value, hh represents hour, mm represents minutes, ss represents seconds, nnn represents nanoseconds.

When you want to return the current date time value in YYYY-MM-DD hh:mm:ss:nnn format, then you can use this method/function.

Let's take an example, check out the following query:

```
SELECT SYSDATETIME()
```

In the above query we have used SYSDATETIME function. If we run the above query, we will get the following output:

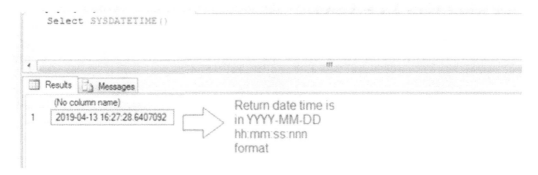

In the above screenshot we can see the returned date time is in YYYY-MM-DDhh:mm:ss:nnn.

SYSDATETIMEOFFSET

This function is similar to the previous function; additionally, it also returns current date time offset value of the machine, where SQL server instance is installed.

When you want to return the current date time offset value of the machine where, SQL server instance is installed, and then you can use this method/function.

Let's take an example, check out the following query:

```
SELECT SYSDATETIMEOFFSET( )
```

In the above query we have used SYSDATETIMEOFFSET function. If we run the above query, we will get the following output:

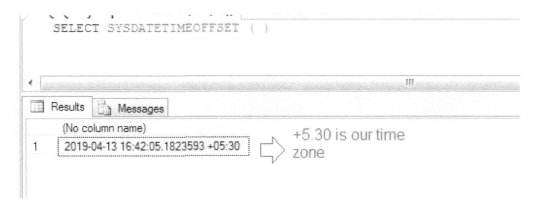

In the above screenshot we can see the returned date time is in YYYY-MM-DD hh:mm:ss:nnn and +5.30 is the time zone of the current system where SQL server instance is installed.

SYSUTCDATETIME

This function is used to return date and time but as per the **UTC** time (UTC time is a **Coordinated Universal Time** which is the world's standard regulated clocks and time).

When you want to return current date time in UTC format, then you can use this method/function.

Let's take an example, check out the following query:

```
SELECT SYSUTCDATETIME( )
```

In the above query we have used SYSUTCDATETIME function. If we run the above query, we will get the following output:

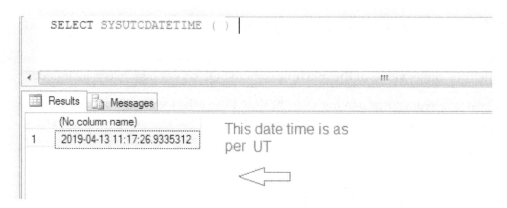

In the above screenshot we can see the returned date time is in UTC format.

CURRENT_TIMESTAMP

This function is used to return current date and time stampof system where SQL is installed. We cansay this function works same as SYSDATETIME but the difference is that this function has less precision in time format.

When you want to return current date and time stamp of system where SQL is installed, then you can use this method/function.

Let's take an example, check out the following query:

```
SELECT CURRENT_TIMESTAMP
```

In the above query we have used SYSUTCDATETIME function. If we run the above query, we will get the following output:

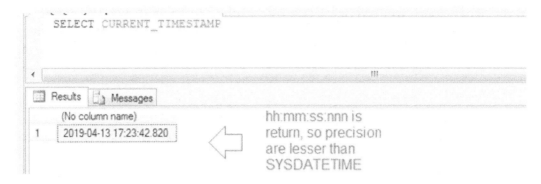

In the above screenshot we can see system date timestamp has returned in YYYY-MM-DD hh:mm:ss:nnn format.

GETDATE

This function is used to return current date and time stamp of system where SQL is installed but it will not include time zone.

When you want to return current date and time stamp of system but without time zone, then you can use this method/function.

Let's take an example, check out the following query:

```
SELECT GETDATE()
```

In the above query we have used GETDATE function. If we run the above query, we will get the following output:

In the above screenshot we can see system date timestamp has been returned, but time zone is not included. To fetch only date from above datetime format, you need to use CONVERT method and pass date datatype to it, see the following query:

```
SELECT CONVERT (date, GETDATE())
```

In the above query we have used **CONVERT** method to convert datetime format to fetch date value. If we execute the above query, we will get the following output:

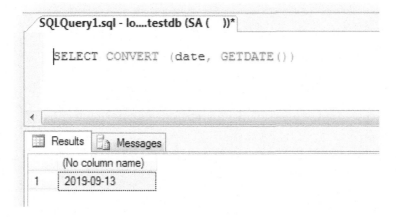

Similarly, we can fetch only time from datetime value with the help of the following query:

```
SELECT CONVERT (time, GETDATE())
```

In the above query we have used **CONVERT** method to convert datetime format to fetch time value:

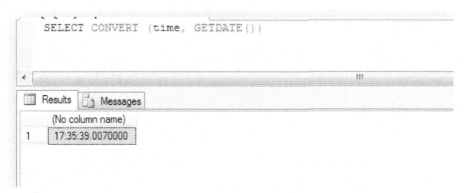

DATENAME

This function is used to return only date or time part from the datetime value; we can even retrieve year, month, day value from the date and hour, minutes, seconds value from time.

When you want to return only date or time part from the datetime value, then you can use this method/function.

Let's take an example, check out the following query:

```
SELECT DATENAME (year, getdate())
```

This function requires two parameters; one isdatatype (which date part we need to fetch from date) and the other parameter is date variable. So in the above query we have used `DATENAME` function with year as a return part and `GETDATE` is standard function that returns date. If we run the above query, we will get the following output:

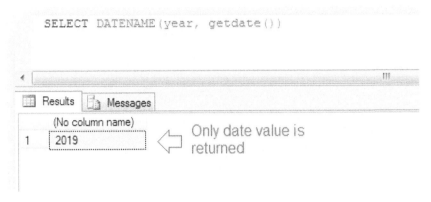

In the above screenshot we fetched only year value from date, similarly we can fetch below parts from date: these datapart are not case sensitive

Sr No	Date part	Description
1	Year	Return year from datetime.
2	Month	Return month from datetime.
3	day of year	Return day of year in numeric format.
4	day	Return day from datetime.
5	Week	Return number of weeks from date datetime.
6	Hour	Return hour from datetime.
7	Minute	Return Minute from datetime.
8	Seconds	Return seconds from datetime.
9	Millisecond	Return milliseconds from datetime.

DATEPART

This function is used to return different parts of date or time from datetime value. This function always returns integer value.

When you want to return different parts of date or time from datetime value, then you can use this method/function.

Let's take an example, check out the following query:

```
SELECT DATEPART(day, getdate())
```

This function requires two parameters; one is datatype (which date part we need to fetch from date), and the other parameter is date variable. So in the above query we have used `DATEPART` function with dayof month (in numeric format). If we the run above query, we will get the following output:

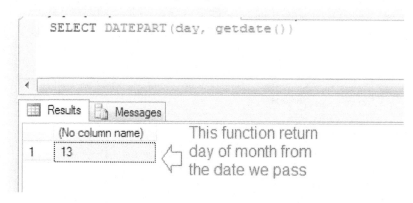

In the above screenshot we fetched only day from the date value, same way if we want to fetch the day of year, then we can use the same method but this time the `DATEPART` parameter will be `DAYOFYEAR` check out the following query:

```
SELECT DATEPART(DAYOFYEAR, getdate())
```

The above query will return the numeric value. Basically it is the value between **1** and **365**, where **1** is the `1st JAN` and 2 is `2nd JAN` and so on. Let's fire the above query and see what the output is:

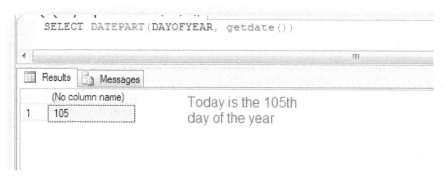

Date part can be used with where, having group by, orderby.

YEAR/MONTH/DAY

Basically, these are small separate functions that will return year, month, and day of the date that we pass to the function.

When you want to return year, month, or day of the date, then you can use this method/function.

Let's take an example, check out the following query:

```
SELECT YEAR(GETDATE())
```

In the above query we have selectedyear from the current date. If we fire the above query we will get the following output:

In the above screenshot, we can see it returns 2019 as the current year (as we have pass current date only, I mean we have used GETDATE() method which returns current date). Similarly, we can use MONTH method as follows:

```
SELECT MONTH(GETDATE())
```

In the above query we have selected month from the current date. If we fire the above query will get the following output:

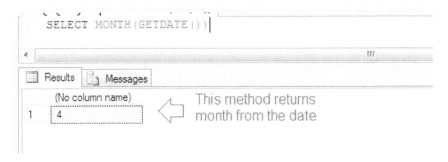

In the above screenshot, we can see MONTH function return 4, which is the current month April (GETDATE method return current date that is 15th APRIL 2019).

We can also use these functions in a single query. Want to see how? Check out the following query:

```
SELECT YEAR(GETDATE()), MONTH(GETDATE()), DAY(GETDATE());
```

In the above query we have used all these functions in the same query, it will return year, month and day for current date. (Today's date is 15th APRIL 2019).

If we fire the above query, then we will get the following output:

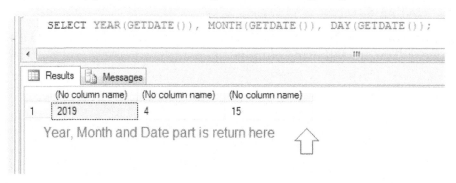

DATEDIFF

This function is used to get the difference between the start and end date. This will return the numeric value that represents the difference in year, month or day dependupon DATEPART we pass to the function. Even we can get the difference in hour, minute, or seconds also.

When you want to get the difference between the start and end date, then you can use this method/function.

Let's pass some random dates to the method and calculate the difference in days. Check out the following query:

```
SELECT DATEDIFF(day, '4/14/2019','4/15/2019')
```

In the preceding query we have passed two different dates to the function, which returned the result in day part. If we fire the preceding query will get the following output:

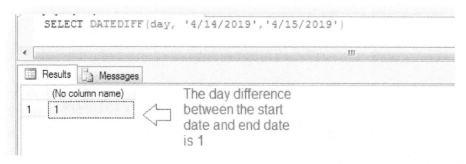

In the above screenshot, we have passed the start date as 14th APRIL 2019 and the end date as 15th APRIL 2019, and if we calculate the difference between these two dates in terms of day, then the answer would be **1** and the same has been returned by the query.

If we run the same query and return month part then the answer would be **0** (zero) as there is the same month, see the following query:

```
SELECT DATEDIFF(MONTH, '4/14/2019','4/15/2019')
```

In the above query we have passed `MONTH` as a return parameter, now let's execute the above query, we will get the following output:

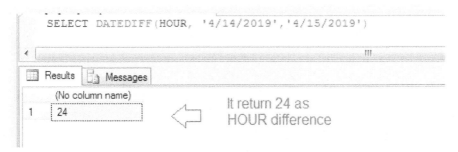

If we run the same query and return `HOUR` part then the answer would be **24** as there is **24** hours difference between these two dates, see the following query:

```
SELECT DATEDIFF(HOUR, '4/14/2019','4/15/2019')
```

In the above query we have passed `HOUR` as a return parameter, now let's execute the above query, we will get the following output:

If there is a large difference between the two dates, then you can use `DATEDIFF_BIG`. Now let's see what is `DATEDIFF_BIG`.

DATEDIFF_BIG

This function returns the counter of the given datepart between two input dates. The syntax would be as below

```
DATEDIFF_BIG ( datepart , startdate , enddate )
```

- `datepart` is the bit different than `DATEDIFF` function. Here `datepart` means part of the start and end date that specifies the boundary.

`startdate` could be of type date, datetime, datetime offset, datetime `2enddate` could be of type date, datetime, datetimeoffset, datetime 2 The return type of this function is signed `bigint`.

DATEADD

This function is used to add date part to a date. In simple words, we can add year, month, day, hour, minute, or seconds to date. This function accepts date part and number of counts of date part as a parameter and adds these values to the date that we pass to function, (confused? Check out the sample in the example section).

When you want to add year, month, day, hour, minute, or seconds to date, then you can use this method / function.

Let's add some days to current date, check out the following query:

```
SELECT DATEADD(DAY,1, GETDATE())
```

In the above query we have passed DAY and 1 parameter to DATEADD function. Here it will add 1 day to the current date (current date is 15th APRIL 2019). If we fire the above query, we will get the following output:

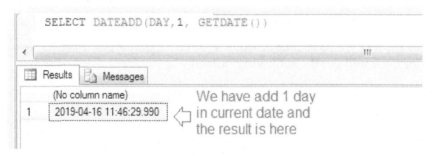

Similarly, if we try to add 3 years in the current date then the query we will be as follows:

```
SELECT DATEADD(YEAR,3, GETDATE())
```

In the above query we have passed YEAR and 3 parameters to DATEADD function. Here it will add 3 years to the current date (current date is 15th APRIL 2019). If we fire the above query, we will get the following output:

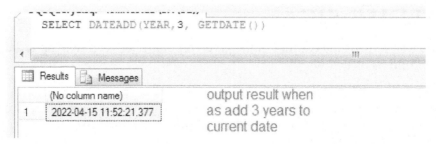

In the above screenshot, we can see DATEADD function adds 3 year in the current year and returns 2022.

ISDATE

This function is used to check if the date is valid or not. This function returns 1 if the date is a valid date, otherwise it returns 0.

When you want to check if the date is valid or not, then you can use this method/function.

Let's take any random date, check out the following query:

```
SELECT ISDATE('04/02/2017')
```

In the above query we have used ISDATE method to check if date 04/02/2017 is valid. Now it seems the date looks valid, so the output should be 1. If we fire the above query we will get the following output:

Similarly, if we fire the query with some invalid date, the output will be 0. Let's checkout the query first:

```
SELECT ISDATE('2017/02/2017')
```

Now we can see that 2017/02/2017 seems to be a wrong date. If we fire this query, we will get the following output:

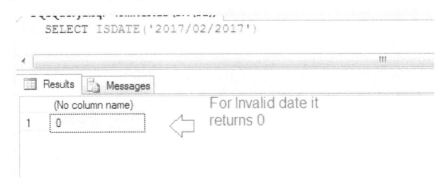

SQL joins

As the name suggests, SQL join is a combination data / rows from two or more tables fetched by applying different conditions on them. There are different types of joins exist in SQL, here is the list of joins:

- Inner join
- Left outer join
- Right outer join
- Full outer join
- Cross join

Let's trace them one by one.

Before playing with JOIN concepts, we first need to create two tables (as JOIN concept is applicable on two or more tables).

We will create 2 tables as EmpMaster and Department by firing the following queries:

- Query1 to create EmpMaster table:

  ```
  CREATE TABLE [EmpMaster](
  [EMPID] [numeric](4, 0) NULL,
  [Name] [varchar](50) NULL,
  [Address] [varchar](50) NULL,
  [DeptID] [numeric](4, 0) NULL
  ) ON [PRIMARY]
  ```

- Query2 to create Department table:

  ```
  CREATE TABLE [Department](
  [DeptID] [numeric](4, 0) NULL,
  [DeptName] [varchar](50) NULL
  ) ON [PRIMARY]
  ```

If we fire these queries, both tables get created. Now we will fire INSERT queries on them to fill-up records. Here is the list of INSERT queries:

- Insert queries for EmpMaster table:

  ```
  INSERT INTO EmpMaster (EMPID, Name, Address, DeptID) VALUES (1,
  'Prasad', 'Pune', 10)
  INSERT INTO EmpMaster (EMPID, Name, Address, DeptID) VALUES (2,
  'Manavya', 'Pune', 20)
  INSERT INTO EmpMaster (EMPID, Name, Address, DeptID) VALUES (3,
  'Anil', 'Mumbai', 20)
  ```

INSERT INTO EmpMaster (EMPID, Name, Address, DeptID) VALUES (4, 'Manas', 'Delhi', 30)

INSERT INTO EmpMaster (EMPID, Name, Address, DeptID) VALUES (5, 'Aryana', 'Delhi', 30)

INSERT INTO EmpMaster (EMPID, Name, Address, DeptID) VALUES (6, 'Manasi', 'Mumbai', 60)

- Insert queries for Department table:

INSERT [Department] ([DeptID], [DeptName]) VALUES (10 , 'Marketing')

INSERT [Department] ([DeptID], [DeptName]) VALUES (20 , 'Development')

INSERT [Department] ([DeptID], [DeptName]) VALUES (30 , 'Sales')

INSERT [Department] ([DeptID], [DeptName]) VALUES (40 ,'Supply')

INSERT [Department] ([DeptID], [DeptName]) VALUES (50 ,'Accounts')

INSERT [Department] ([DeptID], [DeptName]) VALUES (60 , 'HR')

After executing these queries if we open these tables, we will get the following output:

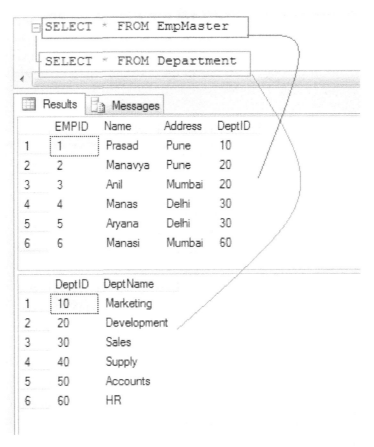

From now onwards we will call our first table `EmpMaster` as *left-side* table and second table `Department` as *right-side* table.

Inner join

Inner joinis used to select all common records from both tables. It basically creates a new set of records with the common records from both tables. Each record from left table (`EmpMaster`) scans each record of right table (`Department`) to match rows and fetch the value. Though this join fetches only common rows but still due to each row combination it will fetch duplicate rows.

When you want to fetch common rows from one or more tables, then you can use join.

Let's use `INNER JOIN` on our left and right tables, see the following query:

`SELECT EmpMaster.EMPID, EmpMaster.Name, department.DeptName`

`FROM EmpMaster INNER JOIN department ON`

`EmpMaster.DeptID = department.DeptID`

In the above query we have selected `EMPID`, `NAME` from `EmpMaster` table and `DEPTNAME` from `Department` table (here we have used allies' concept where to identify column separately we have added its table name before column name, it helps to avoid redundancy), and we have used `INNER JOIN` on `DeptID` column. (As this column is common in both left and right table), if we fire the above query, we will get the following output:

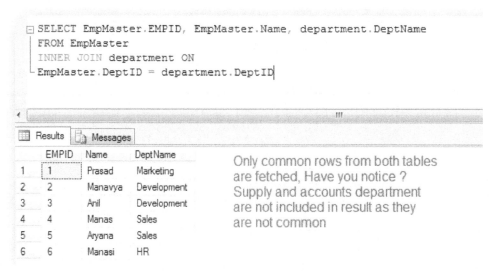

In the above screenshot, we got the record with the department name `Supply` and `Accounts` are not present in output as these records are not common in both tables.

To put more focus on concept, let us place it in pictorial format, see the following diagram:

Common rows from both
tables are fetched in
INNER JOIN

In the above diagram, we can see only common rows between table **A** and **B** have been fetched in INNER JOIN.

Left-outer join

First let's understand what outer join is. Outer join always fetches rows from both tables even if no common rows are present. Further, this outer join is divided in left outer, right outer and full outer joins. When we fire Left outer join on two tables then it will fetch all rows from left side tale and common rows from both table.

When you want to fetch all rows from the left table and common rows from both tables, then you can use this join.

Let's use LEFT OUTER JOIN on our left and right tables, see the following query:

```
SELECT EmpMaster.EMPID, EmpMaster.Name, department.DeptName FROM
EmpMaster LEFT OUTER JOIN department ON

EmpMaster.DeptID = department.DeptID
```

In the above query we have used `LEFT OUTER JOIN` to select all rows from the left table (`EmpMaster`) and common from both the tables. So if we fire the above query, we will get the following output:

In the above screenshot, we can see all rows from left table and common rows from right table have been fetched, but `Supply` and `Accounts` department have not been fetched as both the entries are not from the left table as well as they are not common in both tables.

To put more focus on the concept, let's place it in pictorial format, see the following diagram:

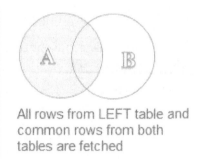

All rows from LEFT table and
common rows from both
tables are fetched

In the above diagram, can see all rows from table **A** and common rows between table **A** and **B** have been fetched in `LEFT OUTER JOIN`.

Right-outer join

As the word suggests, this join will fetch all rows from the right table and common rows from both tables.

When you want to fetch all rows from the right table and common rows from both tables, then you can use this join.

Let's use `RIGHTOUTER JOIN` on our left and right tables, see the following query:

```
SELECT EmpMaster.EMPID, EmpMaster.Name, department.DeptName FROM
EmpMaster RIGHT OUTER JOIN department ON

EmpMaster.DeptID = department.DeptID
```

In the above query we have used `RIGHT OUTER JOIN` to select all rows from the right table (`Department`) and common from both the tables. So if we fire the above query, we will get the following output:

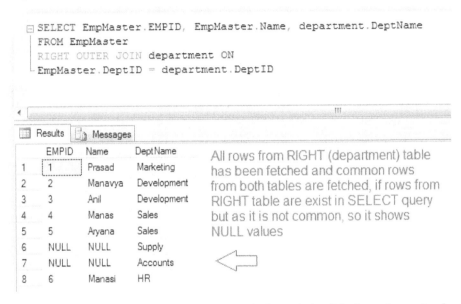

In the above screenshot, we can see all records from left table have been fetched, as well as the combination of common rows from the both tables have been fetched.

To put more focus on the concept, let's place it in pictorial format, see the following diagram:

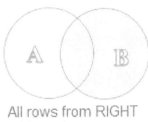

All rows from RIGHT
table and common
rows from both
tables are fetched

In the above diagram, we can see all rows from table **A** and common rows between table **A** and **B** have been fetched in LEFT OUTER JOIN.

Full-outer join

This join is the combination of left and right outer join; it will fetch all rows of left and right outer join result.

When you want to fetch combine effect of left and right outer join, then you can use this join.

Let's use FULL OUTER JOIN on our left and right tables, see the following query:

```
SELECT EmpMaster.EMPID, EmpMaster.Name, department.DeptName FROM
EmpMaster FULL OUTER JOIN department ON

EmpMaster.DeptID = department.DeptID
```

In the above query we have used FULL OUTER JOIN that will select all rows from left, right tables and common rows from both. If we fire the above query, we will get the following output:

Cross join

The CROSS JOIN produces the result by combining each row from left table to each row from right table. Basically, this concept is known as Cartesian product.

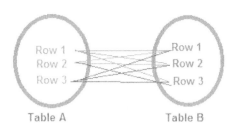

Table A   Table B

In above image we can see each row from Table **A** is linked with each row from table **B**.

When you want to fetch the Cartesian product from result, then you can use this join.

Let's use CROSS JOIN on our left and right tables, see the following query:

```
SELECT * FROM EmpMaster CROSS JOIN Department
```

The query is a bit simple, it just applies CROSS JOIN on both tables. If we fire this query, we will get the following output:

```
SELECT * FROM EmpMaster CROSS JOIN Department
```

	EMPID	Name	Address	DeptID	DeptID	DeptName
1	1	Prasad	Pune	10	10	Marketing
2	2	Manavya	Pune	20	10	Marketing
3	3	Anil	Mumbai	20	10	Marketing
4	4	Manas	Delhi	30	10	Marketing
5	5	Aryana	Delhi	30	10	Marketing
6	6	Manasi	Mumbai	60	10	Marketing
7	1	Prasad	Pune	10	20	Development
8	2	Manavya	Pune	20	20	Development
9	3	Anil	Mumbai	20	20	Development
10	4	Manas	Delhi	30	20	Development
11	5	Aryana	Delhi	30	20	Development
12	6	Manasi	Mumbai	60	20	Development
13	1	Prasad	Pune	10	30	Sales
14	2	Manavya	Pune	20	30	Sales
15	3	Anil	Mumbai	20	30	Sales
16	4	Manas	Delhi	30	30	Sales
17	5	Aryana	Delhi	30	30	Sales
18	6	Manasi	Mumbai	60	30	Sales
19	1	Prasad	Pune	10	40	Supply
20	2	Manavya	Pune	20	40	Supply
21	3	Anil	Mumbai	20	40	Supply
22	4	Manas	Delhi	30	40	Supply

Each row from LEFT table combine to each row from RIGHT table

CASE statement in SQL

SQL CASE statement is like IF and THEN condition in common programming languages. See its structure below; we can say it's a typical syntax:

```
CASE

WHEN condition1 THEN statement

WHEN condition2 THEN statement

WHEN condition N THEN statement

ELSE statement

END;
```

In above syntax, SQL will check a particular condition, if that condition is true then SQL will execute THEN statement, otherwise it will slipup to the next condition. In case, not a single condition is true then it will execute ELSE part, and if there is no ELSE part then it will return NULL, the CASE statement should be concluded with END.

CASE statement is very flexible and can be used with SELECT, DELETE, UPDATE, WHERE, ORDER BY.

When you want check multiple conditions and execute the query accordingly, then you can use this join.

Let's use CASE statement on EmpMaster table, see the following query:

```
SELECT Name, Address,

CASE  DeptID

WHEN 10 THEN 'Marketing'

WHEN 20 THEN 'Development'

WHEN 30 THEN 'Sales'

WHEN 40 THEN 'Supply'

WHEN 60 THEN 'HR'

END

FROM EmpMaster
```

In the above sample we have fetched Name, Address, and DeptID column values from EmpMaster table. We have used CASE statement for DeptID column and check the WHEN condition; if DeptID column has value 10 then it will return text Marketing, if DeptID column has value 20, then it will return text Development and so on. If we execute the above query, we will get the following output:

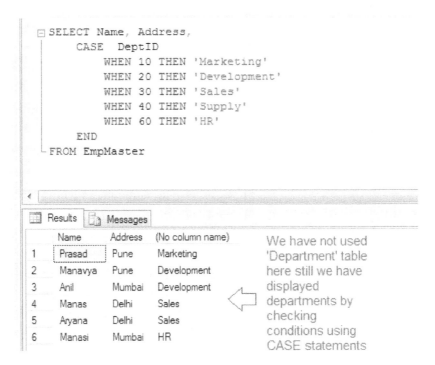

```
SELECT Name, Address,
     CASE   DeptID
          WHEN 10 THEN 'Marketing'
          WHEN 20 THEN 'Development'
          WHEN 30 THEN 'Sales'
          WHEN 40 THEN 'Supply'
          WHEN 60 THEN 'HR'
     END
FROM EmpMaster
```

	Name	Address	(No column name)
1	Prasad	Pune	Marketing
2	Manavya	Pune	Development
3	Anil	Mumbai	Development
4	Manas	Delhi	Sales
5	Aryana	Delhi	Sales
6	Manasi	Mumbai	HR

We have not used 'Department' table here still we have displayed departments by checking conditions using CASE statements

In the above screenshot, we can see 3rd columns have been returned with the textual values depending upon the conditions. SQL allows only 10 level of nesting in CASE.

Conclusion

In this chapter, we have seen the various SQL functions that represent DATE and TIME values, we have seen how to fetch system date, how to get current time zone, and how to calculate date and time difference. SQL gives us the flexibility in playing with date and time related operations. Additionally, we have also seen the different joins that can be applied on two or multiple tables to filter and fetch data. INNER JOIN helps us to fetch common records between two tables, LEFT OUTER JOIN helps us to fetch all records from left table and common records from both tables whereas RIGHT OUTER JOIN helps us to fetch all records from right table and common records from both tables. We also have a FULL OUTER JOIN in which we have records from left and RIGHT OUTER JOIN. We have also learnt about CASE statement where SQL queries are executed by checking different conditions.

In the upcoming chapter, we will learn SQL data definition, data control, and data transaction statements. We will see how to modify existing SQL databases, tables and rows definition. Additionally, we will learn about access control over databases and table, we will also learn about transaction related statements. So, stay tuned.

Rapid fire questions and answers

1. **What are the different SQL functions related to datetime operations?**

   SQL has a plenty of functions that deal with date and time operations. Following is the list of SQL date time functions:

Sr No	Function	Description
1	SYSDATETIME	Used to fetch system date time.
2	SYSDATETIMEOFFSET	Used to fetch system date time with time zone.
3	SYSUTCDATETIME	Used to fetch system date time in UT format.
4	GETDATE	Used to fetch current system date time.
5	DATEPART	Used to fetch different date time parts from specific date.
6	DAY	Used to fetch Day from specific date.
7	MONTH	Used to fetch Month from specific date.
8	YEAR	Used to fetch Year from specific date.
9	DATEDIFF	Used to fetch difference between start and end date.
10	DATEADD	To add specific date time part in specific date.

2. **How to get difference between two dates?**

   We can use DATEDIFF function to get the difference between two dates. This will return the numeric value that represents the difference in year, month or day depending upon the DATEPART we pass to the function. We can even get the difference in hour, minute, and seconds.

3. **How to fetch only year from SQL?**

   You can use YEAR method to fetch only the year from SQL date. This function accepts date from which we need to exclude year value. The typical syntax is as follows:

   ```
   YEAR(date)
   ```

4. **What are SQL joins?**

   SQL join is a combination of data/rows from two or more table fetched by applying different conditions on them.

5. **What is INNER JOIN?**

   INNER JOIN fetches the common records between left and right tables. Basically, it creates a new set of records with the common from both tables. Each record from the left table scans each record of the right table for matching rows and fetches the values.

6. **What is LEFT OUTER JOIN?**

LEFT OUTER JOIN fetches the common records between left and right tables. Additionally, it fetches all records from left table.

7. **What is RIGHT OUTER JOIN?**

RIGHT OUTER JOIN fetches the common records between left and right tables. Additionally, it also fetches all records from right table.

8. **What is CASE statement in SQL?**

SQL CASE statement is like IF and THEN condition in common programming languages. SQL will check a particular condition, if that condition is true then SQL will execute THEN statement, otherwise it will slipup to the next condition. In case, not a single condition is true then it will execute ELSE part. If there is no ELSE part then it will return NULL, the CASE statement should conclude with END. See its structure below, we can say it's a typical syntax:

```
CASE
WHEN condition1 THEN statement
WHEN condition2 THEN statement
WHEN condition N THEN statement
ELSE statement
END;
```

Do you know (lights on facts?)

- To fetch date and time value of current system, SQL uses Windows inbuilt API method GetSystemTimeAsFileTime() Windows.

- While using INNER JOIN you should use common column for joining.

- SQL allows up to 10 levelsof nesting in CASE statement.

- If the first condition is satisfied in CASE statement, then it will not execute other conditions and skip to the end.

CHAPTER 7

SQL DDL, DCL, and DTL Statements

In the previous chapters, we have already seen and learnt **Data Definition Language (DDL)**, **Data Control Language (DCL)**, and **Data Transaction Language (DTL)** concepts. Now the question arises what extra will we learn here? What added knowledge will we get here. Basically, this chapter will be a deep dive into DDL, DCL and DTL concepts. This chapter is at an advanced level than *Chapter 2: SQL Statements, Keywords, and Datatype* and *Chapter 3: SQL Statements and Clauses*, and we will not discuss about the syntax and samples of commands belonging to DDL, DCL, and DTL statements here.

Prerequisite for this chapter: Before walking through this chapter you should have the knowledge of SQL DDL, DCL, and DTL concepts. You should know about their syntax and samples.Additionally, you should have a laptop/desktop with SQL server installed.

Structure
- DDL, DCL, and DTL statements
- CREATE and DROP commands
- ALTER and TRUNCATE commands
- GRANT, REVOKE, and transaction commands
- COMMIT, ROLLBACK, and transaction commands
- Attaching and de-attaching a database

Objective

So, the objective of the chapter is to take a deep dive intothe concepts of DDL, DCL and DTL. We will learn about the different usages of CREATE, DROP, ALTER, and TRUNCATE commands. Additionally, we will focus on GRANT and REVOKE commands and transaction-related commands, like COMMIT and ROLLBACK. We will also look into database-related operations, including how to attach and de-attach database and how to take its backup.

So, let's begin!

DDL, DCL, and DTL statements

In the earlier chapters, we have learnt about DDL statement, where we can create, change, delete and rename database objects like table, column datatypes, view, stored procedure, database, with the help of DDL statement.DDL contains commands like CREATE, DROP, and TRUNCATE.

We have learnt about DCL statement, which are used to control data access through various data control commands, DCL contains commands like GRANT and REVOKE.

We have learnt about TCL statement; these statements are used to control data transactions between two or more databases or database tables. Transaction is a set of SQL operational queries that are logical in order and fire for a specific work flow. COMMIT, ROLLBACK, and SAVE POINT like commands belonging to TCL statement, START and END TRANSACTION are also part of TCL commands.

We have seen their syntax and samples. In this chapter we will see more different things about these statements.

CREATE statement

CREATE can be used to create any database objects like table, keys (will see these concepts in later chapters), database, database encryption key (this key is used to encrypt the database, this makes the whole database encrypted), function (function is a set of code that can be used multiple times to save code redundancy), index, procedure, schema, table, trigger, type, view, user, and many more.

See some basic CREATE sample with some business scenario:

- **Scenario 1 -Create database user**

  Following query will be used to create database user:

  CREATE LOGIN prasad WITH PASSWORD = 'pra123&'

  In above query we have created user ID prasad with password pra123&.

- **Scenario 2 - Create simple database table**

  Following query will be used to create database table:

  `CREATE TABLE emptable (name(25), city(25))`

  In above query we have created `emptable` with columns `name` and `city`.

- **Scenario 3 - Create table with FILESTREAM column**

  Following query will be used to create table with `FILESTREAM` column

  ```
  CREATE TABLE emp
  (
    empid int,
    emp_pic varbinary(max) FILESTREAM
  );
  ```

  In above query we have created `emp` table with columns `empid` and `emp_pic` (which is used to store employee picture).

- **Scenario 4 - Create table with encrypted column**

  Following query will be used to create table with encrypted column:

  ```
  CREATE TABLE emp (
  Name nvarchar(60)
  ENCRYPTED WITH
  (
  COLUMN_ENCRYPTION_KEY = key1,
  ENCRYPTION_TYPE = RANDOMIZED,
  ALGORITHM = 'AEAD_AES_256_CBC_HMAC_SHA_256'
  ),
  Age int
  );
  ```

  In above query we have created `emp` table with columns `Name` (which is encrypted with `key1` as key, and algorithm as `AEAD_AES_256_CBC_HMAC_SHA_256` and `Age`.

- **Scenario 5 - Create database**

  See following syntax `CREATE DATABASE databasename`

  In the above syntax `databasename` is name of the database that needs to be created.

  Following query will be used to create database:

  `CREATE DATABASE testEMP`

  In we fire the above query, it will create new database with name `testEMP`.

We will come back to CREATE scenario once we go through the identity and keys concept.

DROP statement

DROP can be used to delete/remove any database objects like table, keys (will see these concept in later chapters), database, database encryption key (this key is used to encrypt the database, this make the whole database encrypted), function (function is nothing but a set of code that can be use multiple times to save the code redundancy), index, procedure, schema, table, trigger, type, view, user, and many more.

DROP table cannot be used on the table whose column is reference as foreign key. If we delete all the rows from the table still the table exists until we fire DROP command.

One thing to note iswe should not be execute CREATE and DROP query in the same batch on same database, it may lead to error.

See some basic DROP sample with some business scenario:

- **Scenario 1 - Remove SQL login account**

  Following query will be used to remove SQL login account:

  ```
  DROP LOGIN prasad
  ```

  In above query we have removed login for prasad user.

- **Scenario 2 - Drop SQL table**

  Following query will be used to drop SQL table:

  ```
  DROP TABLE emp;
  ```

  In above query we have delete/remove emp table from database.

- **Scenario 3 - Dropping table of another database**

  Following query will be used to drop table of another database:

  ```
  DROP TABLE testdb.dbo.EmpMaster
  ```

  In above query we have delete/remove EmpMaster table from testdb database (dbo is the standard keyword for table).

- **Scenario 4- Drop a database**

  Following query will be used to drop a database:

  ```
  DROP DATABASE testDB;
  ```

  In above query we have deleted testDB database.

- **Scenario 5 - Dropping multiple databases in single query**

  Following query will be used to drop multiple databases in single query:

```
DROP DATABASE emp, department;
```

In the above query we have dropped emp and department table using single query.

- **Scenario 6 - Drop a function**

  Following query will be used to drop a function:

  ```
  DROP FUNCTION func;
  ```

  In above query we have dropped func function from current database.

ALTER statement

ALTER can be used to edit or change/modify any database objects like table, table definitions, adding or removing table columns, keys, database, database encryption key, function, index, procedure, schema, table, trigger, type, view, user, and many more.

See some basic ALTER sample with some business scenario:

- **Scenario 1 - Add column in existing table**

  Following query will be used to add column in existing table:

  ```
  ALTER TABLE EmpMaster ADD City_Col VARCHAR(50) NULL;
  ```

  In the above query we have added column city_colin table EmpMaster with datatype as varchar that can store size up to 50 characters (NULL represent; this column can also hold NULL values).

- **Scenario 2 - Delete column from existing table**

  Following query will be used to delete column from existing table:

  ```
  ALTER TABLE EmpMaster drop column City_Col;
  ```

  In the above query we have removed column city_col from EmpMaster table.

- **Scenario 3 - Add column in an existing table with DEFAULT constraint**

  Following query will be used to add column in an existing table with DEFAULT constraint:

  ```
  ALTER TABLE EmpMaster ADD City_Col VARCHAR(50) DEFAULT 'A';
  ```

  In the above query we have added column city_col in table EmpMaster with datatype as varchar that can store size up to 50 characters (here, DEFAULT means whenever any new record is added in database table, this newly added column will add A as a default).

- **Scenario 4 - Modify column size**

  Following query will be used to modify column size:

```
ALTER TABLE EmpMaster ALTER COLUMN City_Col VARCHAR(100)
```

In the above query we have changed the `city_col` column size to `100` from `50`.

If we change the column size using `ALTER` command, then the new size should not be smaller than the old column size.

- **Scenario 5 – Add default constraint to existing column**

  In this scenario, `ALTER TABLE` will help you specify the column name for which you want to add default value and add default constraint.

  Following query will be used to `ADD` default constraint to existing column:

```
ALTER TABLE EMP ADD CONSTRAINT emp_default DEFAULT 'StandardEmp'
FOR emptype;
```

  In the above query we have `EMP` as a table name, `emp_default` is the constraint name, `StandardEmp` is the column name to which we have applied constraint.

TRUNCATEstatement

We know `TRUNCATE` helps us to remove all rows from database in single execution.

See some basic `TRUNCATE` sample with some business scenario:

- **Scenario 1 - Delete all data from table and reset all constraints**

  Following query will be used to delete all data from table and reset all constraints:

```
TRUNCATE TABLE EmpMaster
```

  In the above query we have removed all rows from table, reset all keys and its constraints `TRUNCATE` command will not fire on table having foreign key.

GRANTstatement

This command belongs to DCL where we set some access permission to different database users.

See some basic `GRANT` sample with some business scenario:

- **Scenario 1 - Give permission to create table using GRANT command**

  Following query will be used to give permission to create table using `GRANT` command:

```
GRANT CREATE TABLE TO prasad;
```

  In the above query we have `GRANT` permission of table creation to user `prasad`.

- **Scenario 2 - Give database control permission to user**

  Following query will be used to give database control permission to user:

  `GRANT CONTROL ON DATABASE:testDB TO prasad;`

  In the above query we have `GRANT` control permission of `testDB` database to `prasad` user.

- **Scenario 3 - Transfer of database control permission from user to user**

  Following query will be used to transfer of database control permission from user to user:

  `USE testdb;`

  `GRANT CONTROL ON USER::prasad TO Manavya;`

  In the above query we have transferred control permission of `testDB` database from user `prasad` to user `Manavya`.

REVOKE statement

This command belongs to DCL where we remove some access permission from different database users which were earlier set by `GRANT` command.

See some basic `REVOKE` sample with some business scenario:

- **Scenario 1: Give permission to create table using REVOKE command**

  Following query will be used to give permission to create table using `REVOKE` command:

  `REVOKE CREATE CERTIFICATE FROM prasad;`

  In the above query we have removed permission of `CREATE CERTIFICATE` using `REVOKE` command from user `prasad`.

- **Scenario 2-REVOKE the permission from user to user**

  Following query will be used to `REVOKE` the permission from user to user:

  `USE testdb;`

  `REVOKE CONTROL ON USER::prasad FROM Manavya;`

  In the above query we have `REVOKE` control of database `testdb` from user `prasad` to user `manavya`.

- **Scenario 3-Remove SELECT permission on database using REVOKE command**

  Following query will be used to remove `SELECT` permission on database using `REVOKE` command:

  `REVOKE SELECT ON OBJECT::EmpMaster FROM prasad;`

  In the above query we have removed `SELECT` permission of `EmpMaster` table for user `prasad`.

COMMIT TRANSACTION statement

This command belongs to TCL where it indicates the end of transaction. The `commit` word indicates that transaction is successful and changes are done in database permanently.

See some basic `COMMIT` sample with some business scenario:

- **Scenario 1-COMMIT a simple transaction**

  Following query will be used to `COMMIT` a simple transaction:

  ```
  BEGIN TRANSACTION;
  DELETE FROM EmpMater WHERE ID = 7;
  COMMIT TRANSACTION;
  ```

  In the above query we have to execute a `DELETE` command and then committrans action, that is the indication of successful transaction.

- **Scenario 2 – How to commit a work in case of distributed transactions. Distributed transactions are managed by Microsoft Distributed Transaction Co-coordinator (MSDTC)**

  Take an example where there are 3 servers and we want to do the distributed transaction. Then the controlling server (in our case it's server A) will connect to MSDTC and start executing `BEGIN DISTRIBUTED TRANSACTION` statement, then the session calls a stored procedure (`sp_configure` remote `proc` trans) on server B and server C. Then it will execute the distributed queries, here each server first completes the local transaction and then passes the session to controller for commit message.

  In the following example we have deleted rows from 2 different databases using distributed transaction concept:

  ```
  BEGIN DISTRIBUTED TRANSACTION;
  DELETE Emp.eMaster
    WHERE emp_id = 23; DELETE Org.eDepartment
    WHERE dept_id = 33; COMMIT TRANSACTION;
  ```

  In the above sample, `BEGIN DISTRIBUTED TRANSACTION:` this is the start of the distributed transaction. We have deleted data from two different databases here.

ROLLBACK TRANSACTION statement

This command belongs to TCL where it indicates the rollback of all operation fire/ execute on database due to the failure in execution.

See some basic `ROLLBACK` samples with some business scenario:

- **Scenario 1- ROLLBACK a simple transaction**

  Following query will be used to ROLLBACK a simple transaction:

  ```
  BEGIN TRANSACTION;
  DELETE FROM EmpMater WHERE ID = 7;

  ROLLBACK TRANSACTION;
  ```

In the above query we have executed a DELETE command and then rolled back transaction, due to which the DELETE command is rolled back and changes will not be permanently saved in database.

Attaching and de-attaching a database

To store data in database, SQL takes use of **MDF (meta data file)** file. It has all records stored in it and with this file we do have more file, **LDF (log data file)** which logs all operations of database (whatever operations we executed on database are audited in LDF file).

Attaching a database

So, if you want to move whole database from one machine to another, then you need to move your MDF and LDF files. You can also move only MDF file and LDF file will be auto-generated again but your old audit logs will be lost in this case. So, the recommended step is to attach with MDF and LDF file only. To attach any database, we need to satisfy the following conditions:

- Database must be in de-attach state, which means that once the database is attached, it can-not be re-attached again. First you need to de-attach it and then re-attach again.
- The MDF and LDF should reside in the same directory. If you want to put them in different directory then that directory should not be a shared location (which means that you should not store one of the files in \\ip\foldername location)

There are two ways to attach a database:

- Using SQL Management Studio
- Using SQL Query analyzer

Let's trace them one by one.

Using SQL Management Studio

1. You just need to log into SQL management studio (always use a user who is having attachment rights to the database). Check out the following step-by-step screenshot of database attachment:

2. Click on the `Attach...`:

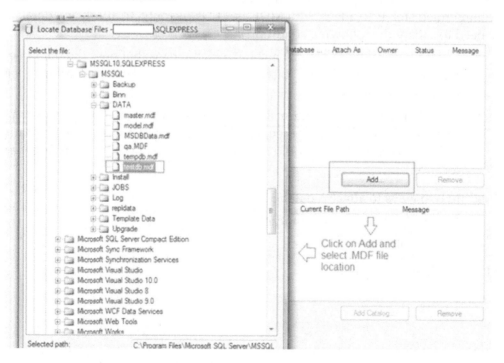

3. On this window, click on **Add...** button to select MDF file location, once MDF file is located and selected, you can click on **OK** button:

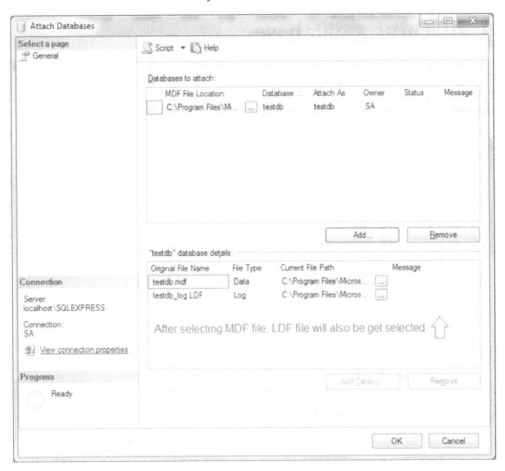

4. After selecting MDF file, the LDF file will be automatically selected; you will see it in the previous screenshot. After selecting these files, just click on **OK** button.

Using SQL Query analyzer

We can attach database with the help of SQL analyzer as well, see the following query:

```
CREATE DATABASE testDB

  ON (FILENAME = 'E:\Database\test.mdf'),

  (FILENAME = 'E:\Database\test_Log.ldf')

FOR ATTACH;
```

In the above query we must first create database using CREATE DATABASE command and then pass the file path of MDF and LDF database.

De-attaching a database

De-attaching of a database means removing it from SQL instance and making it available for re-attachment to any SQL instance (attach only to higher or same version of SQL instance). Before de-attachment of database, we need to follow some conditions:

- To de-attach replicated database, you must be first unpublish it.
- A suspect database cannot be de-attached.
- System database cannot be de-attached.
- If there are active connections to database, then the database cannot be de-attached.

There are two way to de-attach a database:

- Using SQL Management Studio
- Using SQL Query analyzer

Let's trace them one by one.

Using SQL Management Studio

1. You just need to log into SQL Management Studio (always use a user who has de-attach rights to the database), check out the following step-by-step screenshot of database de-attachment:

2. Right click on the database that you want to de-attach, then click on `Tasks` and click on `Detach`...:

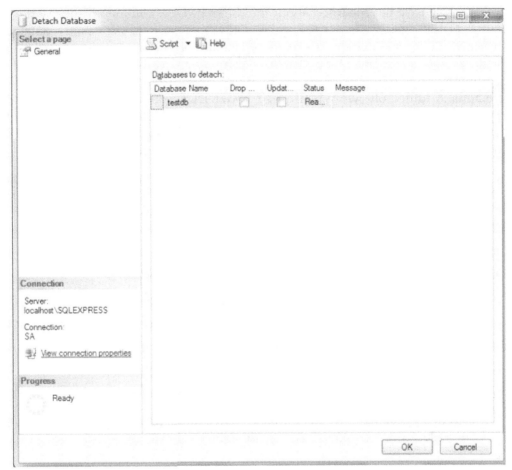

3. Click on `OK` button to de-attach database.

Using SQL Query analyzer

We can attach database with the help of SQL analyzer also, see the following query:

```
EXEC sp_detach_db 'testdb';
```

In the above query we have used standard stored procedure `sp_detach_db` for database de-attach, `testdb` is the database name.

> **Stored procedure: We will learn about stored procedure in the upcoming chapter.**

Conclusion

In this chapter we have learned about the different DDL commands, like CREATE, DROP, ALTER, and TRUNCATE, where CREATE is used to create any database object, DROP is used to delete or remove database object, ALTER is used to modify database objects like table, table structure, column structure and adding, removing of columns.TRUNCATE is used to remove all records from database and reset its structure. Additionally, we havelearned about DCL commands, like GRANT and REVOKE which are used to grant or remove different access permission from or to database, database table or roles. We have also learned about DTL commands like COMMIT and ROLLBACK commands which supporttransaction related operations.

In the upcoming chapters, we will learn what SQL stored procedures is, why to use them and how it will be helpful to us. We will also learn about what is SQL trigger, how to use it and why it is important in SQL, additionally we will learn what is views and SQL transactions. So, stay tuned.

Rapid fire questions and answers

1. **What are the different commands belonging to DDL?**

    DDL have different commands like CREATE, ALTER, TRUNCATE, and DROP.

2. **What are the different commands belonging to TCL?**

    TCL have different commands like COMMIT and ROLLBACK.

3. **How to delete whole database?**

    To delete database, we need to use DDL command, DROP command is used to delete or remove database, see the following example:

    ```
    DROP DATABASE testdb
    ```

    In the above query testdb is the database name that we want to drop.

4. **How to add a column in existing table?**

    To add column in database we need to use DDL command, ALTER command is used to add column to existing database table, see the following example:

    ```
    ALTER TABLE Employee ADD Name VARCHAR(50);
    ```

    In the above query we have added column Name in table Employee with datatype as varchar that can store size up to 50 characters.

5. **What is the use of COMMIT and ROLLBACK commands?**

    These are the DCL commands that can be used in transaction. COMMIT is used when the transaction is successful and the changes can be made in database permanently, whereas ROLLBACK can be used when the transaction fails and we want to roll back all operations that are executed on database.

6. **How to attach database?**

    To attach database, we need MDF and LDF files, where MDF is a meta data file that contains actual data and LDF is log data file that contains log of all database transaction. We at least need MDF for database attachment; there are two ways by which we can attach database:

    - Using SQL Management Studio
    - Using Query analyzer

    Following query can be used to attach database:

    ```
    CREATE DATABASE EmpDB
    ON (FILENAME = 'E:\test\empDB.mdf'),
    (FILENAME = 'E:\test\empDB_Log.ldf')
    FOR ATTACH;
    ```

    In the preceding query we have used `CREATE DATABASE` to create database and attach our MDF file to it.

7. **How to de-attach database?**

    To de-attach database we can use the following ways:

    - Using SQL Management Studio
    - Using Query analyzer

    We have in-built stored procedure that can be used to de-attach database:

    ```
    EXEC sp_detach_db 'Empdb';
    ```

    In the above query we have used standard stored procedure `sp_detach_db` to de-attach database, `Empdb` is the database name.

Do you know (lights on facts?)

- A login cannot be removed or dropped when you are logged in. So first you need to log in with another user and then use `DROP LOGIN` command.
- `CREATE TABLE` and `DROP TABLE` should not be executed in the same query bunch as it may lead to unhandled exception.
- `DROP DATABASE` command is not used on a currently logged in database.
- For Windows Azure (MS cloud), you should connect to master database only to drop other databases.
- If there are inter related functions, `DROP` function command will fail to drop function.
- Database user name is not case sensitive.
- `TRUNCATE` table is not used drop/delete the table or database.
- `TRUNCATE` command is not allowed inside transaction.

CHAPTER 8

SQL Stored Procedure and Triggers

Nowadays, SQL stored procedures are widely used as they are faster in execution and good for security reason. In this chapter we will learn about SQL stored procedures, SQL triggers and SQL Views. Additionally, we will focus on ACID and transaction operations.

Prerequisite for this chapter: Before we walk through this chapter, you should have knowledge of SQL DDL, DCL, and DTL concepts. Additionally, you should have a laptop/desktop with SQL server installed.

Structure

- SQL stored procedure and its types
- Usage of stored procedure
- SQL triggers and its types
- Usage of SQL triggers

Objective

So, the objective of the chapter is to learn about stored procedure, triggers and views. If you want to run some group of SQL statements again and again then we can use stored procedure and if you want to automatically fire/execute those SQL statements depending upon the database changes, then we can use triggers. In this chapter we will see how to use SQL triggers and stored procedure. Additionally, in this chapter we will learn how to create virtual table in SQL and how to use it. We will also dive into SQL transaction and ACID concepts.

So, let's begin.

SQL stored procedure

Stored procedure isa set of or say a bunch of SQL statements, but popular due to the following capabilities:

- Faster in execution
- Can be re-usable
- Supports Microsoft .NET CLR
- Accept input parameters and return multiple values in the form of output parameter
- Can be called from other programming languages
- Returns success or failure status with exception message

The advantages of SQL stored procedure are as follows:

- SQL stored procedure execute a bunch of SQL statements in a single shot. This will really be helpful in reducing traffic as full bunch will travel at once from client to server and execute procedure, instead of sending each query at a time. It will save network traffic and speed up the execution performance.

- SQL stored procedure has to follow an execution plan that is created at first run. In short, when we execute stored procedure for the first time, it compiles and creates an execution plan, and later for each execution it just executes the predefined plan and saves compilation time.

- SQL stored procedure allows separation of database layer and execution layer, as only procedure needs to be updated for any change in database or columns and rest of the things are kept untouched.

- SQL stored procedure follows *'write one time and execute many time'* approach, it leads to reduction in code redundancy and improves code re-usability.

- SQL stored procedure hides table and database structure as we only call direct procedure, so the user will not interact with database and its structure directly. It helps to increase security.

Types of SQL stored procedure

There are multiple types of stored procedures, including the following types:

- System/inbuilt stored procedure
- User defined
    - o Temporary stored procedure

System/inbuilt stored procedure

As the name suggests, these stored procedures are inbuilt and come with SQL instance only. If you go to `msdb` database under system database then you can see all system stored procedure there. All system stored procedure will start with `sp_` word. When we want to execute any stored procedure then the syntax would be as follows:

`EXECUTE ProcedureName [parameters]`

In the above syntax `EXECUTE` is the reserved keyword and it is used to execute stored procedure. `ProcedureName` is the name of the procedure we want to execute and `parameters` is the list of input values that we are going to pass to our procedure.

See following screenshot to check where the inbuilt stored procedure is stored:

Figure 8.1

In the above screenshot, we can see there are multiple procedures that exist in stored procedure folder. Each procedure has its own set of SQL queries designed for specific purpose. From SQL 2017 version, many SQL inbuilt management operations can be handled by system stored procedures only. These stored procedures are again categorized under the following sub types:

Sr No	Subtype	Description
1	**Catalog SP**	This procedure is used to get the information about database, tables and its design.
2	**Change Data Capture SP**	This procedure category is used to fetch details about data history and changes done due the operation carried out by DML.
3	**Cursor SP**	This procedure category is used to implement cursor functionality.
4	**Data collector SP**	This procedure category is used to work with data collection.
5	**Db Engine SP**	This procedure category is used for general information and maintenance of the SQL database engine.
6	**DB Mail SP**	This procedure category is used for different operation related to mail.
7	**DB Maintenance SP**	This procedure category is different than Db Engine SP as it plays with different operations related to database; whereas Db Engine SP plays with different operations related to SQL engine.
8	**Distributed Queries SP**	This procedure category is used to operate and manage distributed queries.
9	**File SP**	This procedure category is used to play with different operation related to file stream and file table.
10	**Firewall SP**	This procedure category is used in Azure database only and is used to configure Azure DB firewall.
11	**Log Ship SP**	This procedure category is used to maintain, monitor operations related to log shipping.
12	**Data Ware house SP**	This procedure category is used to maintain operation related to data ware house.
13	**Replication SP**	This procedure category is used to manage replication related operation.
14	**Security SP**	To manage all security related SQL stuff we can use this procedure category.

| 15 | **Snapshot backup SP** | As the name suggests, this procedure category will help you to monitor and maintain all activities related to snapshot and backup of database. |
| 16 | **XML SP** | All XML relatedoperations can be managed using XML SP stored procedure category. |

Now, all these categories have their own stored procedure, we will see some popular categories with examples and real time snap, so let's get started.

Catalog SP

As we know, catalog SP is used to get information about database, tables and its design. Some of the poplar procedures from Catalog SP are as follows:

- `sp_columns`: It fetches the number of columns and its details from database tables, this procedure accepts table name as input parameter, see the following sample:

EXECUTE sp_columnsempmaster

In the above query we can see EXECUTE is the reserved keyword and sp_columns is the inbuilt stored procedure and empmaster is the SQL data table from which we need to fetch the column's details. If we execute the above query we will get the following output:

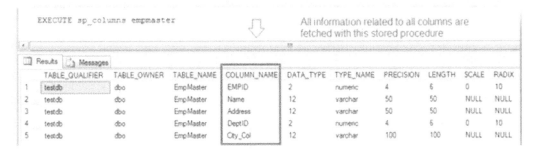

Figure 8.2

In the above screenshot, we can see all the information about empmaster table fetched by sp_columns stored procedure.

- SP_DATABASES: It fetches all database names with its size from current SQL instance, see the following sample:

EXECUTE SP_DATABASES

In the above query we can see `EXECUTE` is the reserved keyword and `SP_DATABASES` is the inbuilt stored procedure. If we execute the above query we will get the following output:

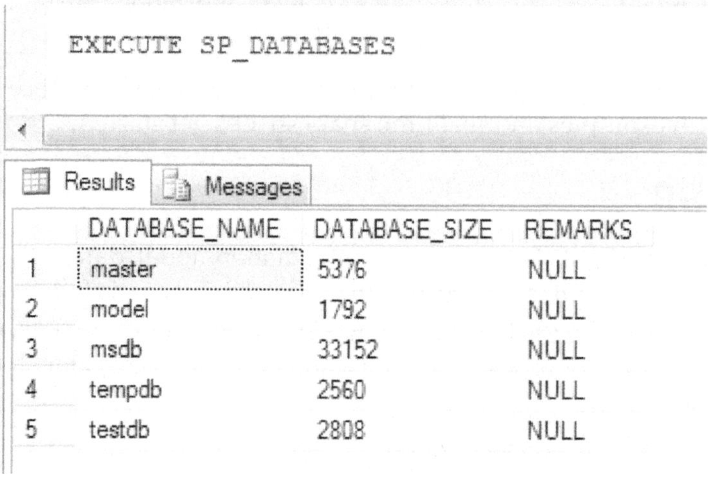
EXECUTE SP_DATABASES
Results
Messages
DATABASE_NAME
DATABASE_SIZE
REMARKS
1 master 5376 NULL
2 model 1792 NULL
3 msdb 33152 NULL
4 tempdb 2560 NULL
5 testdb 2808 NULL

Figure 8.3

In the above screenshot, we can seeall database names from current SQL instance have been fetched by `SP_DATABASES` stored procedure.

- `SP_SERVER_INFO`: It fetches all information related to SQL engine/instance, see the following sample:

  ```
  EXECUTE SP_SERVER_INFO
  ```

In the above query we can see EXECUTE is the reserved keyword and SP_SERVER_INFO is the inbuilt stored procedure. If we execute the above query we will get the following output:

```
EXECUTE SP_SERVER_INFO
```

	attribute_id	attribute_name	attribute_value
1	1	DBMS_NAME	Microsoft SQL Server
2	2	DBMS_VER	Microsoft SQL Server 2008 - 10.0.2531
3	10	OWNER_TERM	owner
4	11	TABLE_TERM	table
5	12	MAX_OWNER_NAME_LENGTH	128
6	13	TABLE_LENGTH	128
7	14	MAX_QUAL_LENGTH	128
8	15	COLUMN_LENGTH	128
9	16	IDENTIFIER_CASE	MIXED
10	17	TX_ISOLATION	2
11	18	COLLATION_SEQ	charset=iso_1 sort_order=nocase_iso charset
12	19	SAVEPOINT_SUPPORT	Y
13	20	MULTI_RESULT_SETS	Y
14	22	ACCESSIBLE_TABLES	Y
15	100	USERID_LENGTH	128
16	101	QUALIFIER_TERM	database
17	102	NAMED_TRANSACTIONS	Y
18	103	SPROC_AS_LANGUAGE	Y
19	104	ACCESSIBLE_SPROC	Y
20	105	MAX_INDEX_COLS	16
21	106	RENAME_TABLE	Y

Figure 8.4

In the above screenshot we can seeall database names from current SQL instance have been fetched by SP_DATABASES stored procedure.

- SP_TABLES: It returns the information about all tables belonging to current database. It also returns TABLE OWNER, TABLE NAME. See the following sample:

EXECUTE SP_TABLES

In the above query we can see EXECUTE is the reserved keyword and SP_TABLES is the inbuilt stored procedure. If we execute the above query we will get the following output:

```
EXECUTE SP_TABLES
```

	TABLE_QUALIFIER	TABLE_OWNER	TABLE_NAME	TABLE_TYPE	REMARKS
1	testdb	dbo	Department	TABLE	NULL
2	testdb	dbo	EmpMaster	TABLE	NULL
3	testdb	dbo	test	TABLE	NULL
4	testdb	INFORMATION_SCHEMA	CHECK_CONSTRAINTS	VIEW	NULL
5	testdb	INFORMATION_SCHEMA	COLUMN_DOMAIN_USAGE	VIEW	NULL
6	testdb	INFORMATION_SCHEMA	COLUMN_PRIVILEGES	VIEW	NULL
7	testdb	INFORMATION_SCHEMA	COLUMNS	VIEW	NULL
8	testdb	INFORMATION_SCHEMA	CONSTRAINT_COLUMN_USAGE	VIEW	NULL
9	testdb	INFORMATION_SCHEMA	CONSTRAINT_TABLE_USAGE	VIEW	NULL
10	testdb	INFORMATION_SCHEMA	DOMAIN_CONSTRAINTS	VIEW	NULL
11	testdb	INFORMATION_SCHEMA	DOMAINS	VIEW	NULL
12	testdb	INFORMATION_SCHEMA	KEY_COLUMN_USAGE	VIEW	NULL
13	testdb	INFORMATION_SCHEMA	PARAMETERS	VIEW	NULL
14	testdb	INFORMATION_SCHEMA	REFERENTIAL_CONSTRAINTS	VIEW	NULL
15	testdb	INFORMATION_SCHEMA	ROUTINE_COLUMNS	VIEW	NULL
16	testdb	INFORMATION_SCHEMA	ROUTINES	VIEW	NULL
17	testdb	INFORMATION_SCHEMA	SCHEMATA	VIEW	NULL
18	testdb	INFORMATION_SCHEMA	TABLE_CONSTRAINTS	VIEW	NULL
19	testdb	INFORMATION_SCHEMA	TABLE_PRIVILEGES	VIEW	NULL
20	testdb	INFORMATION_SCHEMA	TABLES	VIEW	NULL

Figure 8.5

In the above screenshot, we can see all database names from current SQL instance have been fetched by SP_TABLES stored procedure.

Db Engine SP

This procedure category is used for general information and maintenance of the SQL database engine; some of the popular procedures from Db Engine SP are as follows:

- SP_ATTACH_DB: It is used to attach database, it needs database name, MDF, and LDF path; see the following sample:

```
EXEC SP_ATTACH_DB
@dbname =N'testDB',
@filename1 =N'D:\test_Data.mdf',
```

```
@filename2 =N'D:\test_Data.ldf';
```

In the above query we can see, EXECUTE is the reserved keyword and SP_ATTACH_DB is the inbuilt stored procedure, @dbname is the database name, @filename1 is the physical path of MDF file name, @filename2 is the physical path of LDF file name.

- SP_DATATYPE_INFO: This stored procedure is used to fetch the datatypes that is OS supported by the currently installed SQL, see the following sample:

```
EXEC SP_DATATYPE_INFO
```

In the above query we can see EXECUTE is the reserved keyword and SP_ DATATYPE_INFO is the inbuilt stored procedure. If we execute the above query we will get the following output:

	TYPE_NAME	DATA_TYPE	PRECISION
1	sql_variant	-150	8000
2	uniqueidentifier	-11	36
3	ntext	-10	1073741823
4	xml	-10	1073741823
5	nvarchar	-9	4000
6	sysname	-9	128
7	date	-9	10
8	time	-9	16
9	datetime2	-9	27
10	datetimeoffset	-9	34
11	nchar	-8	4000
12	bit	-7	1
13	tinyint	-6	3
14	tinyint identity	-6	3
15	bigint	-5	19
16	bigint identity	-5	19
17	image	-4	2147483647
18	varbinary	-3	8000
19	binary	-2	8000
20	timestamp	-2	8
21	text	-1	2147483647

Figure 8.6

In the above screenshot we can see supported datatypes in currently installed SQL.

- **SP_RENAME:** This stored procedure is used to rename database object like table, column, index, column datatype, and more. See the following sample:

```
EXEC SP_RENAME 'Department','Department2'
```

In the above query we can see EXEC is the reserved keyword and SP_RENAME is the inbuilt stored procedure that is used to change the name of the stored procedure, in above sample Department2 is the new name of the Department stored procedure, if we fire above query the output will be as follows:

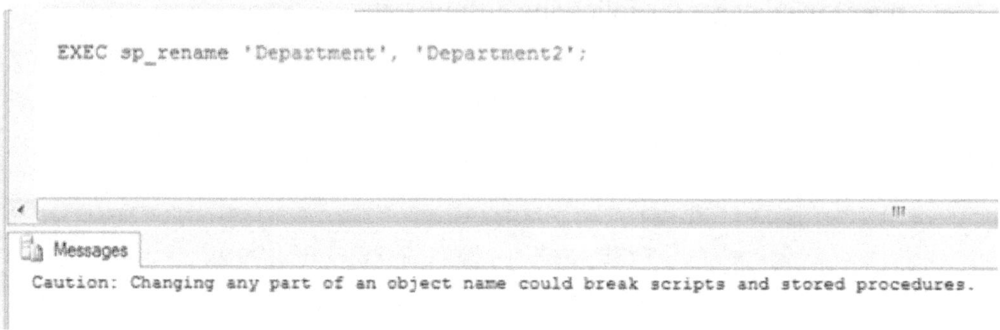

```
EXEC sp_rename 'Department', 'Department2';
```

◢   ⁝

▤ Messages

Caution: Changing any part of an object name could break scripts and stored procedures.

Figure 8.7

In above screenshot we can see, after executing sp_renme SQL showing caution but still it is executed successfully. SP_RENAMEDB: This stored procedure is used to rename database. See the following sample:

```
EXEC SP_RENAMEDB 'testDB','RenamedDB'
```

In the above query we can see EXECUTE is the reserved keyword and SP_RENAMEDB is the inbuilt stored procedure, testDB is the database name that we need to rename, and RenamedDB is the new database name.

Security SP

To manage all security related SQL stuff, we can use this procedure category. Some of the popular procedures are as follows:

- **sp_addapprole:** It is used to add role in current database, see the following sample:

```
EXEC sp_addapprole 'testRole','PwD'
```

In the above query we can see EXECUTE is the reserved keyword and SP_ADDAPPROLE is the inbuilt stored procedure, testRole is the database role name, Pad is the password. To execute this stored procedure you need ALTER permission on database.

- `sp_helprole`: It is used to retrieve all active roles in current database, see the following sample:

`EXEC sp_helprole`

In the above query we can see `EXECUTE` is the reserved keyword and `sp_helprole` is the inbuilt stored procedure. If we execute the above stored procedure, we will get the following result:

```
EXEC sp_helprole
```

	RoleName	RoleId	IsAppRole
1	public	0	0
2	db_owner	16384	0
3	db_accessadmin	16385	0
4	db_securityadmin	16386	0
5	db_ddladmin	16387	0
6	db_backupoperator	16389	0
7	db_datareader	16390	0
8	db_datawriter	16391	0
9	db_denydatareader	16392	0
10	db_denydatawriter	16393	0

Figure 8.8

In the above screenshot, we can see `sp_helprole` returns all active role in current database

- `sp_helprolemember`: It is used to retrieve information about current logged in user role, see the following sample:

`EXEC sp_helprolemember`

In the above query we can see `EXECUTE` is the reserved keyword and `sp_helprolemember` is the inbuilt stored procedure. If we execute the above stored procedure, we will get the following result:

Figure 8.9

In the above screenshot, we can see my current logged user has db_owner role for this database.

User defined stored procedure

As the name suggests, these stored procedures are not built-in but we need to create them. These procedure are a set of sequence of SQL statements that can be enabled to accept input and produce output.

Also, temporary procedures are the part of user defined procedures. Let's see what are temporary procedures.

Temporary procedure

Temporary procedures are created just like normal stored procedure but their names begin with #. Temporary procedures have two types

- **Local temporary procedure:** Local temporary procedure names start with #, they are not dropped after the current session gets over.
- **Global temporary procedure:** Global temporary procedure names start with ##, and they are accessible to all session till user session is closed.

You can create temporary procedure for following use:

- For code re-use.
- Temporary procedure can be used to test actual/permanent store procedure before deployment.
- Convenient for connection to earlier version of SQL.

Here we will see how to create, modify, execute, and rename stored procedure:

- Creating stored procedure (SP)
- Modifying stored procedure (SP)
- Deleting stored procedure (SP)
- Executing stored procedure (SP)
- Renaming stored procedure (SP)

Let's trace them one by one.

Creating stored procedure (SP)

We have two ways to create stored procedure, which are as follows:

- **Using SQL Management Studio:** Follow the below steps to write/create stored procedure using SQL Management Studio:
    1. Open database on which you want to create stored procedure.

2. Select `Programmability` and then select stored procedure, right click on it and click on `New Stored Procedure`.... See the following screenshot:

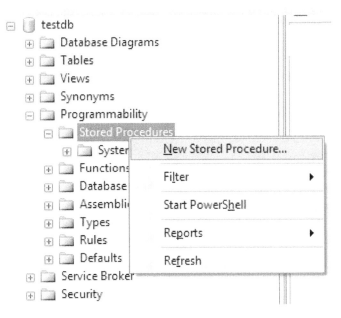

Figure 8.10

3. In the right side window, you will get a default query template, to fill template value click on template value icon on top of the query analyzer, see the following screenshot:

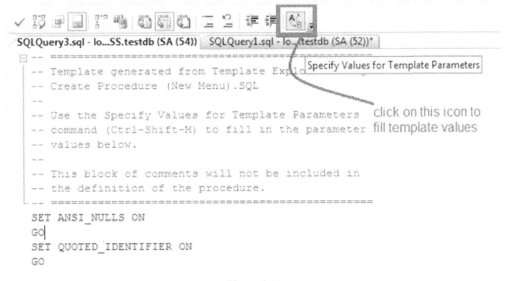

Figure 8.11

4. Click on fill template icon as shown in above screenshot, now fill things in template window, and see the following screenshot:

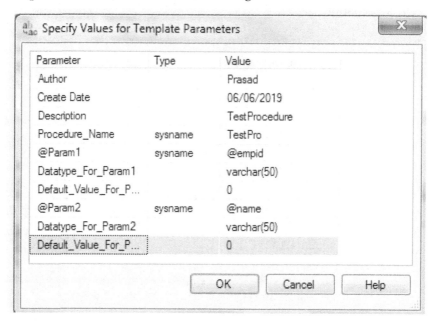

Figure 8.12

5. In above screenshot,we can see Author, Create Date, Description, procedure_name (TestPro) is given and for Param1 and Param2 we have declared variable @empid, @name, respectively, now click on OK to create query.

6. Now, if we execute that query, my stored procedure will be created in Database | Programmability | Stored Procedure section. See the following screenshot:

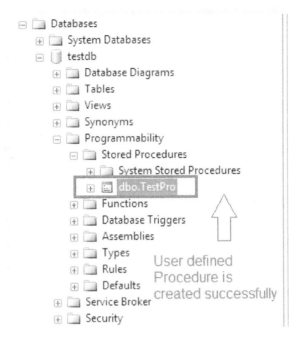

Figure 8.13

This is how we can create user defined procedure

- **Using SQL Query analyzer:** The other way of creating stored procedure is to use SQL Query analyzer, where we can put direct query in analyzer and create stored procedure. Let's create same stored procedure but this time with query. See the following query:

```
CREATE PROCEDURE TestPro
@empid varchar(50)= 0,
@name varchar(50)= 0
AS
BEGIN
SET NOCOUNTON;
SELECT @empid, @name
END
```

In above sample `CREATE PROCEDURE` is the reserved keyword for creating procedure, `TestPro` is the name of the procedure that we want to create, `@empid`, `@name` are the parameters that we are going to pass to procedure, `BEGIN` and `END` indicate the scope of the procedure. Now, if we execute that query, my stored procedure will be created in `Database | Programmability | Stored Procedure` section.

Here we have used SETNOCOUNTON which helps us to avoid/prevent extra row set added in final result.

- Some of the best practice for stored procedure are as follows. To improve readability use proper indentation

- Do not rename your stored procedure to start with SP_ as it is reserved for system stored procedure only.

- Stored procedure are famous for compile one and use multi behavior, so it is not recommended to use `temp` table in stored procedure, otherwise it will compile each time

- Try avoiding cursor in stored procedure.

Modifying stored procedure (SP)

We do have two ways to modify stored procedure, which are as follows:

- **Using SQL Management Studio:** Steps to modify stored procedure using SQL management studio is so simple:

  1. Connect to database engine and open database.

  2. Expand the database to `Programmability | StoredProcedure`.

  3. Select the stored procedure you want to modify.

  4. Right click on stored procedure.

  5. Click on `Modify`. See the following screenshot:

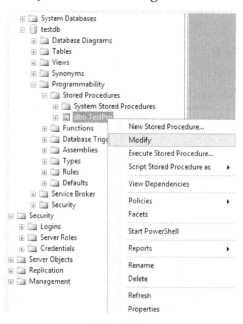

Figure 8.14

6. In the above screenshot we have selected `Tester` for modification.

7. When you click on `Modify` option, the stored procedure opens up in query analyzer window for modification, you can modify the text and save it later.

- **Using SQL Query analyzer:** The other way to modify stored procedure is to use the query analyzer. Use `ALTER` command to modify the procedure, see the following sample:

```
ALTER PROCEDURE [dbo].[TestPro]

@empid varchar(30)= 0,

@name varchar(30)= 0

AS

BEGIN

SET NOCOUNTON;

SELECT @empid, @name

END
```

In the above query we have used `ALTERPROCEDURE` to modify the procedure and we have changed the datatype (`varchar`) length from `50` to `30`. If we execute the above sample, the stored procedure gets modified.

Deleting stored procedure (SP)

We have two ways to delete stored procedure, which are as follows:

- **Using SQL Management Studio:** Steps to delete stored procedure using SQL management studio are as follows:
  1. Connect to database engine and open database.
  2. Expand the database to `Programmability | StoredProcedure`.
  3. Select the stored procedure you want to delete.
  4. Right click on stored procedure.

5. Click on `Delete`. See the following screenshot:

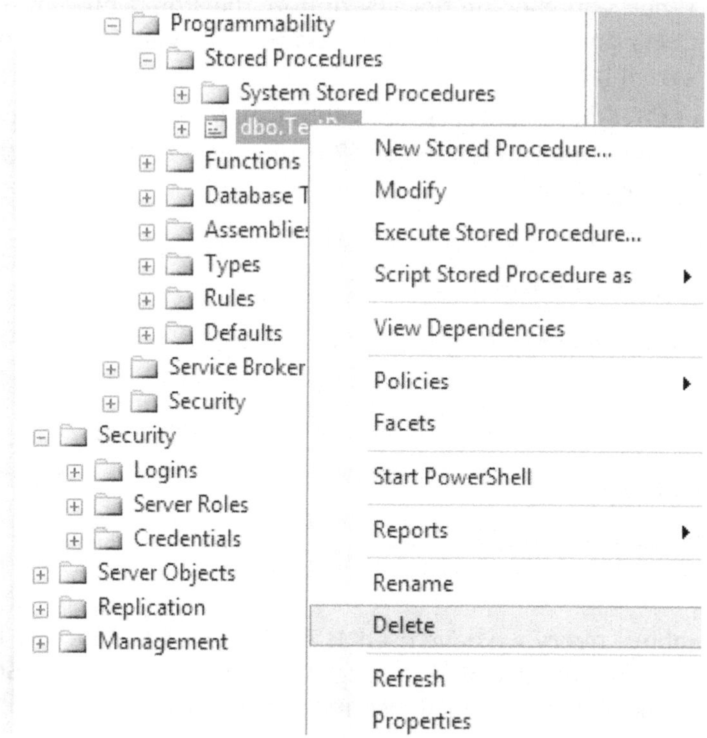

Figure 8.15

6. In the above screenshot, we have selected out `TestProf` or deletion.

7. When you click on `Delete` option, you can delete stored procedure and save later.

- **Using SQL Query analyzer:** The other way to delete stored procedure is to use the query analyzer. Use `DROP` command to delete the procedure, see the following sample:

```
DROP PROCEDURE [TestPro]
```

In the above query we have used `DROP PROCEDURE` to delete/remove the procedure and if we execute the above sample, the stored procedure gets deleted.

Executing stored procedure (SP)

The stored procedure can be executed either by calling it from external sources like any programming languages or by running automatically, or by using any other stored procedure or we can explicitly call it by using `EXEC` command.

We can call it explicitly by using following ways:

- **Using SQL Management Studio:** Steps to execute stored procedure using SQL Management Studio through following the steps:

  1. Connect to database engine and open database.

  2. Expand the database to `Programmability | StoredProcedure`.

  3. Select the stored procedure you want to execute.

  4. Right click on stored procedure.

  5. Click on `Execute Stored Procedure....` See the following screenshot:

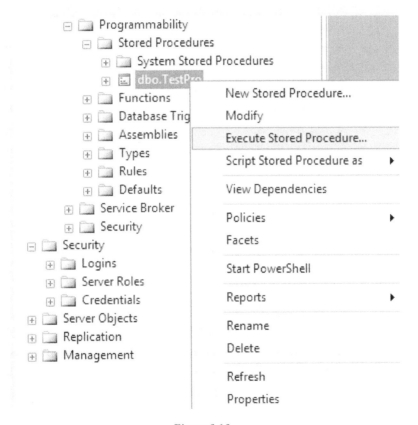

Figure 8.16

6. In the above screenshot, we have selected out `TestPro` for execution. When you click on `Execute Stored Procedure.` It will get executed.

7. If we are trying to execute it then following will be the output, observe the following screenshot:

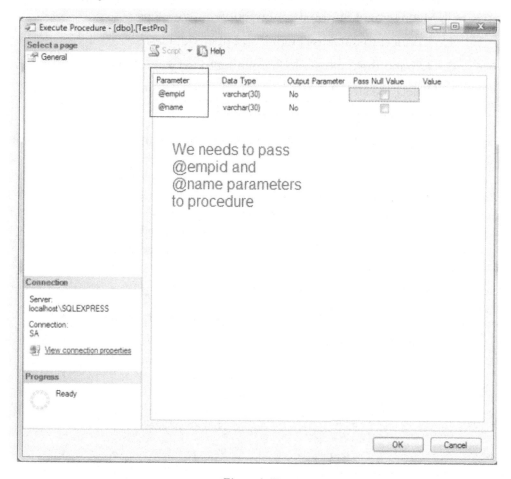

Figure 8.17

8. In the above screenshot, we have to pass @empid and @name parameters. Let's input 2 as empid and Manavya as name, now on clicking OK button, the procedure gets executed with the following final result:

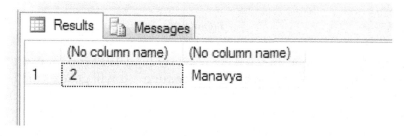

Figure 8.18

9. In the above screenshot, we can see stored procedure fetches result from database for matching entity (Here we have pass EmpID as 2 and Name a Manavya).

- **Using SQL Query analyzer:** The other way to execute stored procedure is to use the query analyzer. Use EXEC command to execute the procedure, see the following sample:

```
EXEC @return_value = [TestPro]
@empid ='2',
@name ='Manavya'
```

In the above query we have used EXEC to execute the procedure; if we execute the above sample, the stored procedure gets executed and returns the same output (same as SQL Management Studio pattern), which is as follows:

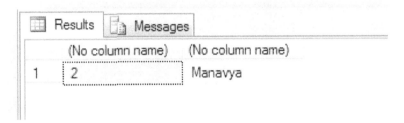

Figure 8.19

Renaming stored procedure (SP)

The stored procedure can be easily be renamed in the following ways:

- **Using SQL Management Studio:** Steps to execute stored procedure using SQL management studio. Here are the steps:

  1. Connect to database engine and open database.

  2. Expand the database to Programmability | StoredProcedure.

  3. Select the stored procedure you want to rename.

  4. Right click on stored procedure.

5.   Click on **Rename** and provide a new name. See the following screenshot:

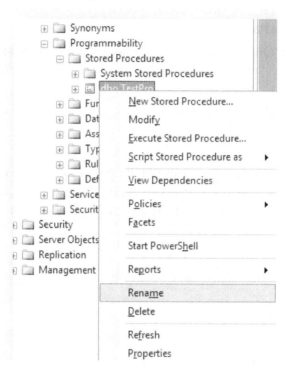

Figure 8.20

6.   In the above screenshot, we have selected **Rename** option to rename stored procedure.

- **Using SQL Query analyzer:** The other way to rename stored procedure is to use the query analyzer. Use **sp_rename** (which is inbuilt system procedure) procedure to rename the procedure, see the following sample:

```
EXEC sp_rename 'TestPro', 'NewTestPro'
```

In the above query we have used inbuilt stored procedure **sp_rename to** rename existing stored procedure; if we execute the above sample, our stored procedure gets renamed.

SQL triggers

A trigger is a set of queries or a special type of stored procedure that is fired automatically when an event occurs. An event may be DML queries (like **INSERT**, **UPDATE**, **DELETE** operations), DDL queries (like **CREATE**, **TRUNCATE**, **DROP** operations) or at the time of logon operation like user logged in database and connect to database.

Triggers are of following types:

- DML triggers
- DDL triggers
- Logon triggers

Let's trace them one by one.

DML triggers

As the name suggests, these triggers are fired when any DML event occurs, this event may be INSERT, UPDATE, and DELETE statement.

DML triggers help us prevent malicious/hacking INSERT/UPDATE/DELETE operation and enforce the security policy. DML triggers can easily track position/state of the table BEFORE and AFTER execution of the triggers and it helps to take action depending on the difference.

DML triggers are of the following types:

- AFTER: To fire DML queries these triggers are used. If we execute a group of DML statement then for each DML statement AFTER trigger is fired.
- INSTEAD OF: The INSTEAD OF triggers are like *before action triggers*. They are used to check exception or error that occurs after executing DML statement. So, they always check errors/exception before they occur. They can check value for one or more column at a time.

To clear the concept, let's take one example:

Suppose in a sugar factory application, table TempTB is updated hourly to record how much sugar is produced; now at the same time on the record insertion of TempTB, two more supporting tables are also filled. Now, if there is some error that occurs while inserting record in TempTB, then that supporting table is also left empty. To avoid this, if we have INSTEAD OF trigger then it catches error before actual execution. INSTEAD OF triggers can be applicable for both table and VIEW.

- CLR: These triggers are executed by **CLR (common language runtime)** and they are carried out by programming languages like .NET. *After* triggers or *instead of* triggers are called by a managed code methods.

Creating a trigger

We can create trigger by using SQL Management Studio or by using SQL Query analyzer. Let's create some sample trigger:

- **Using SQL Management Studio:** Go through the following steps:
    1. Connect to database engine and open database.

2. Expand the database tables.

3. Select the table on which we want to create triggers.

4. Right click on Triggers and select New Trigger....

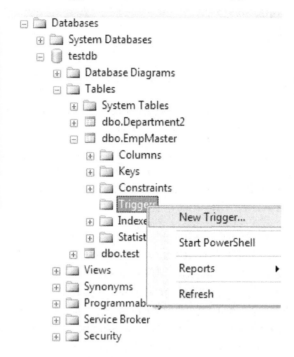

Figure 8.21

5. Expand the database tables. Like stored procedure, click on Specify Values for Template Parameter icon, see the following screenshot:

```
SQLQuery1.sql - lo...SS.testdb (SA (52))
                                                      Specify Values for Template Parameters
-- Template generated from Template Explorer using:
-- Create Trigger (New Menu).SQL
--
-- Use the Specify Values for Template Parameters
-- command (Ctrl-Shift-M) to fill in the parameter
```

Figure 8.22

6. After clicking on the above icon, fill all values, see the following screenshot:

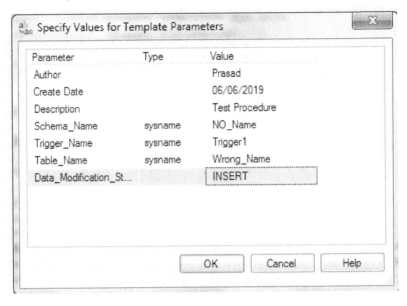

Figure 8.23

7. After making the necessary changes in query, we will get the following query:

```
CREATE TRIGGER Trigger1

ON EmpMaster

AFTER INSERT

AS

BEGIN

SET NOCOUNT ON;

INSERT INTO Department2(DeptID, DeptName)VALUES(10,'testEMP');

END
```

8. Now if we execute the above query, our trigger will be created, see the following query:

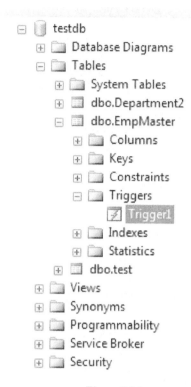

Figure 8.24

- **Using SQL Query analyzer:** It is a bit easier process, where you need to just put a query and execute it, use the following query to create trigger:

```
CREATE TRIGGER Trigger1

ON  EmpMaster

AFTER INSERT

AS

BEGIN

SET NOCOUNT ON;

INSERT INTO Department2(DeptID, DeptName)VALUES(10,'testEMP');

END
```

Here is the explanation for the above query:

- `CREATE TRIGGER` is the reserved keyword
- `Trigger1` is the trigger name.
- `ON` is the reserved keyword.
- `EmpMaster` is the table name on which we need to put a trigger.
- `AFTER INSERT` reserved keyword.

And rests of the contents are the `INSERT` statements. The above query will fire when `INSERT` event occurs in `EmpMaster` table and `INSERT` query will fire `Department2` table. After executing the above query, our trigger gets created

Now let's see how to create nested trigger. When one trigger initiates another trigger then it is called a nested trigger. You can nest these trigger up to 32 levels. Trigger is so intelligent that if any linked trigger from nested family goes in loop then nesting level is exceeded and triggers get terminated. The triggers which are executed in transaction scope, a single failure in a nested trigger will cancel the whole transaction.

Executing trigger

This is a bit confusing question, there is no need to execute trigger as it is automatically executed when an event occurs. Now, if you notice, our trigger will automatically fire when `INSERT` event happens in `EmpMaster` table. Now let's try the same.

We will fire `INSERT` query on table `EmpMaster` and database, and see if the following query is automatically fired on `Department2` table. First of all, see both table records:

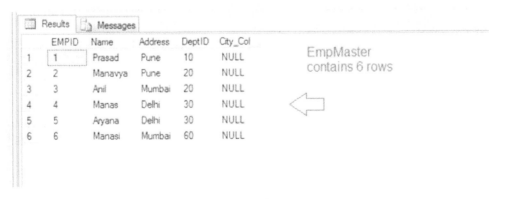

Figure 8.25

In the above screenshot, we can see data stored in table `EmpMaster` and the following table shows data entries in `Department2` table:

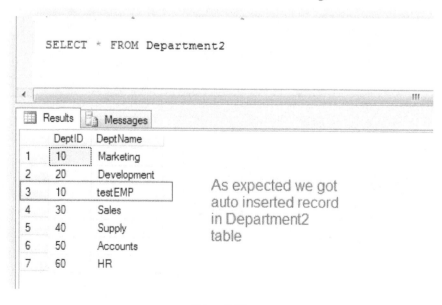

Figure 8.26

Now let'sinsert 1 record in `EmpMaster` table and see when happens to `Department2` table. See the following query:

```
INSERT INTO EmpMaster(EMPID, Name, Address, DeptID, City_Col)VALUES
(100,'Anil','Delhi', 20,'DEL')
```

Now if I fire the above query, 1 record will be added to `EmpMaster` table, but what happens with `Department2` table, let's see in the following screenshot:

```
SELECT * FROM Department2
```

	DeptID	DeptName
1	10	Marketing
2	20	Development
3	10	testEMP
4	30	Sales
5	40	Supply
6	50	Accounts
7	60	HR

As expected we got auto inserted record in Department2 table

Figure 8.27

We can see, we got record inserted in `Department2` table (This insertion is carried out by trigger)

Deleting and renamingtrigger

There are two ways to rename the trigger:

- Using `sp_rename` stored procedure
- Using `DROP` and `CREATE` statement

But SQL recommends against using `sp_rename` procedure as it may break the procedure or trigger statements. SQL always recommends to `DROP` and `RE-CREATE` the trigger.

`DROP` action can be completed by using SQL Management Studio or Query Analyzer.

If you want to use the SQL Management Studio then here are the steps:

1. Connect to database engine and open database.
2. Expand the database tables.
3. Select the table on which we want to create triggers.
4. Right click on `Triggers` and select `Delete`. Refer to the following screenshot:

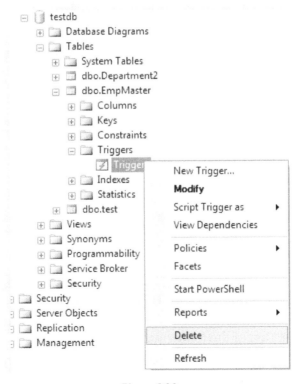

Figure 8.28

Using Query Analyzer, you need to fire DROP query as the following text:

```
DROP TRIGGER trigger1
```

If you fire the above query, `trigger1` will delete from database. So to create NEW trigger you need to use CREATE statement. If you don't want to use DROP and CREATE trigger again, then you can use MODIFY option from SQL Management Studio, check out the following screenshot:

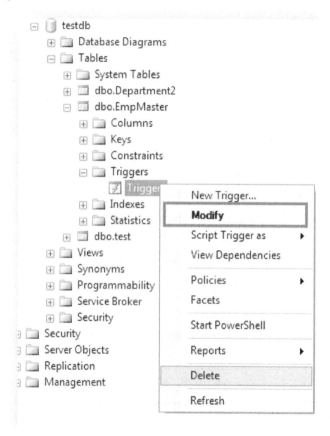

Figure 8.29

DDL triggers

As the name suggests, these triggers are fired when any DDL event occurs. This event may CREATE, DROP, ALTER, and TRUNCATE statement. If you want to prevent the database architecture changes by someone else, then you can take use of DDL triggers. DDL triggers are of the following types:

1. **TRANSACT-SQL DDL trigger:** This is a special type of trigger that executes a series of SQL commands/statements if any DDL event occurs, like CREATE,

ALTER TABLE, DATABASE, DROP, or TRUNCATE event. Check out the following sample:

```
CREATE TRIGGER testTrigger

ON testDB

FOR ALTER_TABLE

AS

BEGIN

    INSERT INTO EmpMaster(EMPID, Name,Address, DeptID, City_Col)

END
```

The above query represents DDL trigger where the trigger is fired on database testDB if any ALTER TABLE action is fired on it and as a result it will fire INSERT query on EmpMaster table.

2. **CLR DDLtriggers:** As we know, these triggers are executed by CLR carried out by programming language. CLR DML and DDL triggers are the same, except that DDL triggers are fired only after DDL statements are executed, similarly DML triggers are fired only after DML statements are executed.

The creation, modification and deletion of the DDL triggers are the same like DML triggers; we can use either SQL Management Studio or can use Query analyzer to operate them.

Do you know how to enable and disable triggers? Yes, we can enable and disable triggers. Basically, triggers are enabled by default when they are created. When we disable them, they just turn mute but do not get dropped from the database, they are not executed when any related statements get fired.

The syntax is as follows:

```
Disable Trigger :

DISABLE TRIGGER trigger1 ON EmpMaster;
```

If we fire the above query then it will disable trigger1 which is associated with EmpMaster table. We can disable all triggers at once with the help of the following query:

```
DISABLE Trigger ALL ON ALL SERVER;
```

If we fire the above query then it will disable all triggers of the current database.

```
Enable Trigger:

ENABLE TRIGGER trigger1 ON EmpMaster;
```

If we fire the preceding query, then it will enable `trigger1` which is associated with `EmpMaster` table. We can enable all triggers at once with the help of the following query:

```
ENABLE Trigger ALL ON ALL SERVER;
```

If we fire the preceding query then it will disable all triggers of the current database.

Conclusion

In this chapter, we have learned about what is stored procedure, and their advantages. We also learned inbuilt and user defined stored procedures. Additionally, we have seen how to create, modify, execute, rename and delete stored procedure, with a number of samples. We also learned about SQL triggers and their usage. We have seen DML and DDL triggers which are fired when DML events occur (like `INSERT`, `UPDATE`, `DELETE`) and DDL events like (`CREATE`, `ALTER`, `DROP`) occur.

In the upcoming chapters, we will learn SQL `VIEW`, its usage, with database samples. Additionally, we will learn about the SQL transaction ACID properties. We will also learn about the different SQL keys, constraint and design concepts. So, stay tuned.

Questions

1. **What is SQL stored procedure?**

   Stored procedure is just a set of or a bunch of SQL statements, executed, or called by outer sources as well.

2. **What are the different types of stored procedure?**

   We have the following types of stored procedure:
   - System / inbuilt stored procedure
   - User defined stored procedure

3. **How to CREATE stored procedure using query? Explain with example.**

   We need to use `CREATE PROCEDURE` statement to create stored procedure, as can be seen in the following sample:

   ```
   CREATE PROCEDURE Test
   AS
   BEGIN
   SELECT* FROM EmpMaster
   END
   ```

   In the above sample we have created a trigger which selects record from `EmpMaster` table.

4. **How to attach a database using stored procedure?**

As we know, we have inbuilt stored procedure to attach database. We can use `SP_ATTACHDB` stored procedure to attach database, as can be seen in the following sample:

```
EXEC SP_ATTACH_DB
@dbname = N'myDB',
 @filename1 = N'E:\databasefile_Data.mdf',
 @filename2 = N'E:\databasefile_Data.ldf';
```

In the above query we can see `EXECUTE` is the reserved keyword and `SP_ATTACH_DB` is the inbuilt stored procedure, `@dbname` is the database name, `@filename1` is the physical path of MDF file name, `@filename2` is the physical path of LDF file name.

5. **What is SQL trigger?**

A trigger is a set of queries or a special type of stored procedure that is fired automatically when an event occurs. An event may be DML queries (like `INSERT, UPDATE, DELETE` operations), DDL queries (like `CREATE, TRUNCATE, DROP` operations) or at the time of logon operation, like user logged in database and connect to database.

6. **What are the types of SQL triggers?**

Triggers are of the following types:

- DML triggers
- DDL triggers
- Logon triggers

Do you know (lights on facts?)

- If you change the table structure or design then it is always beneficial to re-compile the stored procedure and build a new execution plan to save time.
- Before deleting any stored procedure you need to check the data dependency otherwise the data object can go in failed state. SQL management gives you show dependencies option to check possible dependencies on stored procedure before deleting it.
- `CREATE` trigger can apply to only one table.
- `ALTER, CREATE, DROP` operations related to database are not allowed in trigger.
- User-defined triggers are not allowed on system tables.

CHAPTER 9

SQL Views, Keys, Indexes, Injections, and Constraints

SQL speed, performance, data storage technique depends on how you design the database, table, and database structure. In this chapter we will discuss all about the design structure of the database and SQL views, keys, indexes, injections, and constraints concepts.

Prerequisite for this chapter: Before we walk through this chapter you should have knowledge of SQL DDL, DCL, and DTL concepts. Additionally, you should have a laptop/desktop with SQL server installed.

Structure

- SQL view
- Create SQL view
- Alter/update SQL view
- Delete SQL view
- Identity column
- SQL keys and its types
- Primary key
- Candidate key
- Unique key

- Composite key
- Foreign key
- Super key
- Alternate key
- SQL indexes and their types
- Clustered index
- Non-clustered index
- SQL injection
- Injection example
- Injection prevention
- Types of SQL constraints

Objective

So, the objective of this chapter is to learn what is SQL view, how to create and use it. We will also go through the concept of SQL keys, different types of SQL keys, and how to use them. Basically, we will learn about primary, candidate, unique, and composite key, we will also learn about cluster and non-cluster index, SQL injection and how to avoid SQL injection.

So, let's begin.

SQL view

A view is a temporary virtual table; it consists of a combination of rows and columns. Basically, view is the result of a query where we can store it in a virtual table that can be used later. The view can be created using multiple table or multiple databases. View can also provide us security by giving access permission. SQL view is used to improve performance as query is compiled and run only once, but the result is accessible all the time via virtual table.

A view can have max 1024 columns. If there are any changes done in view then you can run `sp_refresh` view procedure to reflect the changes.

Types of SQL view

A SQL view has the following types:

- Indexed views
- Partitioned views
- System views

Let's trace them one by one.

Indexed views

Indexed views are common views, and can be created with the execution of the query and stored as a normal table. Here we have used the clustered index (it helps SQL to filter and fetch values faster, we will learn about this concept in this chapter itself). These views are faster in execution but they are recommended to be used in an environment where data is not frequently updated.

Partitioned views

As the name suggests, partitioned views are created by joining data across tables or across multiple databases, but the data will appear as a single table.

System views

As the name suggests, these views are inbuilt view, you can use this view to return current SQL instance information. This view includes the following:

- System catalog views
- System compatibility views
- System dynamic management views
- System information schema views

Creating a SQL view

You can create view by combination of one or more tables or one or more databases, let's checkout the following sample query, which will clear our doubts:

```
CREATE VIEW firstView

AS

SELECT EmpMaster.Name, EmpMaster.Address, EmpMaster.EMPID

FROM EmpMaster, Department2

WHERE EmpMaster.DeptID = Department2.DeptID
```

In the above query `CREATE VIEW` is the reserved keyword for creating view, `firstview` is the view name. We have fired the query by joining two tables. (Confused? Yes, we can join multiple table in single SQL query by putting the table name before column name, it helps to differentiate and resolve the conflicts between the column names, if you notice we have used `EmpMaster` and `Department2` table and fetched column from `EmpMaster` table.)

If you fire the above query, we will get the following output:

```
CREATE VIEW firstView
AS
SELECT EmpMaster.Name, EmpMaster.Address, EmpMaster.EMPID
FROM EmpMaster, Department2
WHERE EmpMaster.DeptID = Department2.DeptID
```

Messages

Command(s) completed successfully.

In the above screenshot, we can see query has been successfully executed, and in the following screenshot we can see our view (firstview) has also been created successfully:

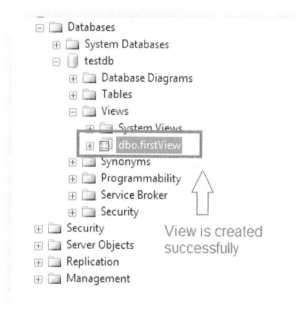

If you right click the view and try to open it then you will see the result is already stored in view, let's right click it and select Select Top 1000 Rows, we will get the following output:

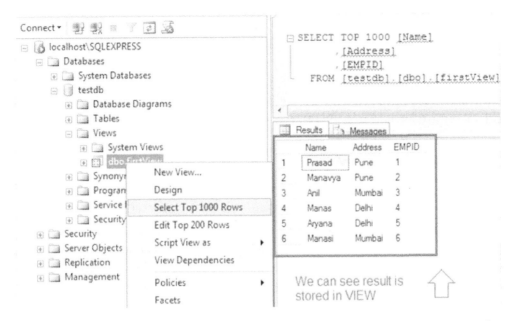

In the above screenshot we can see view is already stored as a result in it, so when you fire view, it just collects the records runtime and displays them.

Updatableview

Views are not only used to fetch data but also to update data (Yes! we can update data using view), but there are some conditions for it. Let's discuss them:

- There should be only one base table mentioned in view. In short, view should only contain one base table.

- The column that needs to be update through view should not be derived through aggregate functions like SUM, AVG, MIN, MAX, among others.

- The columns should not be affected by GROUP BY and HAVING clause.

Partitioned view

Partitioned view contains combination of different tables and are defined by UNION ALL clause, but stored separately as multiple tables. We can define the sample as following:

Consider we have a student data and it is spread across 3 tables, and those tables also span across 3 different servers, then the view which is used to fetch all data is called as partitioned view, checkout the following sample:

```
SELECT * FROM server1.stud1

UNION ALL
```

```
SELECT * FROM server2.Stud2

UNION ALL

SELECT * FROM server3.Stud3
```

In the above example, we can see all queries are combined with UNION ALL clause and values are fetched from 3 different tables and from 3 different servers.

Modifying view

Already created view can be modified using SQL Management Studio or by using Query analyzer.

Modification of view will not affect any object as it is a temporary storage of data. The modification of the view can be done using ALTER VIEW statement, in which database engine locks the current view so that no active user uses it and then deletes all copies of the view from database and re-generates the new view. So basically, it's a delete-create operation.

View can be modified using SQL Management Studio, check out the following steps:

1. Open object explorer in database, select Views and navigate to your view (you want to modify), check the following screenshot:

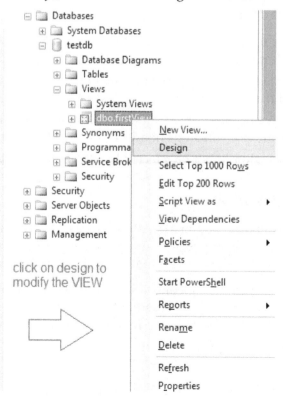

Now, right click on the view and click on design, as shown in the following screenshot:

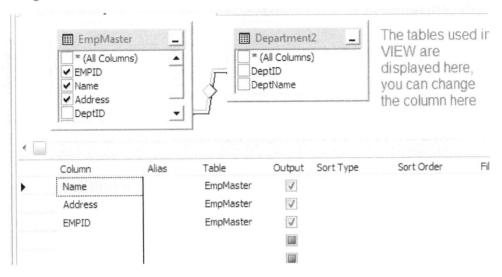

In the above screenshot you can see a graphical interface with the tables used in view. All ticked columns are the columns that we have SELECT in result. Here you can change your column selection, change the linking, you can even add new table in view, using Add Table... option. See the following screenshot:

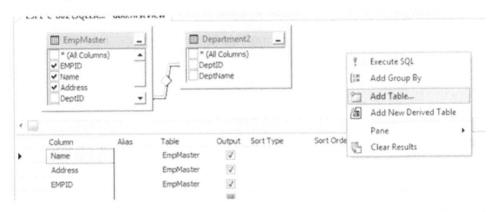

View can be modified using SQL Query Analyzer. ALTER VIEW statement is used to modify the current view, check out the following query:

```
ALTER VIEW firstView

AS

SELECT EmpMaster.Name, EmpMaster.Address, EmpMaster.EMPID, EmpMaster.
DeptID

FROM EmpMaster, Department2

WHERE EmpMaster.DeptID = Department2.DeptID
```

In the above query we have used ALTER VIEW, which is the statement used to alter/modify current view, and then we can re-generate the view.

Deleting view

You can delete or drop a view by using SQL Management Studio or by using SQL Query analyzer. To delete a view, we need ALTER permission on the view.

Deleting a view using SQL Management Studio

Let's check out how to delete a view using SQL Management Studio:

1. Open object explorer in database, select Views and navigate to your view (you want to delete), check the following screenshot:

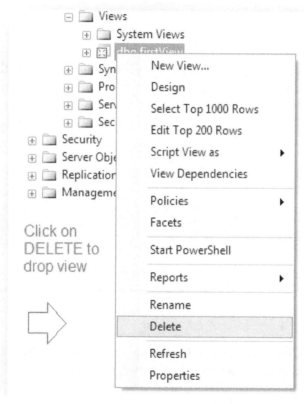

2. Select Delete to drop view.

Deleting view using SQL query analyzer

Check out the following query to delete view:

```
DROP VIEW firstView
```

In the above query we have used DROP VIEW statement to delete view from table.

Identity column

Identity column is the column with the numeric field (datatype), and it has the auto number features, which means when you insert any record in a table, which has identity column, its value is incremented automatically. It has two properties--seed and increment--which are as follows:

- Seed indicate the value that is loaded for the very first time, so if we keep seed as 2 then the first data entry will be with 2.

- Increment is the value that is added to the identity column, the default value of increment is 1.

Let's check the set identity column with increment and seed field. We can set it through SQL Management studio and SQL Query analyzer.

Using SQL Management Studio

Open SQL Management studio and select the table for which you want to set identity column. See the following screenshot:

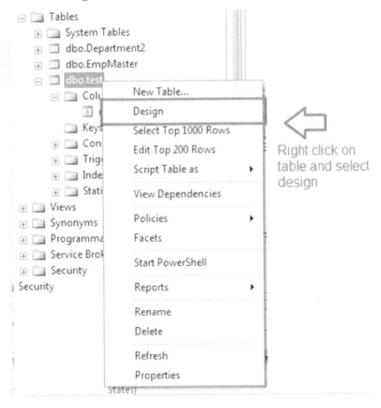

Now, on the next window add a column with the data type numeric, I have added No column with numeric datatype, see the following screenshot:

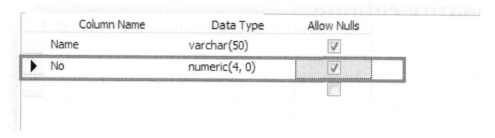

Now, go to column properties and set Is Identity to Yes. Identity Increment is 1, Identity Seed is 1.

Here you can notice that when I set Is Identity to Yes, Allow Nulls is automatically unchecked (allow nulls means this column can contains null values, one thing to remember is null is not a blank value). See the following screenshot:

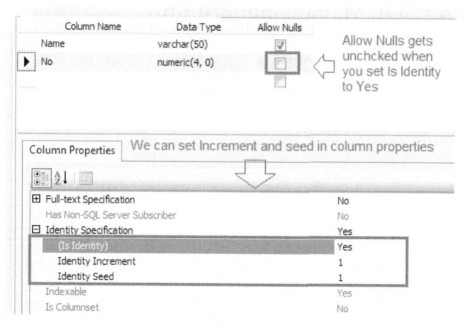

In the above screenshot, we have set identity and increment seed.

Using SQL Query analyzer

Using query, we can add column with identity constraint.

The syntax is as follows:

```
IDENTITY [ ( seed , increment ) ]
```

Here, seed indicates the starting value of the column, the default value is 1.

increment indicates the incremental value that is added in previously added increment seed, and each new value is generated based on the current seed & increment.

Let's go through the following query:

```
ALTER TABLE test ADD [No] [numeric](4, 0) IDENTITY(1,1) NOT NULL
```

In the above query we have used `ALTER TABLE` statement to edit table and add column No with datatype as `numeric (4)` and `IDENTITY` is reserved keyword for identity column, `(1,1)` denotes identity increment and identity seed, respectively.

If identity column is used in a transaction, and due to any issue the transaction fails, then the identity column value will not get rolled back.

@@identity

It is related to identity column concept but basically it is a function that returns last inserted seed value. This function is applicable to current scope of SQL server. If there is no identity column then this function returns NULL value. If you want last inserted identity value from remote SQL server, then you need to take help of stored procedure. Here, we need to use `SCOPE_IDENTITY()` function, which helps us to return the last inserted latest identity used within the scope.

SQL keys and its types

In database management system, a key is the field which helps us to sort data, put index, avoid duplication, and speed up search operation among records. There are following types of keys present in SQL:

- Primary key
- Candidate key
- Unique key
- Composite key
- Foreign key
- Super key
- Alternate key

Let's dig them one by one.

Primary key

As we know, a SQL table contains one or more columns. Now, a set of columns (may be one or more) that defines sole data or guarantee unique data is called as primary key. Mostly, the columns are also defined as identity column (which will not accept nulls but auto values only).

Let's set a column as primary key constraint, we can do it using SQL Management Studio or SQL Query analyzer.

Using SQL Management Studio

Open SQL Management Studio and select the table for which you want to set primary column. See the following screenshot:

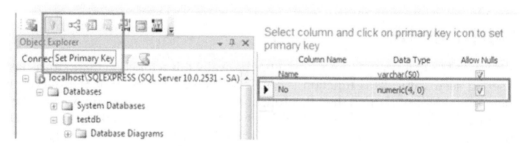

In the above screenshot, we can seeby selecting column you just need to click on `Set Primary Key` icon, on left side of the pane. After setting the primary key we can see key icon on left side of column, see the following screenshot:

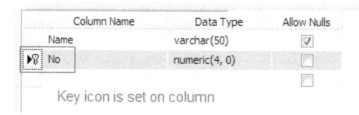

Using SQL Query analyzer

Here we have two different scenarios:

- If the column does not exist in table and we need to add column with primary key.
- If the column is already present in the table and we need to set it as primary key.

In both the cases we can fire the following query, let's trace them one by one.

- If the column is not present in table then you can use the following query:

  First add column to table, with the help of following query

  `ALTER TABLE test ADD no numeric(4,0)`

  In above query we have added new column to query, now we will add primary key in it, see the below query

  `ALTER TABLE test ADD PRIMARY KEY (No)`

  In the preceding query we have used `ALTER TABLE` statement to edit table and `ADD PRIMARY KEY` is a reserved keyword to add primary key to column, No is the name of the column.

- If the column is already present in the table and you want to add the primary key, then you can use the following query:

  `ALTER TABLE test ADD PRIMARY KEY (No)`

  In the above query we have used `ALTER TABLE` statement to edit table and `ADD PRIMARY KEY` is a reserved keyword to add primary key to column, `No` is the name of the column.

  Please note that all primary keys must be defined as NOT NULL. To modify the primary key, you must first delete the existing `PRIMARY KEY` constraint and then re-create it with the new definition.

Candidate key

If you want to identify the record uniquely then you can use candidate key. So a candidate key is a set of columns that identify the records uniquely, multiple primary key forms candidate key.

Let's take an example. We have created a table `StudentMaster` with 3 columns `Name`, `No` and `PRN_No`. Here we have formed candidate key as `No` and `PRN_No` are primary key. See the following screenshot:

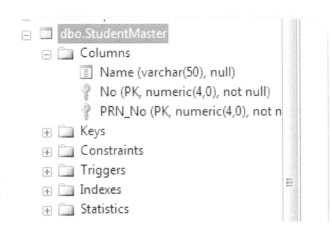

In the above screenshot, we can see No and PRN_No columns are primary keys and uniquely identify the record, this is known as `candidate key`.

Unique key

Unique key is a bit confusing. This key is a set of one or more columns and also identifies record uniquely. It also helps us to avoid duplication of records. So what is the difference between primary key and unique key. Let'shave a look on them:

- The main and the first difference is that primary key *does not* accept *null* values, whereas unique keys accept *only one null* value.
- We can have only one primary key in table, but we can have multiple unique keys.

Let's create a table with unique key using SQL Query analyzer, go through the following query:

CREATE TABLE TestEmp

(

EmpID int PRIMARY KEY,--This is PRIMARY key

EmpName varchar (100) NOTNULL,

LibraryCard_No int UNIQUE,--This is UNIQUE key

Department varchar (50) NOT NULL,

SubDept varchar (50) NULL,

)

In the above query we can see column EmpID is the primary key, EmpName column is a column with varchar datatype and cannot accept NULL values (so for each record we should have a value in it), column LibraryCard_No is unique key, column Department is varchar by datatype and does not accept NULL, whereas, SubDept is varchar and accepts NULL values.

If we fire the above query, we will get the following output:

```
CREATE TABLE TestEmp
  (
      EmpID int PRIMARY KEY, --This is PRIMARY key
      EmpName varchar (100) NOT NULL,
      LibraryCard_No int UNIQUE, --This is UNIQUE key
      Department varchar (50) NOT NULL,
      SubDept varchar (50) NULL,
  )
```

Messages

Command(s) completed successfully.

The resultant table structure will be as follows:

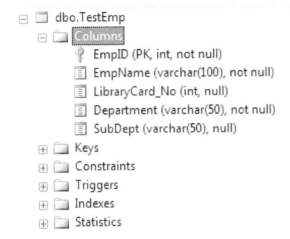

In the above screenshot, we can see `EmpID` is the primary key column and `LibraryCard_No` is the unique key column. If you check in the keys section of database table, then you can see that the primary key and the unique key are defined.

Go through the following screenshot:

In above screenshot, you can check **PK (primary key)** and **unique key** are defined.

Composite key

A combination of two or more columns forms composite key, and that combination identifies record uniquely. Now the confusion is what is the difference between unique key and candidate key? The main difference is that each column of candidate key can identify the record uniquely, but in the case of composite key, each column of candidate key *may not* identify the record uniquely.

Go through the following screenshot:

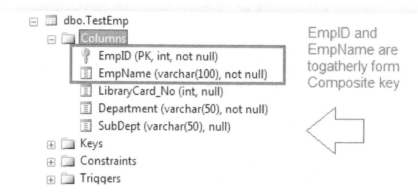

In the above screenshot, `EmpID` and `EmpName` can together form composite key. Here `EmpName` does not identify record uniquely because name of the employee can be repeated but combination of `EmpID` and `EmpName` can identify the record uniquely.

Foreign key

A primary key of one table can be foreign key of another table, but a foreign may have duplicate values in it and can also contain null values (if the column definition permits). In other words, if you want to relate two tables or create a relationship between two tables then you can use this key. We can have multiple foreign keys in one table if that table is linked/related with multiple tables.

Foreign key can be created in two ways:

- Using SQL Management Studio
- Using SQL Query analyzer

Using SQL Management Studio

Connect SQL Server and open table. Right click on table of which you want to give foreign key (foreign key column table), see the following screenshot:

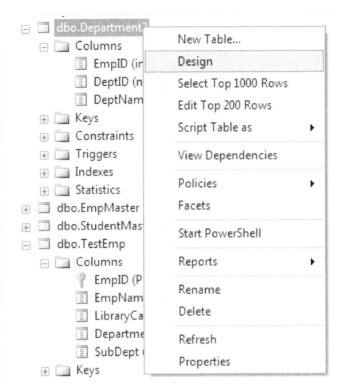

Click on `Relationships`..., see the following screenshot:

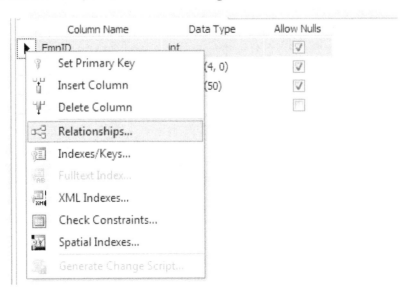

On click on `Relationships`...we will get the following screen, click on `Add` button to add foreign key relationship:

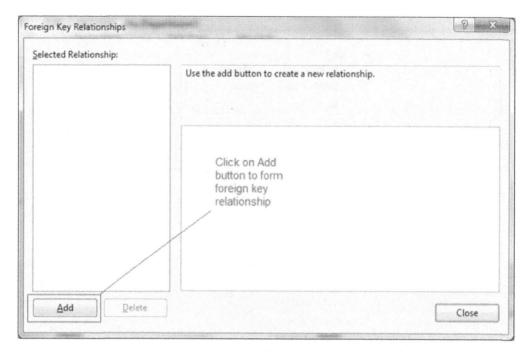

In the following screenshot, we have clicked on Add button to add FK_relationship. Now we will add a primary and foreign key on Tables And Columns Specification:

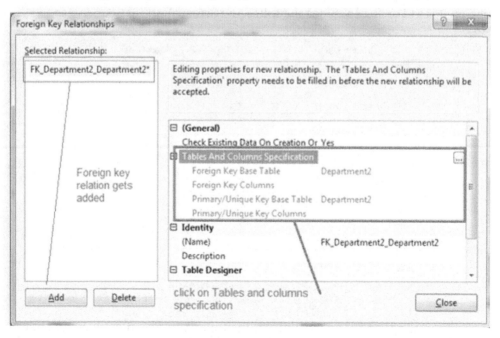

Now, in the following screenshot, we have selected primary and foreign key tables and columns:

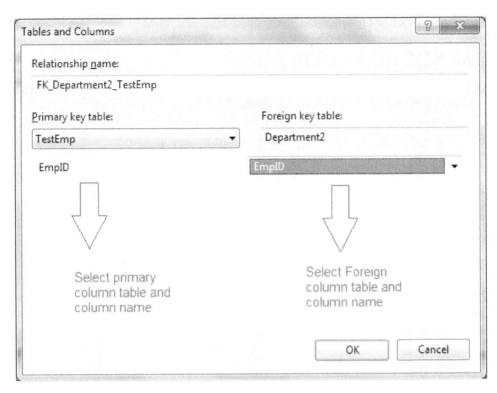

Click on OK button to set the relationship. In the next window, we can see primary and foreign key relationship have been set successfully, see the following screenshot:

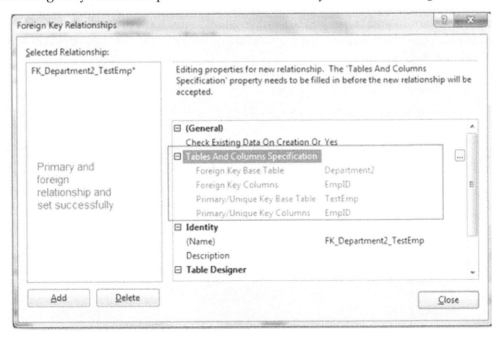

This is how we can set foreign key.

Using SQL query analyzer

You can set foreign key using SQL query analyzer as well. Just take a use of FOREIGNKEYREFERENCES keyword to set the particular column as foreign key. Now in the earlier example, we have added EmpID column as foreign key, if we do the same using SQL analyzer then the query would be as following:

```
CREATE TABLE Department (

OrderID int NOT NULL PRIMARYKEY,

OrderNumber int NOT NULL,

EmpID int FOREIGN KEY REFERENCES TestEmp(EmpID)

);
```

In the above query, Department is these condary table in which we have pull EmpID column as a foreign key from TestEmp table, for this we have used FOREIGN KEY REFERENCES as keyword.

Superkey

Superkey is the set of columns on which the functionality is dependent upon (the record is uniquely identified). You can say it is the set of columns that can identify there the record uniquely. Primary key is the minimal superkey as it is functionally very important.In our case EmpID and EmpName are the columns on which the functionality is dependent on, so we can say; it is the superkey for TestEmp table. See following screenshot:

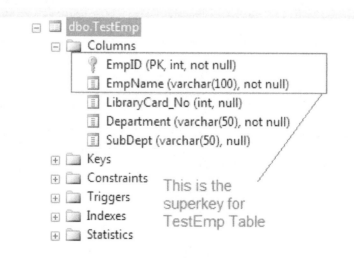

In the above screenshot, we can see `EmpID` and `EmpName` are the minimal required columns to run functionality, so we can say that, these columns are the superkey of the table.

Alternate key

Alternate key is a candidate key, which is currently not selected as primary key. In our case `LibraryCard_No` is the alternate key.

Let us have a sample picture where we try to include all types of keys in a single picture to make it clearer:

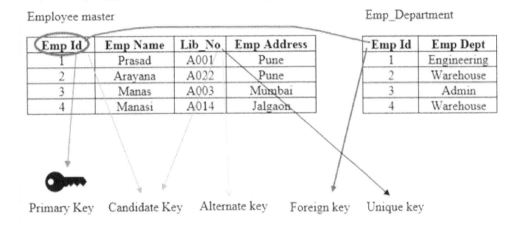

SQL indexes and its types

As name suggest index is the like a list, or we can say a catalog or a dictionary which is used to find records, sort them and to filter them. Same way SQL has also indexes present in database, which is used to filter and fetch records accordingly; this filtration can be done with the help of different SQL keys (keys like primary, candidate, foreign, and more.). When we define those keys on columns or tables then these will be stored in a tree like structure, that structure is called as B-Tree, and it helps SQL to find the row and records with quick and efficient manner.

Further SQL indexes are divided into following types:

- Clustered index
- Non-clustered index

Clustered index

This index helps us to sort and store the rows based on their key values, so when we fetch data it can be fetched quickly. The data can be stored in only one order and that is why we do have only one clustered index per table. This index helps database to stored data in sorted order, and the resultant table is called as clustered table. By default, the data stored in table in unstructured format and this is known as heap. There are multiple benefits of clustered index that we can use, following are some of them:

- Clustered index helps us to improve query execution performance.
- It help store build the index.
- It can control table fragmentation.

When you any create any primary key then clustered index associated with that columns is also get created automatically, here one point to note is, you can create a clustered index on non-primary key also but for that you first need to make the primary key as non-clustered index.

Check out following screenshot where we can see clustered index for primary key is automatically created:

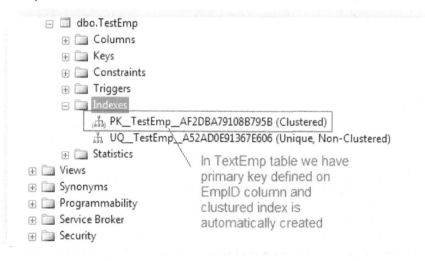

In the preceding screenshot, we can see for primary key column `EmpID` in clustered index is automatically created under `Indexes` folder.

Non-clustered index

Non-clustered index having different structure than clustered index, basically this index contains a non-cluster index values that are pointing to the row that contains value, each point is called as row-locator. Both the cluster and non-cluster index are unique in values. Indexes are always automatically maintained.

Non-clustered indexes are created when you create unique key, see following screenshot where we have unique key in table:

So, well designed keys and indexes are good in performance, disk operation and IO operations and finally that leads to overall query performance improvement.

SQL injection

Data security is the big thing in data/IT industry, attackers are always search for the loop holes in your application, to enter and steal data, same way SQL Injection is the code insertion technique that allows attacker to steal data, dump user data, and disturb the sensitive data by inserting some malicious INSERT statements.

SQL injection also harms transaction data, temper user identity, destroy the data or make it hidden.

How SQL injection attack carried out?

Generally, attacker finds vulnerable SQL input in web application, and then tries to INSERT some malicious script in input page. That malicious can run directly on database, as database is unknown for the source of the scripts. As we know SQL query can add, modify or delete data from database, the attackers also use these queries to disturb your data. By this way attacker can gain a complete access of your data. By using admin related scripts, it is easy to find the admin rights user and change the password easily.

In case of sensitive application like banking SQL injections can alter transactions, balance, transfer money, or steal passwords.

The following section has some SQL injection examples.

Using OR 1=1 condition

Let's look at the following sample where we have tries insert SQL injection in login web page. Normally to check user we use following SQL query:

```
SELECT * FROM EmpMaster WHERE NAME='Manavya' AND PASS='man'
```

In the preceding query we have select user from `EmpMaster` table with the help of name and password, now if attacker want to break this security then he will take use of `OR 1=1` technique, `OR 1=1` condition is always true and with the help of this query he will fetch all username and password from the database. Now if we run above query we will get following result, before that first see the database records:

EMPID	Name	Address	DeptID	City_Col	Pass
1	Prasad	Pune	10	NULL	pras
2	Manavya	Pune	20	NULL	man
3	Anil	Mumbai	20	NULL	ani
4	Manas	Delhi	30	NULL	mana
5	Aryana	Delhi	30	NULL	ary
6	Manasi	Mumbai	60	NULL	ma
	NULL	NULL	NULL	NULL	NULL

In preceding screenshot, we can see, we have Name and pass column exist and we can fetch records with the help of these columns, now if attacker wants to steal the data then the user just enters `OR 1=1` condition in **userID** textbox as given in following screenshot:

In preceding screenshot, we have entered dummy user ID as `402` and `OR 1=1` condition. If we submit this page the following query will get formed:

```
SELECT * FROM EmpMaster WHERE NAME='105' OR 1=1;
```

Same query will get fire on database and the result will as follows:

```
SELECT * FROM EmpMaster WHERE NAME='105' OR 1=1;
```

	EMPID	Name	Address	DeptID	City_Col	Pass
1	1	Prasad	Pune	10	NULL	pras
2	2	Manavya	Pune	20	NULL	man
3	3	Anil	Mumbai	20	NULL	ani
4	4	Manas	Delhi	30	NULL	mana
5	5	Aryana	Delhi	30	NULL	ary
6	6	Manasi	Mumbai	60	NULL	ma

In previous screenshot, we can see all records with password get fetched and attacker is successful in his attempt.

Using "or" "="

The other way to insert SQL injection is to use "or""=" character, just put these characters in username and password and see the result:

In the preceding screenshot, we have use "or""=" characters in userID and password field respectively. When we click on Sign in button it will create following SQL query internally and fire it on database:

SELECT * FROM EmpMaster WHERE Name='""""or'""""='"""' AND Pass='""""or'""""='"""'

Now, if we fire the preceding query, we will get following output:

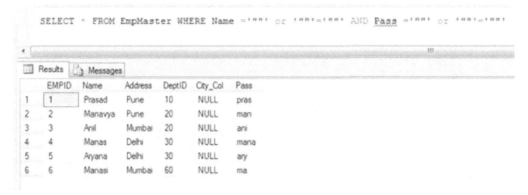

In the preceding screenshot, we can see all our data fetched from database without username and password, and in this case also attacker is successful to fetch the values.

Using batch SQL queries

Another way of SQL injection is to use SQL batch queries in which two or more SQL queries separated with semicolon is send to database, and that queries may contains DELETE like condition to destroy data.

Consider following sample where we have provided batch query in user id field, see the following screenshot:

In the preceding screenshot, we have entered Anil; DROP TABLE test data in user ID field, now when I click on Sign in button then application will form following query:

```
SELECT * FROM EmpMaster WHERE Name='Anil'; DROP TABLE TEST
```

If we run above query then all details for user Anil gets fetched but at the same time DROP statement is also fired on database and it will destroy our table with data.

Preventing SQL injection

We can avoid SQL injection by using SQL parameters, basically these parameters add value to the SQL query at the time of query execution, and while execution SQL engine examine each query and make sure that all the values are syntactically correct, so no invalid input is entertained. These parameters can be controlled and called using different programming languages.

See the following sample, where we have collected values from web form and with the help of parameters, we have added them in INSERT statement, we use @ sign as parameter notation:

```
szName=GetString("EmpName");

szAddress=GetString("EmpAddress");

szCity=GetString("City");

szSQL="INSERT INTO Customers(EmpName, Address, City)Values(@0,@1,@2)";

//Fire szSQL Query
```

Following are the additional ways to avoid SQL injection:

- You can use stored procedure to avoid SQL injection.
- You can validate user inputs before processing the request.
- Keep antivirus and firewall updated.
- Keep the data username and password encrypted and secure.

SQL constraints

SQL constraint is nothing but a set of rules that is bound to table or some specific columns; they are mostly used to restrict the datatype, length and specific culture data.

Following types of SQL constraints are available in SQL. These constraints are basically like SQL keys:

- NOTNULL: These constraints make sure that column should not accept any null value.
- INDEX: Indexing constraints is used to fetch, filter the data from database but with the good speed, so for speed and performance we can use this constraint.
- UNIQUE: These constraints make sure that column should have a different record in that specific column.
- DEFAULT: These constraints set the given default value to the column if we don't specify any value to it.

- `PRIMARYKEY`: These constraints are the combination of `NOTNULL` and `UNIQUE` constraint where primary key constraint column should not contain any null value and that column should not have duplicate data value.

- `CHECK`: This is the different constraint where this column ensures that all the record of these columns should satisfy the specific condition.

Conclusion

In this chapter we have seen about SQL view and how we can store a query result as a temporary table, we also seen how to delete, modify SQL view. We also check about the column that can be auto incremented its value which is known as identity columns. SQL Keys are playing very vital role in SQL database management, in this chapter we also go through various SQL keys including primary, foreign, candidate, unique, and alter keys. We have also seen about SQL Cluster index and non-cluster index concepts that help to sorting and filter rows and records. We have also seen how attacker steals our data and put malicious entry our database, we have also seen about different database injection and away to prevent SQL injection.

Incoming chapters, we will learn about how SQL can connect to JSON and interchange data, we will also learn more on SQL and JSON connection, SQL reporting and integration services. We will learn how to host your SQL to cloud server (Azure), How to control it. So, stay tuned.

Questions

1. **Can you explain SQL view?**

   An SQL view is a temporary virtual table that consists of a combination of rows and columns that can store query result further, which will be used to fetch the data.

2. **What is identity column?**

   A SQL table column with numeric data type and has the auto incremented number features, is called as identity column. It has two properties, seed and increment.

3. **What are SQL keys and its types?**

   In data base management system a key is the field which helps us to sort data, put index, avoid duplication, and speed up search operation among records.

   There are following types of keys present in SQL:
   - Primary key
   - Candidate key
   - Unique key

- Composite key
- Foreign key
- Super key
- Alternate key

4. **What is candidate key?**

Candidate key is a set of columns that identify the records uniquely, multiple primary key forms candidate key. So we can say it's a set of combination of primary keys.

5. **What is primary key?**

A column that defines or guarantees data uniqueness is called as primary key. Mostly the columns are also identity column.

6. **What is foreign key?**

A primary key of one table can be foreign key of another table but a foreign may have duplicate values in it and can also contain NULL values, one table may contain multiple foreign keys.

7. **What is clustered index?**

This index helps us to sort and store the rows, based on their key values, so when we fetch data it can be fetched quickly, the data can be stored in only one order and that is why we do have only one clustered index per table.

8. **What is non-clustered index?**

Non-clustered index having different structure than clustered index, basically this index contains a non-cluster index values that are pointing to the row that contains value, each point is called as row-locator.

9. **What is SQL injection?**

Data security is the big thing in data/IT industry, attackers are always search for the loop holes in your application, to enter and steal data, and same way SQL Injection is the code insertion technique that allows attacker to steal data, dump user data.

Do you know (lights on facts?)

- A view can have maximum of 1024 columns.
- SQL will produce the error if you try to use the view, which tables are dropped/removed.
- If there is a change in SQL table on which view is built, then you need to drop and re-create the view.

- You cannot use ORDERBY clause in SELECT VIEW. If you want to use it then you should use TOP clause with SELECT.

- Modifying a view does not affect any dependent object like table, database, and stored procedure as it is temporary/virtual table.

- DROP table will not drop/delete view of the table; we need for fire DROP VIEW statement explicitly on the view.

- SQL injection attack was first publicly discussed in 1998.

CHAPTER 10

SSRS, SSIS, SQL Cloud Database (Azure) and JSON Support

SQL is not only good at storing data but it also has good capacity to generate report from stored data, analyze them and integrate with other systems too. SQL also has good support over cloud connection and support to **JavaScript Object Notation (JSON)** data.

Prerequisite for this chapter: Before we walk through this chapter you should have knowledge of basic SQL concepts. Additionally, you should have a laptop/desktop with SQL server installed.

Structure

- SQL Server reporting services
- SQL server integration services
- Cloud DB (Azure DB)
- JSON support

Objective

So, theobjective of the chapter is to learn about reporting system supported by SQL, which is also known as SSRS. Additionally, this report also works for mobile and smart devices, as well as web portals. We will also learn about integration services and its data migration techniques. We will go through connection and working of cloud database like AZURE DB and support to JSON technology.

So, let's begin.

SQL reporting services (SSRS)

As the name suggests, it is the reporting services that are server based and designed by Microsoft. These services are quite useful for creating interactive, user friendly and printable reports; basically, it is linked with Visual studio so that a developer can directly interact with the reporting tool. This tool provides us report builder to design reports.

In earlier days, SSRS was used with report definition language for report design but now, it uses SQL server data tools for business intelligence (SSDT BI). In this new technique you can drag and drop icons to build reports. Additionally, SSRS will give facility to download reports in different formats, including PDF, Excel, CSV, and many more. SSRS will offer report in all formats, including legacy paginated report, modern web-based report, and report for mobile portal that supportsresponsive layout. SSRS supports only vb.net for embed code. Let's trace these points in detail:

- **Paginated reports:** As discussed, earlier SSDT supported paginated reports which were ideal for fixed layout. SSDT applies new style to legacy paginated report to make them more interactive. Now, you can export data directly to Power point slides which are editable.

- **Modernweb-based reports:** In this new portal, web report manager has been designed so that it can support single page, HTML 5 designs that can run on modern advanced browsers like Microsoft Edge, Firefox, and Chrome. These reports are capable of handling reports, excel sheets, different data sources. Access permissions are also supported by these web-based reports. Web portal supports the following tasks:

  o   View, print, search and export reports.

  o   Functionality, like send feedback, which is inbuilt in this portal.

  o   Linked reports.

  o   View report history and parameters.

  o   Group by functionality for different categories, like Excel, dataset, data sources.

Go through the following screenshot to see the interface of SQL server reporting services for web portal:

Mobile reports

Mobile reports are more popular these days as fixed layout reports are not compatible with modern devices and hence user community looks forward to responsive reports. To make these reports responsive SQL uses DataZen technology, which is a year old and has now been merged into reports. SQL has given mobile report publisher app that can be compatible in Windows 10, Cloud database, iOS, or Android.

Basically, SSRS has the following components:

- **Report designer:** As the name suggests, designer is used to develop and build simple and complex report. Basically, it is a tool that can be used using Visual Studio or you can host with business Intelligence Development Studio.

- **Report builder:** This is ready to use drag and drop tool used to design report, it is always executed on client computer.

- **Report manager:** This tool is used to access web-based reports, the default path is `http://server/reports`.
- **Report server:** As the name suggests, this is the report server that is used to manage interaction and data transfer between user request and data sources.
- **Data sources:** This is the base of data that can be in the form of different data set like relational, multi dimensional data.

For better understanding of SSRS' working, go through the following snap. Here, the user requests for the report to be fetched from data sources. The request is first served by report server, which is responsible for data that is transferred to the user. Report server acts like a bridge between user request and data sources.

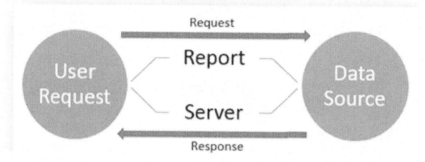

Let's see the concept of drill down and drill through in SSRS. These two features are used to get detailed information of data. As the name suggests, **drill down** function allows user to get deeper into data to fetch specific layer information.

Say for example, we have data of different business list in country, so when we use drill down approach we will get the data of state and city too.

Drill through isa bit different from drill down. This approach takes the user to analyze relevant data ratherthan going deeper into the same data. Say for example, we have data of different business list for each state, then instead of going deeper into any one state we can analyze different states' data at the same time.

SSRS benefits and drawbacks

The following are the benefits of SSRS:

- Easy access to different report formats.
- Ready-made tool is provided for report designer.
- SQL server reporting services has different chart types, including pie chart, bar chart, line chart and more.
- Filter options are available.
- Complex report can easily be rendered into different devices and browsers.

- Sub report is also possible in the main report.
- Due to central data warehouse, SSRS is more flexible than any other reporting tool.
- Rendering of SSRS is the easy part as compared to other reporting alternatives.
- Report designer is included in Visual Studio, so no extra add-on tool is required.

Every reporting tool has advantages as well as drawbacks. Let's see some drawbacks of SSRS:

- SSRS requires knowledge of SQL.
- You need to maintain extra server for SSRS.
- There is no way to protect exported report (like password protection, encryption).
- Bit costlier than other reporting solutions.

SSRS allows user to export in different formats like:

- HTML
- Excel
- Image format
- XML
- CSV

Now, the most important question is when to use this reporting tool. Let's discuss that.

We do have different types of data sources in SSRS:

o Microsoft SQL server
o Microsoft power pivot and tabular models
o Microsoft Azure SQL DB
o SAP
o Oracle
o Teradata

You can directly bind stored procedure in SSRS. Let's check out how it works. Basically, SSRS accepts dataset as a data source and SSRS dataset can be created by using query text, SQL table or stored procedure (the stored procedure has to be saved in database first). SSRS gives you the facility to change the query parameter if you want.

Alternative to SSRS

There are a plenty of alternatives to SSRS. Some of them are listed below:

- **Pentaho:** It's an opensource software, which provides us reporting tools, data integration services

- **SpagoBI:** This is also an open source software, which comes with Business Intelligence suite, including reporting and integration services

- **Crystal report:** This is a popular reporting tool, and with its help you can create powerful and rich reports

- **Telerik:** This is a third party reporting tool, which allows us to produce large number of report formats and export options

Usage of SSRS

As the name suggests, SSRS is used not just for creating report but also the following:

- When you want print copy control, formattingcontrol, then you should go for SSRS.

- When you have a complex data and want to put it in graphical report then you should go for SSRS.

- When you want to export data in different formats then you should go for SSRS.

- SSRS is better fitted with SQL. If you are good at SQL and want to put SQL data in reporting services then you should go for SSRS.

- If you want to show data on different devices like desktop, mobile and smart devices then you should go for SSRS.

SQL Integration Services (SSIS)

SSIS was introduced with SQL 2005. Basically, Microsoft team had decided to change the functionality of DTC and renamed it to Integration services. Later on, in SQL 2008, they had made a lot of improvement and announced new sources. In later releases of SQL (like SQL 2000) they introduced project deployment module with SSIS. If you moved to SQL 2014, you would have found that the SSIS transformation could be downloaded using Code Plex. In SQL 2016, you could deploy entire projects with additional facilities like cloud connectivity and big data sources.

SSIS is a data integration, migration, and transformation tool that helps us to analyze, clean, extract, and transform data from one form to another. This tool extracts and transforms data from different formats like XML, flat files, relational database. You can transform that data in ETL*, data warehouseor any other storage space.

*ETL is the short form of **Extraction, Transformation, and Loading**. Basically, it is the process of replicating data from different sources to one central place that may be a data warehouse. It is more useful to move data across databases. SSIS also has graphical tools that are used to handle email messages, FTP operations.

SSIS architecture

SSIS has the following model in its architecture:

- Data flow
- Control flow
- SSIS package

Let's trace out these points.

Data flow

In data flow model, data is first extracted and saved into server memory and then transformed into another form, and finally converted to destination type. Data flow is responsible for handling data.

After the data has been transformed, a package is created which further can be saved to SQL, or package catalog data.

Control flow

Control flow handles execution of all tasks that are carried between data transformation. A task is an individual work or a set of work that needs to be carried out.

SSIS package

SSIS package is used to merge data from different sources into a package so that they can transform into another format. So, we can say control flow + data flow = package

Here is the diagrammatic representation for the same:

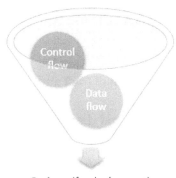

Package (for deployment)

SSIS is responsible for carrying out different tasks, some of which are listed as follows:

- **Execute SQL task:** This task is used to execute different SQLoperations on relational databases.
- **Data flow SQL task:** As the name suggests, this task is used to read data from different sources and transform them. This task is also used to write data in memory.
- **XML task:** This task is used to perform different operations on XML, like editing and re-formatting.
- **FTP task:** This task is used for simple FTP related functionalities.

The following are the benefits of SSIS:

- SSIS has multiple capabilities to transform data;in short, it can handle heterogeneous data sources and link them easily to fetch data. Many a times, it can fetch data that can't be handled by SQL and FTP like services.
- SSIS has the functionality to identify the irrelevant data and send it for further investigation
- SSIS can connect to different data providers, including SQL, OLEDB, SAP, and Oracle.
- It has relevant data integration function.
- It is easy to use.
- It has tight coupled relationship while integration with other Microsoft products like Excel.
- It is highly tested with enterprise level application.
- It has good community support.

Now, we let us go through the disadvantages of SQL, which are as follows:

- SSIS takes high memory and resources if we load multiple packages parallelly.
- As SSIS is the feature of SQL server, the licensing is a bit confusing.

A question comes to mind, which is why to use SQL integration services. Let's discuss.

Usage of SSIS

- SSIS is useful when we need to extract and migrate data from multiple data sources.
- SSIS automates data loading and data reports.
- SSIS helps us clean data and make it easily available for furtherfiltering.
- SSIS helps us to transform data from one form to another, without writing a code.

- SSIS can handle a large volume of data in very less time.

SSIS supports the following connection managers:
- **ADO:** It directly connects with active data objects.
- **ADO.NET:** It can connect to .NET based active data object.
- **EXCEL:** It can connect to EXCEL workbook.
- **FILE:** It can connect to any file or folder.
- **HTTP:** It can connect to webserver.
- **FTP:** It can connect to FTP server.
- **SMTP:** It can connect to SMTP mail server.

Apart from the above connection manager we do have OLEDB, ODBC, WMI to connect to SSIS

Cloud DB (Azure DB)

Basically, Azure DB is a cloud database services that provides wide range of data functionality and compatibility. As it is a clouds database, so you can access it from anywhere regardless of location connectivity.

Let's have a walkthrough of features of Azure database:
- You can easily migrate to your on-going on premises database to cloud without single code change in your production application.
- It has inbuilt machine learning technique that will help us enhance database security.
- Simple and straight forward solution for database.
- It's cost effective compared with alternative cloud database solutions.
- Bigger scale possible, you can use up to 100TB.
- Encrypted technology will give you advanced security to database.
- Multilayered safety provided by Microsoft across the world.
- Large customer support, including multi-location datacenter and operation facilities.
- Deployment is easy and manageable.

You can use Cloud Azure database in the following cases:

- If your customer is globally distributed and you need to connect your database from different parts of the world.
- If you want a managed relation database that can be accessed on the fly with security.
- If you want a MySQL of PostgreSQL, then you can go for Azure database.
- If you want to host a large enterprise level application.
- If you want to build data warehouse that is hosted on cloud.
- If you want to migrate, you're on-premises database to cloud but you don't want to change your application code.

JSON support

JSON is a popular lightweight textual format datathat is used widely to store and handle data. JSON also helps us to store unstructured data (like NoSQL, Cosmo Db), Now a days, REST services mostly return JSON data in the form of key and value pair, same like Azure also supports JSON to consume and transfer data between webpages.

We can use JSON in SQL to connect different databases like NoSQL to SQL. We can use JSON to format text to relational data and vice versa.

With the help of JSON we can do the following things:

- Transform JSON array object into table format.
- You can run SQL query on JSON objects (here JSON objects are nothing but the table data that is converted to JSON objects).
- Parse JSON data.

SQL has the following inbuilt JSON functions to deal with data:

- `ISJSON`: This function is used to check if the given string contains JSON data. The syntax is as follows:

`ISJSON (expression)`

In the above syntax, the expression is the string that we need to test.

- **JSON_MODIFY:** This function helps is us to change the value in JSON string. The syntax is as follows:

  `JSON_MODIFY(expression, path, new_value)`

  In the above syntax, expression is the string that contains JSON text path is JSON path new value is new value for property.

- **JSON_VALUE:** This function helps is us to change the value in JSON string. The syntax is as follows:

  `JSON_QUERY(expression, path)`

  In the above syntax, expression is the string that contains JSON text path is JSON path.

- **JSON_QUERY:** This function helps us to extract an object from a JSON string. The syntax is as follows:

  `JSON_QUERY(expression, [path])`

  In the above syntax, expression is the string that contains JSON text path is JSON path (square bracket around path indicates optional variable)

Conclusion

In this chapter, we have seen that SQL server has its own report generation tool, named as SSRS. It has its own report server with report designer facility. The reports created by SSRS can be rendered on web browsers as well as desktop. We can also view them on different smart devices like mobile, laptops, and palm tab. SSRS givesus the facility to drag and drop control to design the desired port with support to graphical layouts, like pie chart, bar chart, histogram etc. Additionally, we have seen that SSIS is a Microsoft created integration tool (basically we can call it is ETL tool) that is used to extract data from different data sources and transform them into desired form and finally load it into the system. We also learnt about the Azure database system which is a cloud database that is widely used due to always and anywhere available features. We also checked outhow JSON is connected and supported by SQL.

In the upcoming chapter, we will learn about the new features of SQL 2016, 2017 and some features of CTP-2019 and few SQL performance improvement tips that will helps boost application performance.

Questions

1. **What is SSRS?**

   SSRS is a SQL server reporting tool that is suitable for creating high definition, user interactive reports that can be rendered on web browser and a range of smart devices. We can export our reports in different formats.

2. **Can we have Crystal reports in SSRS?**

Crystal reports are run and handled by IIS server whereas SSRS is itself an SQL server. Crystal reports can be run in cache server where SSRS reports are available for report history.

3. **What are the different data sources that SSRS can support?**

SSRS supports a wide range of data sources. Let's go through them:

- Oracle
- ODBC
- SQL server
- Report server model
- XML

4. **What are the modules of SSRS?**

Modules of SSRS are report manager, report designer, report server, data sources, among others.

5. **What is SSIS?**

SSIS is an integration ETL tool that is used to extract data from different sources and transform them to desired format and finally load them to database.

6. **What are the features of SSIS?**

Following are the features of the SSIS:

- Secure to use
- Ease of use
- Less costly than any other alternative ETL tool
- Supports wide range of data sources

7. **What is the difference between control flow and data flow?**

The very first thing to keep in mind is that control flow is for designing and as the name suggests, data flow is for data transformation process (ETL process). So we can say that data flow is a subset of control flow, data flow and control flow can together bind to create a package of SSIS.

8. **Can SSIS run with the SQL express version?**

SSIS can run with SQL Enterprise, Standard, Datacenter and web version, with operating server support from Windows client OS 8, 8.1, 10 and Windows server OS Win server 2012, 2016 and 2019.

9. **What is SQL Azure DB?**

   SQL Azure DB is a cloud based relational database that can be used when you have multiple database access locations spread globally.

10. **How many database servers you can create at Azure DB?**

    Azure database is subscription license and for each license you can create up to 6 different database servers.

11. **How Azure DB maintains security?**

    Azure database has its own Azure database firewall, which will accept a request from a specific IP address; alternatively, Azure SQL will accept only SSL connections by default.

12. **What steps are required to migrate our data from on-premises to Azure DB?**

    Azure database has its own migration wizard like SSIS or BCP or you can use simple SQL script generation wizard to migrate your data (with tables and schema) from on-premises to Azure database.

Do you know (lights on facts?)

- SSRS web portal is not supported on SharePoint integrated mode.

- SSIS tool is mainly used for data migrations.

- SSIS can connect to EXCEL and XML.

- SSIS package can be stored at SQL server, File system or at package store.

- SQL Azure DB is a remote cloud database server that is available for geographically scattered locations.

CHAPTER 11

New Features of SQL 2016, 2017, 2019

Introduction

Nowadays, data storage and its extraction with good performance is a big challenge, where SQL server has been serving with ease and good routine from past many years. It has travelled a lot from Version 2000 to 2019 (the current one) and so on. SQL is an industry lead enterprise level database that helps us to manage store, fetch and secure our data.

Prerequisite for this chapter: Before we walk through this chapter, you should have knowledge of basic SQL concepts. Additionally, you should have a laptop/desktop with SQL server installed.

Structure

- New features of SQL 2016
- New features of SQL 2017
- New features of SQL 2019

Objective

So, the objective of the chapter is to learn the new features of SQL 2016, 2017 and 2019.

So, let's begin.

New features of SQL 2016

SQL 2016 was released on 1st June 2016 with a few things in mind Basically, this build of SQL was released for Cloud connect, support to JSON technology, Connectivity to Windows server 2016, transaction handling at ROW level, non-relational database connectivity like NoSQL and some performance improvements. Let's trace them one by one.

SQL Server edition

This build of SQL server comes with different editions, which are as follows:

- **Enterprise Edition:** As the name suggests, this is the highest edition and mostly used for enterprise level application. It has high-end capabilities with stunning performance and unlimited users and virtualization techniques

- **Standard Edition:** This is a low level business database intelligent tool compared with enterprise level edition. It also has effective data management tool

- **Web Edition:** This is basically a web hosting edition with low cost solution. It will be useful for small and medium level web hosting applications

- **Developer Edition:** As the name suggests, this edition is for developers and it allows developers to build applications on SQL. It has all the capabilities of Enterprise level edition but the license is limited to only development and testing purposes. It should now be used on the production server

- **Express Edition:** This is an entry level free database edition released by SQL server, which can be good for building, learning and for small server applications.

Secure encryption

This is the new feature that has been introduced in SQL 2016. Here you can keep your data secure by encryption, and this feature is very good and can work on-premise or cloud database and helps us guard our data and sensitive information from users like DBA, database operators and admin rights users. Now let's see how to use this functionality.

This functionality is implemented on individual row, where you need to specify the encryption process and parse phase keys for data guard. Basically, we need to define Encryption key and Master key, where Encryption key is used to encrypt data and Master key is used to encode encryption key.

We can say that it's the double encryption that will protect our data and the interesting thing is that client application will automatically encrypt and decrypt the data.

Let's take an example, where we need to encrypt a column value, first we need to create master key for encryption, which should have a strong password. See the following syntax:

```
CREATE MASTERKEY ENCRYPTION BY

PASSWORD = '<some strong password>';
```

Then we need to create a certificate for key with the following syntax:

```
CREATE CERTIFICATE encryptCER

WITH SUBJECT = 'Database encryption certificate';

GO
```

Then we need to create symmetric key with the following syntax:

```
CREATE SYMMETRIC KEYDBKEY1

WITH ALGORITHM = AES_256

   ENCRYPTION BY CERTIFICATE encryptCER;

GO
```

And, then we will use `ENCRYPTBYKEY` method to encrypt the data.

Data masking

This is a really good feature introduced in SQL 2016. It is basically used for hiding data. It uses MASK to wrap the data inside so that attacker or hacker will be unable to identify the content. It is useful when you have a confidential data store in table and you want to hide the contents. After you have applied this function, you will not be able to see plain text, you will only be able to view masked data. The masking function has to be applied on columns for it to take effect. See the following samples:

Sr No	Data type	Plain text	After masking
1	String, Number	XYZ	XXX
2	Email type	abc@xyz.com	aXXXXXX@XX
3	Text	BLAH BLAH	BXXH XXXH
4	Numbers	123456	001400

In the above table you can see plain text is hidden inside with XXX after applying masking function. The functions that are used for masking are as follows:

- `Default ()`: This function is applied for any datatype, including string, number.
- `Email ()`: This function is applied for email datatype, which means you can store email in this field.
- `Random ()`: This function is applied for masking numbers.
- `Custom String`: This is customized data type used for string.

Check out the following syntax of masking:

```
ALTER TABLE TableName ALTER COLUMN ColumnName MASKED WITH
(FUNCTION=,default()')
```

Support to JSON

From SQL 2016, JSON is supported to SQL, JSON is JavaScript Object notation. SQL now reads JSON format data, it can also load SQL table by JSON data. To store JSON data, SQL uses `nvarchar` datatype. Here the advantage is `nvarchar` is supported by SQL component, and with the SQL script, you can fetch data for JSON from SQL by the following syntax:

```
SELECT column names FROM table1, table2 FOR JSON [AUTO | PATH]
```

When we fire the above query it returns JSON object, SQL has inbuilt function for JSON.

Auto temp DB

When we are working on big crucial data then it is always a good practice to update data in temporary database and then make the change permanently. In the earlier version of SQL (SQL 2014), `temp` DB files were used but you were required to manually add them to database, but as this version automates the things for you, you just need to configure settings to number of temp DB at the time of installation and SQL will do the test of the operation for you. So, you no longer want to create or configure data automatically.

Secure your row

If you are a developer then this is the most awaited feature of the SQL. If you want to set access permission to a specific row then this would be possible from this SQL version. This will be helpful if you want to show only specific data. For example, if you set row level security then employee can view only department specific data.

To implement this functionality, first define security policy (to define this policy we need predicate and function).

To define predicates and function we can use the following syntax:

```
CREATE SECURITY POLICY fn_security ADD [FILTER | BLOCK] PREDICATE
FunctionName ON TableName
```

In the above syntax,

- `FLITER` is the predicate that is applicable to rows that are available for read.
- `BLOCK` is used for blocking rows for operation.
- `FunctionName` is the simple user defined SQL function, but when you write a SQL Function for security policy then here are some rules that you need to follow:
    o Operation with data modification is not possible.
    o A function should return multiple functions.
    o `OUTPUT INTO` clause is not allowed in function.

Stretch database concept for cloud DB

Stretch database concept is applicable to cloud (Azure) database, where we can store at cloud and it can be fetched back to on premise as per the request. The data which is stored at the cloud is called as COLD data, whereas on premise data is called as HOT data. You can use this concept/feature when you want to store data for long term use and it can be accessed whenever you need it, and as the data is stored on cloud so you can access it from anywhere. As far as COLD data storage, it's a cost effective and robust solution . To use this feature, you should have an Azure account and a database should be installed on the server.

Query store

Now, you know every query has its plan. This plan will estimate all the resources and the time needed toexecute the query, but there is no facility in SQL to store that plan for review purpose or for further studies. But SQL 2016 brings the concept of SQL Store that will help you take tour of current query plan, statistics, and more. If you want to use this feature then right click on database, go to `Properties`, you will see `Query Store` option on the left side of properties window, now you can select it and click on enable *true* option. Or you can use the following query:

```
ALTER DATABASE [testDB] SET QUERY_STORE = ON
```

In the aboveduery, syntax test DB is the database name for which we need to enable Query Store.

Temporal database

Each time when you update or change SQL tables, there is no way to keep track of old records or data, but with the help of these features you can keep track of old data. Further, this data can be used for review or compare process. With the help of the version facility, SQL maintains the old and the new data. To support this feature, SQL uses history table with data time columns, one with start data time and another is end datetime. Here, history table contains previous records that have been changed. We can use the following query to fetch data from history table:

```
SELECT * FROM HistoryTable FOR SYSTEM_TIME

BETWEEN date1 AND date2

WHERE condition;
```

In the above syntax, `HistoryTable` is the database table that stores history `date1` and `date2` are the dates for which old data is stored.

Working with R

SQL 2016 has now direct support for R. First let's see what R is. It is the programming language or software which is used for statistical calculations and has graphics support with reporting techniques. R was developed by *Robert Gentleman* and *Ross Ihaka* at NewZealand. R has different scripts that can be run on relational data to get the desired output. Now, with the help of SQL 2016, R scripts can be executed at SQL level.

New features of SQL 2017

SQL 2017 was released in October 2017. This is very a fast and immediate build, which was released to broaden up the deployment edges of SQL to Linux. This means that from this build onwards, SQL can be deployed and run on Linux, additionally, SQL has concentrated on performance improvement for improving database engine, data services, integration services, analysis services, etc. Now we will walk through each of the features of SQL 2017, so let's begin.

Automatic tuning

Nowadays, performance is the major bar for SQL. To tune the performance we need to tune each query. This feature helps us to find out the problem in query performance, it not only identifies the issue but also fixes them to boost performance. This performance tuning follows one of the following techniques:

- **Automatic correction plan:** If we lookout for automatic correction plan then, this technique scans the slow performance query and applies recommend fixes for it.

- **Automatic index plan:** If we lookout for automatic index plan then, this technique scans the order of the indices of the queries and corrects them if it has a problem.

Correct identity

Identity column can contains only auto incremented unique values, (but keep in mind that it is different than primary key). Have you ever faceda problem about identity column? Does your identity increment seed skip next immediate number ? this may happens due to the database connection failure or database crash. Or a problem may occur in case of unexpected server shutdown or failure. If yes, then identity_cache feature will help you resolve this issue. This feature helps avoid discrepancy found in identity column. To enable this feature we need to just set the IDENTITY_CACHE = { ON | OFF } flag to ON, we need to do this settings in 'DATABASE SCOPED CONFIGURATION part, the syntax is as follows:

```
ALTER DATABASE SCOPED CONFIGURATION
{
  { [ FOR SECONDARY] SET <set_options>  }
}
| CLEAR PROCEDURE_CACHE
| SET < set_options >
[;]


< set_options > ::=
{
  MAXDOP = { <value> | PRIMARY}
  | LEGACY_CARDINALITY_ESTIMATION = { ON | OFF | PRIMARY}
  | PARAMETER_SNIFFING = { ON | OFF | PRIMARY}
  | QUERY_OPTIMIZER_HOTFIXES = { ON | OFF | PRIMARY}
  | IDENTITY_CACHE = { ON | OFF }
}
```

Graph database

SQL server 2017 supports many to many relationship model using graphical database skill. Now, first let us see what is graph database. It is the collection of or a group of vertices and relationships, where a single vertices is a node or an entire (it may be living or nonliving thing). Both vertices and edges have different inbuilt properties, so we can say that each edge can be successfully connected to multiple nodes in graph database. Now, the question is when to use graph DB

See the following situation where you can use graph database:

- If you have interconnected data and relationship, and you want to analyze it then you can go for it.

- If you have complex connected many to may data relations and as data flows, more data relations are again added to existing data then you can use graph database to simplify this complexity.

- If your data is in hierarchical format and you want use node with multiple parent then you can go for it.

Cross database connectivity

This feature will allow you to connect and open transaction between different instances of single SQL connection. It also supports DDMS (same SQL instance can be connected to different instances). SQL 2016 also supports cross database connectivity but allows cross database access only on same SQL instance).

DTA (database tuning advisor)

As discussed earlier, SQL 2017 has major improvement in terms of performance, they have introduced database tuning advisor with additional feature. First, let's see what **DTA (Database tuning advisor)** is.

Basically, DTA is a simple database engine which first scans the input query and gives us option to execute the query performance. The option may be to change the table keys or put extra indices or rebuild the index. To use this feature you can use GUI or a command line utility

For GUI use, click on `Tools` menu, and select `Database Engine Tuning Advisor`, and then connect database.

Machine learning

From SQL 2016 version, database has been supporting R language for various statistical calculations. Now, the same services are renamed with SQL server machine learning services, so that you can execute R or python script on SQL. If you want to use this feature but don't want to use SQL then also you can do it with the help of MMLS tools, (MMLS is Microsoft machine learning server), Now you connect Python, R scripts and AI libraries together. SQL has the following solution to use SQL with AI:

- **Using microsomal:** This package comes with Python bindings and machine learning algorithm and transformation. It helps in making decision trees and forests and is also helpful in liner and logistics regression. It also supports large text transformation and streaming.
- **Using revoscalepy:** This solution comes with the library to give and support high performance algorithm.

Wide-ranging Linux support

SQL server 2017 has good support for Linux, this version is predestined to be for Linux deployment. When Microsoft introduced this build then the tag line was *SQL on Linux and Windows*. It supports the following features on Linux:

- Linux can enable SQL engine abilities.
- It does support native Linux path.
- Support to IP version 6.
- Database files support on NFS.
- Transport layer security is also enabled.
- Active directory authentication is possible with Linux.
- Full-text search enabled.
- Log shipping also supported on Linux.
- Mail activities.
- SQL job scheduling and transaction.
- Command line SQL execution tool.
- Support to Visual studio code.
- Support to cross platform script generator.

New string functions introduced in SQL 2017

SQL 2017 has some new string functions. Let's trace them one by one.

STRING_AGG

This is the most-awaited and stunning function which will concatenate string expression and separator between each result, and the good thing is that it will not append any separator at the end of the resultant string. The output is converted into string and then concatenation happens. In this case, if compiler finds any NULL value then it is ignored and corresponding separator is not added.

Checkout the syntax as follows:

```
STRING_AGG ( expression, separator ) [ <order_clause> ]
```

```
<order_clause> ::=  WITHIN GROUP ( ORDER BY <order_by_expression_list> [
ASC | DESC ] )
```

In the above syntax, `STRING_AGG` is the function name, expression is the name of the expression that is passed to query, and separator is the separator field that needs to be added after each expression result. Rest of the parameters are optional.

Let's take an example, if we want to fetch the list of all employees but only the first name and each row should have only one name, then the query will be as follows:

```
SELECT STRING_AGG (FirstName, CHAR (13)) AS Names
```

```
FROM Employee;
```

In the above query `FirstName` is the column name that needs to be fetched from database, `CHAR(13)` is the ASCII keycode of enter char so we need to enter after each result. Here, NULL values are ignored by compiler. If we run the above query the result would be as follows:

Names
Prasad
Manavya
Aaru
MANAS
MANASI

In the same example, if we want to separate them with comma then the query will be as follows:

```
SELECT STRING_AGG (FirstName, ',') AS Names
```

```
FROM Employee;
```

In the above query we can see `CHAR(13)` is replaced by comma sign and the result would be as follows:

```
Prasad, Manavya, Aaru, MANAS, MANASI
```

TRIM

Finally, SQL has `TRIM` function in command, which is also one of the most awaited functions. It is used to `TRIM` spaces, characters, literals, variable from left and right side. By default, the `TRIM` function removes the space character. We can say this function is same as `LTRIM(RTRIM(@string))`. The syntax is as follows:

```
TRIM ([characters FROM] string)
```

In the above syntax TRIM is the function name, characters is the character that needs to be trimmed. Let's take an example where we need to remove spaces from string. The syntax would be as follows:

```
SELECT TRIM('trimME') AS output;
```

In the above case, TRIM is the function name and we need to trim the spaces of string. If we execute the above query the output will be as follows:

```
trimME
```

So we can see that all the spaces have been trimmed. Similarly, we can trim any character too, see the following sample where we have trimmed # from the string:

```
SELECT TRIM( '#' FROM  '#test**#') AS Result;
```

If we fire the above query the output will be as follows:

```
test**
```

In the above output we can see # character gets trimmed and only string without # gets returned.

CONCAT_WS

This function is the same as STRING_AGG, which will return a string by joining two or more input strings separated by character given in syntax. The output is a single string:

```
CONCAT_WS (separator, argument1, argument2 [, and argument]...)
```

In the above syntax, CONTACT_WS is the function name, separator is the separator character and arguments 1, 2 are the arguments that need to be concatenated.

There is one option in CONCAT_WS syntax 'SET CONCAT_NULL_YIELDS_NULL {ON|OFF}, which helps us to ignore the NULL values.

Take an example, go through the following sample:

```
SELECT CONCAT_WS(',','a', 'b', 'C', 102) AS Value;
```

If we execute the above script the output will be as follows:

Value
A,b,C,102

Above, we can see that all the arguments are concatenated with comma.

TRANSLATE

This function is used to replace the input character with given new characters, so basically this method helps us to translate the string to new string.

The typical syntax is as follows:

```
TRANSLATE (inputString, OLD characters, NEW translations)
```

In the above syntax:

- `TRANSLATE`: It is the name of the function.
- `OLD characters`: It is the list of old character that needs to be replaced with.
- `NEW translations`: It is the list of new characters that needs to be replaced with old characters.

Here, we need to keep the `OLD characters` length and `NEW translations` as the same, otherwise this function will return error. See the following sample:

```
SELECT TRANSLATE('A*[B+C]/{D-F}', '[]{}', '()()') as Value;
```

In the above syntax, we have demanded to `replace []{}`with `()()`. If we fire the above query then the output will be as follows:

Value
A*(B+C)/(D-F)

Features of SQL 2019

Index encrypted columns

SQL server 2019 has made a lot of changes interms of security. It has introduced columns with indexes that can be encrypted. To achieve this functionality, it uses random encryption techniques, which will helps us in improving `LIKE` and comparison operator.

As we know, always encrypted functionality in SQL 2016 helped us to protect sensitive data from attackers. Up till now, we have been encrypting the data at frontend and saving it in database, but this will restrict the SQL operations also as SQL is unable to perform pattern matching or other cryptographic operations in encrypted data. To resolve this, SQL 2019 introduced this feature where we are allowing SQL to do the operation in plaintext data inside a safe enclave on the server side. This safe enclave is a secure region of memory and acts as a safe execution environment.

Transparent data encryption scan

If we want to enable **transparent data encryption (TDE)** on a database then SQL server first performs a scan which will read all the pages from the data files and then write the encrypted text back to the disk but this will put additional load on our system. If we are running some heavy task then the system gets slow and that may affect the overall performance of the application.

To avoid this issue, SQL server 2019 gives you the flexibility of having control over encryption scanning. Here you can suspend the encryption at any stage and then start it over again after finishing your task:

```
ALTER DATABASE <db_name> SET ENCRYPTION SUSPEND;

ALTER DATABASE <db_name> SET ENCRYPTION RESUME;
```

SSL/TLS certificates

In SQL server 2019, you can easily add SSL or TSL security certificates to the SQL database. In the earlier versions of SQL, the database team needs to fight for deploying the certificates and spend lot of time on them. But from now on, it will be very easy to integrate the certificates with database. With the help of this feature you can easily view or validate install certificates in SQL server, identify the expired certificates, deploy certificate by using certificate management in SQL server configuration manager.

Big Data cluster

Do you have Big Data with you? Do you want to store it or interact with it to SQL server? Then this new feature, called as Big Data cluster, will help connect to different databases.

This feature will allow you to connect to different Big Data and relational databases with the help of scalable clusters SQL server. It allows you to read and use Big Data from SQL. First, this Big Data is stored in hdfs and then you can query data from multiple data sources for AI, machine learning, and other tasks. So Big Data is nothing but data cluster that can connect to the external data sources moving or copying the data.

New graph function shortest path

As we know, graph is the collection of notes and vertices for showing hierarchical data, it needs to traverse between nodes. Shortest path function, which is used inside the match word, will be helpful in finding the shortest path between any two nodes in a graph, this functionality was introduced by SQL 2019.

Partition tables and indexes

From SQL server 2019, partition table data and indexes will be divided into a number of units, which can read in one or more file group in graph databases.

OPTIMIZE_FOR_SEQUENTIAL_KEY

There is indexes related Optimization improvement taken in SQL server 2019 for the betterment of high accuracy indexes. When we do concurrency on index columns then this feature will help us play with identity columns such as datetime, which needs to be inserted automatically. It helps to avoid problems that occurred while concurrency inserts for identity columns

Build and rebuild online clustered column store index

This feature helps us to create or drop indexes while SQL Server is online. This will be carried out by using SQL server management studio or by using transact SQL. Here we can rebuild the indexes while the user continues to update and query all the specified table or columns, which means that with this feature SQL index rebuilding is possible while the user is working on a database.

Hybrid buffer pool

SQL server 2019 introduced a new functionality named as hybrid buffer pool, which will allow the database to directly have access to the pages that are stored inside the database files. These database files are stored on persistent memory devices.

Before this feature came up, SQL used buffer spaces instead of accessing the page directly from data file, where the database needs to first copy the page into the RAM based portion of the pool but with this new hybrid buffer pool, SQL server skips performing copy operation of the page into DRAM portion and hence leads to performance improvement.

Query external tables

SQL server 2016 and higher have functionality to access the external data but from Hadoop as your blob storage database, but SQL server 2019 has extended their boundaries and now you can use SQL to access external data in Oracle, Teradata, and MongoDB as well. Switcher also allows you to connect to high value relational data in your data bases.

VERBOSE_TRUNCATION_WARNINGS

It is a very basic case where, when you try to insert values more than the length of defined value in a column than database, most of the time we face truncation error. But SQL server 2019 came up with more detailed error. Now you can get new error message, which is assigned for truncation error code 2628 and a detailed message as follows:

```
String or binary data would be truncated in table '%.*ls', column '%.*ls'.
Truncated value: '%.*ls'.
```

To use this feature we need to set to ON. When we set to OFF, truncation error will change and raise the error code 8152, the syntax is as below

```
VERBOSE_TRUNCATION_WARNINGS={ON| OFF}
```

Accelerated database recovery

SQL server 2019 introduced accelerated problem option that resides on premise (not on cloud). As the name suggests, this feature will accelerate or improve the performance of the database recovery, especially in the presence of long running transactions.

Following query will help you to set the database recovery option on database:

```
ALTER DATABASE <db_name> SET ACCELERATED_DATABASE_RECOVERY = {ON | OFF}
```

Conclusion

In this chapter we have seen the new features that were introduced by SQL 2016, 2017, 2019. Data masking like techniques, which will help us hide sensitive information like numbers and email, as well as JSON support is given by SQL. We also learnt about the stretch data concept which allows the on premise database to be connected to cloud database, and temporal database gives us a chance to store data temporarily. With the help of this feature, you can keep a track of old data, further. this data can be used for review or comparing process. Now, SQL is supported by R and you can easily run R queries on SQL.

In SQL 2017, queries can be auto tuned and performance can be improved with ease. This technique scans the slow performance query and applies recommended fixes for it. With the help of correct identity like features we can avoid the inconsistency that can occur due to unusual system failures. Now, Linux is also supported in SQL and we can install SQL server database engine and management studio on Linux. SQL 2019 has released big data cluster concept, which will support different big database for importing and exporting data, it also works with SSL like encryption.

In the upcoming chapter, we will learn about Fuzzy random SQL questions and Performance improvement tips. Till then stay tuned.

Questions

1. **How to hide our data from admin person like database administrator?**

    SQL 2016 has introduced new feature called secure encryption, which is implemented on individual row where you need to specify the encryption process and parse phase keys for data guard. Basically, we need to define

Encryption key and Master key, where Encryption key is used to encrypt data and Master key is used to encode encryption key.

2. **What is data masking?**

   It is basically used for data hiding, it uses MASK to wrap the data inside so that attacker or hacker will unknot be able to identify the content. It is useful when you have a confidential data store in table and you want to hide the content.

3. **Can I secure only one row in database?**

   To implement this functionality, first define security policy (to define this policy we need to predicate and function). To define predicates and function we can use the following syntax:

   ```
   CREATE SECURITY POLICY fn_security ADD [FILTER | BLOCK] PREDICATE
   FunctionName ON TableName
   ```

4. **What is stretch database and how it is helpful?**

   Stretch database concept is applicable to cloud (Azure) database. Where we can store at cloud and can fetch back to on premise as per the request. The data which is stored at the cloud is called as **COLD** data, whereas on premise data is called as **HOT** data. You can use this concept/feature when you want to store data for long term use and access whenever you need itas it is stored on cloud, so you can access it from anywhere.

5. **How to keep track of OLD and NEW data?**

   You can use new database functionality called as temporal database, which is simply like version facility. With the help of version facility, SQL maintains the old and new data. To support this feature, SQL uses history table with data time columns, one with start data time and another is end date time.

6. **Can we work with R in SQL?**

   R has different scripts that can be run on relational data to get desired output. Now with the help of SQL 2016, R scripts can be executed at SQL level.

7. **Can SQL tune script automatically?**

   Yes, SQL 2016 has query auto tune feature, which helps us to find out the problem in query performance. It not only identifies the issue but also fixes them to boost up performance. This performance tuning follows one of the following techniques:

   - Automatic correction plan
   - Automatic index plan

8. What is STRING_AGG function?

This function concatenates string expression and separator between each result, and does not append any separator at the end of the resultant string. The output is converted into string and then concatenation happens. In this case if compiler finds any NULL value then it is ignored and corresponding separator is not added.

9. Can SQL have TRIM function?

This function is used to TRIM spaces, characters, literals, variable from left and right side. By default, the TRIM function removes the space character. We can say this function is same as LTRIM(RTRIM(@string)).

10. What is the use of TRANSLATE function?

As the name suggests, this function input string for a character and replace or we can say translate them to new input characters. The typical syntax is as follows:

```
TRANSLATE (inputString, OLD characters, NEW translations)
```

In the preceding syntax,

- TRANSLATE: It is the name of the function.
- OLD characters: It is the list of old character that needs to be replaced with.
- NEW translations: It is the list of new characters that needs to be replaced with old characters.

Do you know (lights on facts?)

- SQL Express version is entry level free database edition released by SQL server.

- With the help of masking functionality you can hide email and random numbers.

- From SQL server 2016, you can set access permission for a specific row.

- String or binary data truncation error has been made more descriptive from SQL 2019.

- From SQL 2017, SQL database can connect to other big databases and import and export data from it.

CHAPTER 12

Fuzzy Interview Questions and SQL Performance Tips

Now a days, data storage and extraction with good performance is a big challenge, so that is why there is no button in software saying *improve performance*. SQL server is serving us with ease and good routine from past many years, it has travelled a lot from Version 2000 to 2019 (current version). Really, SQL is an industry leading enterprise level database software that helps us to manage, store, fetch and secure our data.

Prerequisite for this chapter: Before we walk through this chapter you should have a good knowledge of SQL concepts. Additionally, you should have a laptop/desktop with SQL server installed.

Structure

- Performance improvement tips for SQL server
- Fuzzy interview questions and answers

Objective

So, the objective of this chapter is to walk through some of the cool performance improvement tips that will help us speed-up application performance. Additionally, in this chapter we will learn about last minute interview questions and answers that will help you clear the interview.

So, let's begin.

Performance improvement tips for SQL server

Now a days,developing a software is a simple thing as good development tools help us to develop software with rapid speed, but performance is everyone's headache. We do have some good performance improvement tips for SQL server that you can follow to develop a decent performance compliant software.

Let's start with its operating system settings:

- Do you know while we think from the performance point of view, not only SQL queries but other factors are also taken under consideration?

- If you are using Windows server 2008 or later version then set the `Power Saving` option to `High Performance`, the default power saving settings is set on 'Balanced' which means the processor and other operating things are set back if the system is not busy and that may affect SQL performance if it is set for heavy load

- In SQL, if we keep auto grow option for SQL data files then we need to add data or log files to an existing database at that point of time. SQL backup user should have access to `Perform Volume Maintenance Tasks` under Windows security policy. It will help create instant file initialization for data file creation

- When we configure antivirus settings then we should exclude the following files from being scanned:
  - SQL data files like `.mdf, .ndf, .ldf` files
  - SQL backup files like `.trn, .bak` files
  - Trace file by SQL like `.trc` files
  - Audit files by SQL like `.sqlaudit` files
  - SQL query files like `.sql` files
  - Remote blob storage files
  - `SQLServr.exe` file from `Bin` folder of SQL folder
  - ReportingServices `Service.exe` file from `Bin` folder of SQL folder
  - `MSMDSrv.exe` file from Bin folder of SQL folder

SQL tips

- To check if the data exists in an SQL table, use `EXISTS` instead of `IN` operator.
- `IN` operator is used to compare each value with a set of data, whereas `EXISTS` tell you whether the query will return a result, which is more quicker than

IN. Where there are static items then you can use IN but for dynamic items (like data from table row) you should use EXISTS. For example,

```
SELECT * FROM Emp WHERE EXISTS ( SELECT * FROM Dept

  WHERE Emp.EmpID = Dept.EmpID)
```

The above query can be executed more quickly than the below one

```
SELECT * FROM Emp WHERE ID IN (SELECT EmpID FROM Dept)
```

- Always avoid * in SELECT statement, it will put extra load on system if we do have a number of columns in our SQL table. For example:

Use SELECT name, last name FROM Customers

Instead of SELECT * FROM Employee

- Avoid using SP_ prefix name to your user defined procedures as SQL first searches for inbuilt procedure and then for the inbuilt database procedure that starts with SP_. So it will slow down the execution process.For example:

Use EmployeeProcedure

Instead of SP_EmployeeProcedure

- Do not keep the transaction block too largeas it will lead to deadlocks and slow down the overall processing.

- Instead of using complex queries, use stored procedures.

- Use schema name before SQL objectwhenever you are connecting to database for executing query.For example:

```
Select * from database1.SP_EmployeeProcedure
```

- Avoid cursor wherever possible as they are slow to process.

Use JOIN instead of subqueries.

Subqueries are slower to execute than join, which can create execution plan and then load the data,but sub queries are run randomly until the last row record is fetched. For example,

```
SELECT firstname, sal FROM Emp, Dept WHERE sal=
(SELECT sal> 10000 FROM Dept) AND (Emp.ID=Dept.ID);
```

The above query is slower than the below one:

```
SELECT firstname, sal FROM Emp E
INNER JOIN
Dept D ON E.ID = D.ID WHERE D.sal> 10000;
```

- It is a better idea to drop the empty indexes of table, you can do it by rebuilding the table indexes, and it will improve the SQL performance.

- Avoid HAVING clause unless it is used with aggregate operator for row filter, use WHERE instead. WHERE restricts the result set before returning the rows and HAVING restricts the result set after fetching rows, so WHERE is faster in execution than HAVING

- Avoid nchar and nvarchar datatypes as they take double the memory space than char and varchar.

- In SELECT statement, always select number column first and then select string later image datatype if it exists. For example,in the following query we have selected numeric column first and then string column. This arrangement will help execute query faster:

```
SELECT EmpID,FirstName, LastName from Employee;
```

- Most of the times, it is observed that SQL performance is degraded by SQL queries. So, avoid using nested or lengthy queries, break them down into small bunch of queries or use stored procedure.

- Use appropriate datatypes, take an example: if you want to store student count in a class room then use tinyint datatype, whose storing range is 0 to 255 instead of intwhich is bigger than tinyint.

- If you have fixed length column then avoid using NULL values in that column.

- If you want to make union of the table then always use UNION ALL instead of UNION as it does not sort the result.

- The default behavior of SQL is to return the number of rows affected but it will slow down the performance. To avoid this problem we can set SETNOCOUNT ON statement and it will not affect the count of rows.

- If you don't want transaction safety access, for example just want to select a table rows, then you can access table with NOLOCK statement, it will help us to improve the SQL performance.

- When we want a single integer value to be returned from database table then use RETURN keyword.

- Do not use DDL (data definition language) inside the stored procedure it will reduce the chance of reusing the execution plan.

- Do not try to put primary key on string column unless it is very necessary.

- Try to use primary and foreign key relationship, it helps to fetch and delete records for dependent tables.

- Avoid using TEMP clause unless it is really required.

- Use LEFT OUTER JOIN instead of NOT IN clause.

- Use SQL Profiler to monitor the execution speed and plan.

- Always build up a good key relationship like primary and foreign key relation between tables. For example, if we have a student and a marks table, then student id should be present in marks table, otherwise without student ID column marks tables is of no use.

- To delete all rows in a table, always use `TRUNCATE` as it is faster than `DELETE`.

- If you want to transfer large number of data from one table to another (where the database table structure is the same) then you can use:

```
INSERT INTO <target table> SELECT <columns> FROM <source table>
```

Fuzzy interview questions and answers

After SQL tips let's move to fuzzy SQL interview questions that confuse you. So let's begin.

1. **In which file does SQL store physical data?**

    SQL has two data files associated with it: MDF file, which stores actual data and the other is LDF file, which stores transaction log information. This means MDF file is used to store actual data

2. **What is locking in SQL?**

    SQL locking is a concept related to transaction handling. When we start any database transaction then database puts some exclusive lock on tables or rows to avoid conflicts. The types of the SQL transaction locks are as follows:

    - Shared
    - Exclusive
    - Schema
    - Intent
    - Update
    - Bulk Update

3. **How can I insert value in table having only one column which is of type integerand set as primary key with identity?**

    You can insert value in table with only column which is identity by firing the following script:

    ```
    INSERT INTO TABLE1 DEFAULT VALUES;
    ```

    Here, `TABLE1` is an SQL table in which we need to insert value and `DEFAULT VALUES` are the reserved keywords to insert identity value in columns

4. **How can I rename database using query?**

    We can rename databaseby firingthe following script:

    ```
    ALTER DATABASE old_database_name MODIFY NAME = old_database_name;
    ```

Here, `ALTER DATABASE` is used to rename the database name, we need to use `MODIFY` keyword to set a new name.

5. How can I take full database backup using query?

Use `BACKUP DATABASE` command to take backup of database. The following script will let you take full database backup:

```
BACKUP DATABASE myDB TO DISK = 'D:\databaseBKP\myDB.bak'
```

In the above query we have taken backup of `myDB` database to disk at location `D:\databaseBKP`.

6. How many columns can I give in SELECT statement?

An SQL query can contain 4096 columns per `SELECT` statement.

7. How many columns can I give in INSERT statement?

An SQL query can contain 4096 columns per `INSERT` statement.

8. What could be a maximum database size per database?

A database size can span up to 524272 TB.

9. How many databases can be attached per single SQL instance?

32767 databases are allowed to be attached to single SQL instance.

10. How many nested sub-queries are allowed per single query?

32 nested sub-queries are allowed per single query.

11. How many nested triggers are allowed per single query?

32 nested triggers are allowed per single query.

12. How many maximum parameters we can pass to stored procedures?

We can pass a maximum of up to 2100 parameters to stored procedure.

13. How many maximum parameters we can pass per user-defined function?

We can pass a maximum of up to 2100 parameters per user-defined function.

14. How many maximum rows can an SQL table contain?

There is no limit for rows per table; it is limited to the available storage.

15. How many maximum rows can an SQL table contain?

There is no limit for rows per table, it is limited to the available storage.

16. How many columns can I give in UPDATE statement?

An SQL query can contains 4096 columns per `UPDATE` statement.

17. How many user connections are allowed per SQL database instance?

32767 user connections are allowed per database instance.

18. How many instance of SQL server does single server has?

Single server can have up to 5 number of SQL server instance.

19. What is NOT NULL related to SQL server columns?

As the name suggests, NOT NULL forces the column to not accept any NULL value, so we cannot leave the cell empty/null.

20. What is PIVOT in SQL?

Basically, it is a relational operator, which is used to produce the output where we can convert the rows into columns and columns into rows, this is often useful when we want some report like data from database.

21. Find the 2nd highest salary from employee table?

This is a frequently asked interview question. We can query in multiple ways, and here are some examples:

```
SELECT MAX(sal) FROM Employee WHERE sal NOT IN (SELECT Max(sal) FROM Employee);
```

In the above query, we have first fetched the highest salary from the employee table and then used NOT IN to remove that salary from subquery. We can get the same output with the below query:

```
SELECT TOP 1 sal FROM (SELECT TOP 2 sal FROM Employee ORDER BY sal DESC) AS table1 ORDER BY sal ASC;
```

22. How can I check if my SQL server database has any transaction locks?

We can use inbuilt stored procedure to check if the SQL server database has any transaction lock associated with it. See the following stored procedure:

```
EXEC sp_lock
```

If you use the above query you will find out if there is any lock on database or not

23. How to get the version of SQL server using query?

You can use the following query to get SQL server version:

```
Select SERVERPROPERTY('productversion')
```

24. What is the use of = (equal) == (double equal) === (triple equal) in SQL?

Following are the usage of the signs:

Sr No	Sign	Verbal	Meaning
1	=	Equal	It is an assignment operator
2	==	Double equal	It is a comparison operator
3	===	Triple equal	It is also a comparison operator but it only compares string with string, and number with number

25. How to delete duplicate rows?

Only DELETE command can delete all rows from the SQL table. If you want to delete only duplicate rows then you can use ROW NUMBER and CTE functions. See the following query:

```
WITH CTE AS
(
SELECT *,ROW_NUMBER() OVER (PARTITION BY col1,col2,col3 ORDER BY col1,col2,col3) AS RN
FROM table1
)
DELETE FROM CTE WHERE RN<>1
```

26. How to delete all rows from SQL tale?

Only DELETE command can delete all rows from the SQL table, you can use Truncate command to delete the rows, but it will reset the table structure.

27. What are the types of SQL server authentication?

There are two types of authentication in SQL:

- SA
- Windows authentication

SA is the system admin user.

28. What are the ways to avoid SQL injection attack?

SQL injection attack can be blocked by the following ways:

- Using parameters in SQL script or stored procedure
- Using dynamic SQL with parameter collation
- Using escape characters

29. Which TCP/IP port is used by SQL?

Port no 1433 is used by SQL.

30. What is log-shipping?

Log shipping is the process where SQL takes backup from one server to another standalone server; it is easy to use and is a low-maintenance activity.

31. How to get the number of records in table?

We can get the number of records in a table using COUNT function. See the following query:

```
SELECT COUNT(*) FROM table1
```

32. What is normalization in SQL?

Normalization is a process where we have to de-compose SQL table and remove redundancy.

33. What are the types of normalization in SQL?

In SQL, we have following types of normalizations:

- **1NF:** This is the basic level normalization where we have defined primary key wherever needed, and focus is on uniqueness.
- **2NF:** This is the second level normalization where we have defined dependencies, and all dependencies should be dependent on only unique identifiers
- **3NF:** This is the third level normalization where we check that no column entry should depend only upon key field or key columns.
- **4NF:** This is the fourth level normalization where we check that tables should not have any multi-value dependency on primary key
- **BCNF:** This is the Boyce-Codd normalization form where we check that for each table the database should have only one primary key.

34. What is XQuery?

In SQL, XQuery is used to query XML data, so if we want data from XML file then we can use XQuery.

35. What is Inner Join?

Suppose we have two tables and we want the common values between left and right table, then we use inner join on them.

36. What is Full Join?

Suppose we have two tables and we want to combine all values in the left and the right table, then we use full join.

37. What is Left Join?

Suppose we have two tables and we want a combination of all values from left table and common values from left and right table, then we use left join on them.

38. What is Right Join?

Suppose we have two tables and we want a combination of all values from right table and common values from left and right table, then we use right join on them.

39. What is Self-Join?

This join is a bit different from the other joins as it is used is used when we need to compare rows from self-table or to querying hierarchical data.

40. What is Cross Join?

Suppose we have two tables and we use cross join on them, then it will become a combination of all rows from right and left table with all rows from both table. This join is required when we need all possible combination of data in both tables.

41. What is data integrity?

Data integrity means the guarantee of accuracy and quality of data over the lifetime of the product (where the database is used), it not only concentrates on quality but also enforces business rules to save and retrieve data as per industry standards.

42. Can we have a multiple primary key in an SQL table?

There is only one primary key per table. If we define more than one primary keys for different columns then it is called as candidate key (which is a set of primary keys). List out some good features of SSRS:

- This report is multi-dimensional report that supports multi-source database.
- You can draw multi format reports in SSRS, including graphs, tabular, charts and many more.
- We can export SSRS reports in multiple formats like XML, CSV, TIFF, HTML, PDF.
- It is easy to deploy.
- As it is user friendly, so no need for any specialist to generate report.

43. What are the components of SSRS?

SSRS components are as follows:

- Report Builder
- Report Designer
- Report Manager
- Report Server
- Report Database
- Data Sources

Types of reports that SSRS can create

- Drill down reports
- Drill through reports
- Sub reports
- Linked reports
- Parameterized reports

44. What is SSIS?

It is a component of SQL server that is used to carry out data migration tasks. It is used as an ETL tool that is used for extraction, transformation and loading.

45. What are the component of SSIS?

SSIS component are as follows:

- Data flow
- Package explorer
- Control flow
- Event handler

46. What is the task concept in SSIS?

It is the part of the integration server that represents individual task, which may be of the following types:

- Control flow task
- Database task

Index

Made in the USA
Middletown, DE
18 October 2020